MEDAL OF HONOR HONOR WARFIGHTER™

PRIMA OFFICIAL GAME GUIDE

Written by Michael Knight & David Knight

Prima Games
An Imprint of Random House, Inc.
3000 Lava Ridge Court, Suite 100
Roseville, CA 95661
www.primagames.com

CONTENTS

BEHIND-THE-SCENES

Welcome to the official game guide for *Medal of Honor Warfighter*. The latest release in this long-running and highly acclaimed series is inspired by and has been developed with Tier 1 Operators from an elite, international community. This personal story was written by actual Tier 1 Operators while deployed overseas. In it, players step into the boots of these warfighters and apply unique skill sets to track down a real global threat, in real international locations, sponsored by real enemies. It doesn't get any more authentic than this. The only game that gives players the ability to be in real world events, *Medal of Honor Warfighter* lets you experience the action as it might have taken place in the field.

GLOBAL WARFIGHTERS

This is Tier 1 on a global scale, featuring real-world hot spots in the single-player campaign and introducing international Tier 1 Operators in multiplayer. This groundbreaking move gives players a window into the look and style of elite soldiers from ten different countries around the world. With *Medal of Honor Warfighter*, gamers can represent their nation's Special Operations Forces on the multiplayer battlefield. Battlelog's Warfigher Nations meta game introduces a new mode where the world's best-of-the-best warriors go head-to-head in online competition. Here's a rundown of the twelve units featured in the game |as well as a brief background of each. Who will you fight for?

AUSTRALIAN SAS-R

Special Air Service Regiment (SAS-R) is a special forces unit of the Australian Army. While it is modeled on the British SAS, with which it shares the motto "Who Dares Wins", the regiment also draws on the experience of World War II Australian special reconnaissance and commando units, particularly Z Special Unit (Z Force/SRD).

BRITISH SAS

Special Air Service (SAS) is a corps of the British Army constituted on May 31, 1950. They are part of the United Kingdom Special Forces (UKSF) and have served as a model for the special forces of many other countries all over the world.

CANADIAN JTF2

Joint Task Force 2 (JTF2) is an elite special operations force of the Canadian Forces primarily tasked with counter-terrorism operations. JTF2 is part of the |operational elements of the Canadian Special Operations Forces Command.

GERMAN KSK

Kommando Spezialkräfte (KSK) is an elite military unit composed of Special Operations soldiers from the ranks of Germany's Bundeswehr and organized as such under the Division Spezielle Operationen (Special Operations Division, DSO).

NORWAY FSK/HJK

Hærens Jegerkommando (FSK/HJK) is a special forces unit of the Norwegian military. It is the armed forces competence center for commando, airborne, and counter-terrorist duty in the Norwegian Army.

POLISH GROM

GROM (Grupa Reagowania Operacyjno-Manewrowego) is one of five special forces units of the Polish Armed Forces. It was officially activated on July 8, 1990. It is deployed in a variety of special operations and unconventional warfare roles, including anti-terrorist actions and projection of power behind enemy lines.

ROKN UDT/SEAL

Naval Special Warfare Brigade (UDT) is a special warfare unit of the Republic of Korea Navy. The UDT are heavily influenced by the United States Navy SEALs, and maintain a strong relationship by regularly undertaking joint cross-training (JCET) several times a year.

RUSSIAN SPETSGRUPPA ALFA

GRUPPA ALFA is an elite, stand-alone component of Russia's special forces and the dedicated counter-terrorism task force of the Russian Federal Security Service (FSB), with an emphasis on hostage rescue and counter-terrorism operations.

SWEDISH SOG

Särskilda Skyddsgruppen (SOG) is a special operations unit of the Swedish military, which became active in 1994. The exact number of operatives is classified, but is thought to be between 60 and 80, with an average age of 31.

U.S. OGA

Other Government Agency (OGA) is the operational arm of the Intelligence Community. These agencies often recruit persons from various special operations units in the United States military and therefore have a diverse set of backgrounds and skills.

U.S. ARMY SFOD-D

SFOD-D is one of the United States' secretive Tier 1 counter-terrorism and Special Mission Units. Commonly known as The Unit, it was formed under the designation 1st SFOD-D, and has been involved in every U.S. ground operation since its inception.

U.S. NAVY SEALS

The United States Navy's Sea, Air, and Land Teams, commonly known as Navy SEALs, are the U.S. Navy's principal special operations force and a part of the Naval Special Warfare Command (NSWC) as well as the maritime component of the United States Special Operations Command.

DANGER CLOSE PROFILE

Welcome to Danger Close Games at the EA Los Angeles complex.

Medal of Honor Warfighter was created by Danger Close Games. This studio was created in 2010 to work on the new incarnation of *Medal of Honor* that was released that same year. However, Danger Close Games has quite a history that goes back almost two decades. Therefore, even though the studio has had a new name for just two years, it has existed in one form or another since 1995. That year the film studio DreamWorks SKG founded a video game development subsidiary known as DreamWorks Interactive LLC. While most of the games were based on movies and other DreamWorks franchises, in 1999, the studio created the first of a new series of games. Created for the Playstation, *Medal of Honor* was a first-person shooter that put players right into the middle of World War II. The game was such a success, that the following year the studio released *Medal of Honor: Underground*–also for the Playstation. The same year, 2000, Electronic Arts acquired the studio and brought it to their Los Angeles offices. In 2003, EA merged with Westwood Studios and EA Pacific to form the EA Los Angeles (EALA) development studios.

These awards for past Medal of Honor games speak for themselves.

The Medal of Honor series is famous for its World War II games, putting players into historical battles and combat situations.

Between 2002 and 2005, EA Los Angeles developed five new *Medal of Honor* titles for the Xbox, Playstation 2, and Game Cube, as well as for the PC. Then the studio revamped for the next-gen consoles, releasing *Medal of Honor: Airborne* in 2007 for the Xbox 360, Playstation 3, and PC. This game was unique to the series since it offered a third dimension to the battle, as players could parachute into missions at various locations rather than progressing linearly through each mission. As Electronic Arts decided to bring the *Medal of Honor* series from the historical battlefields of World War II to the modern combat of today's war on terror, the move was made to create a studio for that sole purpose. As a result, Danger Close Games was born–or more appropriately reborn.

Visitors first enter the reception area at EA Los Angeles, which includes stylish architecture.

As you get off of the elevator at the Danger Close Games floor, you know right away on what this studio is focused.

Housed within the EA Los Angeles studio complex near Marina del Rey, Danger Close Games chose its name after the term used by the military for an artillery or air strike called in very close to friendly units. Units calling in danger close strikes usually have enemy close to them and risk friendly fire since the situation is so dangerous. This name reflects Danger Close Games' commitment to games that are designed to be as authentic as possible as well as respectful to those serving their country. This is apparent to any visitor to the Danger Close Games studio.

The hallways of the studio are lined with concept art, which helps the designers really get into the project and maintain their focus on creating a great game.

Walking into the Danger Close Games studio is like entering another world. This is not just an ordinary office building, though it may appear like that from the outside. Instead, almost every square foot of the area is dedicated to the project. The halls are lined with artwork. Walls have charts and tables to help the designers visualize the organization of units and classes for the multiplayer elements. They even have large action figures to use as models for the various classes in the game. These serve as references for the artists so they can ensure that the game is as realistic as possible.

Large charts and tables on the walls help illustrate the organization of Medal of Honor Warfighter.

Reference models help ensure accuracy so that players feel like they are in the real fight—and experience what it might be like to be a Tier 1 Operator—as much as possible in a game.

Danger Close Games believes in immersing their team in the game. They are surrounded by art, objects, and other items that reflect the game. It is difficult to walk into the offices and work areas and not immediately get excited about *Medal of Honor Warfighter*. As you look around and see models of helicopters, weapons, and other items, you appreciate the level of detail of these objects within the game. Even the quality assurance team gets to know the models so they can ensure they are well represented in the final product.

The quality assurance team works diligently to find bugs in the game so you won't see them in the final product.

The flags hanging over the cubicles reflect the international nature of the war on terror as exhibited within Medal of Honor Warfighter.

While the *Medal of Honor Warfighter* team works hard, they also have opportunities to take a break from the grindstone without having to stray too far from their work. The EA Los Angeles complex features kitchens, break areas, and even sports such as their outdoor basketball and sand volleyball courts and soccer field. By allowing the team to get some physical recreation, they can come back and be ready to work with a refreshed mind and energized body.

Caffeine and energy drinks are close at hand to help fight through the fatigue.

When the team needs a bit more than liquid energy, they can retire to the kitchen and break room for more substantial sustenance.

Sometimes the team needs more than a sports video game. The outdoor sports area offers something for everyone.

Danger Close Games may be working on their second game as a studio, however their history goes back many years. As they work on *Medal of Honor Warfighter*, they continue a tradition of excellence as they tell the story of the men and women who serve our country and at times pay the ultimate price for our security, liberty, and freedom. To the team, this is more than just a game. It is a tribute to those who fight behind the scenes and when they succeed, no one ever knows.

The gaming world anticipates the release of the latest in the Medal of Honor *family.*

This lush courtyard gives the developers a chance to step outside and enjoy the year-round perfect weather.

The studio's lobby and reception area is a relaxing place for visitors to unwind or browse the adjoining employee store, filled with EA merchandise.

This studio lounge is another area where developers can relax and show-off their gaming prowess in the latest console releases. Fighting games are always a big draw.

When the developers need a break, this game room offers plenty of welcome distractions including several arcade games, a pinball machine, as well as a foosball and pool table.

MEDAL OF HONOR LEGACY

The *Medal of Honor* series began with the basic premise of telling a soldier's story. Released on the Playstation back in the fall of 1999, the first title did just that, chronicling the adventures of an OSS field agent fighting behind enemy lines in World War II-era Europe. The success of the first game spawned a long-running and award-winning series of games set in WWII, each telling the story of a soldier risking it all to stem the tide of fascism.

MEDAL OF HONOR

Release: October 31, 1999
Platform: Playstation
Inspired by DreamWorks SKG co-founder Steven Spielberg, *Medal of Honor* marked the first WWII action-adventure game developed for the Playstation system. The game begins on June 5, 1944, the night before D-Day, when the Allied forces launched a massive aerial assault behind German lines. Assuming the role of a young C-47 pilot shot down during the operation, the player is recruited into the OSS and begins a new career as a field agent, participating in various covert operations, search and rescue assignments, and commando raids. Each mission is drawn from pivotal historical events that helped shape the Allied crusade in Europe, including sorties involving the development, capture, and destruction of secret war-making technologies. Upon release, *Medal of Honor* was seen as one of the best first-person shooters of its time, garnering praise for its graphics, level design, and original soundtrack, composed by Michael Giacchino.

MEDAL OF HONOR: ALLIED ASSAULT

Release: January 20, 2002
Platform: PC
In *Medal of Honor: Allied Assault*, players assumed the role of Lt. Mike Powell, member of the famed 1st Ranger Battalion, who gets recruited by the OSS and battles through more than twenty levels that are based on historical military campaigns of World War II. Set during the most trying years of the war, 1942–1945, *Allied Assault* gave players a sense of the courage it took to survive the landings at Normandy, the assault at Arzew, a rendezvous with the French Resistance outside the village of St. Lo, and the push through the heavily defended border of Germany. As the first title in the series on the PC, *Medal of Honor: Allied Assault* was met with critical acclaim and was soon followed by two expansion packs, *Spearhead* and *Breakthrough*.

1999   **2000**   **2002**   **2002**

MEDAL OF HONOR: UNDERGROUND

Release: October 23, 2000
Platform: Playstation
Medal of Honor: Underground begins in 1942, not long after Germany crushed the French military and overran the country. Players are introduced to Manon, who has just witnessed her house destroyed and hometown occupied. With nothing left to lose, she joins one of the many clandestine resistance movements that have taken root throughout her homeland during the early days of the occupation. Over the course of the game, players will experience her ascent from a naive volunteer to a seasoned veteran who is ultimately recruited by the Americans for the Office of Strategic Services (OSS), where she will eventually play a key role in the Liberation of Paris.

SPEARHEAD (EXPANSION PACK)

Release: November 11, 2002
Platform: PC
Spearhead was the first of two expansion packs for *Medal of Honor: Allied Assault*. Players assumed the role of Sgt. Jack Barnes as he endured the final months of World War II, from Operation Overlord to the Battle of the Bulge, and culminating with the fall of Berlin. Set during the last year of the war in Europe, June 1944 to May 1945, *Spearhead* gave players a chance to parachute behind enemy lines during Operation Overlord, halt the German counter offensive during the Battle of the Bulge, and engage the Germans as they desperately tried to defend their capital.

MEDAL OF HONOR: FRONTLINE

Release: May 28, 2002
Platform: Playstation 2, Xbox, GameCube

Medal of Honor: Frontline took players back behind enemy lines with Lt. Jimmy Patterson. In this installment, Patterson and his men used the confusion of the real-world offensive Operation Market Garden to infiltrate the German frontline and steal the HO-IX flying wing, an experimental Nazi weapon so powerful that it could turn the tide of World War II. To help him succeed in his assignment, Lt. Patterson had the assistance of a small squad of soldiers and a slew of new weapons. Together they took on crucial assignments ranging from the assault on Omaha Beach, to the epic battle for control of the Nijmegen Bridge.

MEDAL OF HONOR: RISING SUN

Release: November 11, 2003
Platform: Playstation 2, Xbox, GameCube

Medal of Honor: Rising Sun gave gamers the opportunity to turn the tide in the Pacific, and marked the first time the series expanded beyond the European theater. Playing as Marine Corporal Joseph Griffin, *Rising Sun* told a far-reaching tale of two brothers as Japanese forces sought to expand their dominion over the Pacific. Featuring real-life historical battles like Pearl Harbor and Guadalcanal, *Medal of Honor: Rising Sun* delivered solid action and a compelling story.

2002   2003   2003   2003

BREAKTHROUGH (EXPANSION PACK)

Release: September 22, 2003
Platform: PC

Set in the European Theater of Operations from 1943–1944, *Breakthrough* was the final chapter in the popular *Medal of Honor: Allied Assault* series. As U.S. Army Sergeant John Baker, players joined the battle at Kasserine Pass in North Africa, raced to capture Messina in Sicily, and then finally repelled the German army at the historic battle of Monte Battaglia in the heart of Italy. Armed with a new arsenal of weapons, Sgt. Baker fought alone and with squadmates in a rush to stop the Axis powers by striking at the soft underbelly of Europe.

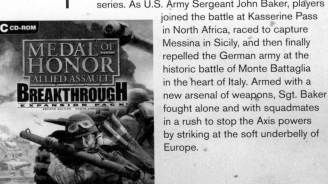

MEDAL OF HONOR: INFILTRATOR

Release: November 17, 2003
Platform: Game Boy Advance

In *Medal of Honor: Infiltrator*, players assumed the role of Corporal Jake Murphy, during several daring missions to defeat the Axis in some of WWII's most famous battles. From sabotaging enemy resources, to capturing key personnel, to all-out firefights, there was never any shortage of action. On foot, in a tank, or even in disguise, Murphy engaged opponents on the battlefield with a variety of WWII-era weapons including machine guns, grenades, and bazookas. The title also offered connectivity with the GameCube version of *Medal of Honor: Rising Sun*, allowing gamers to access a useful overhead map on their Game Boy Advance.

MEDAL OF HONOR: PACIFIC ASSAULT

Release: November 4, 2004
Platform: PC

Medal of Honor: Pacific Assault ushered players into battle against the Imperial Japanese Army, taking them from the shock of Pearl Harbor to triumph on the shores of the Tarawa Atoll. Set in the Pacific Theater of Operations from 1941–1944, players jumped into the boots of Marine recruit Tom Conlin as he survived the attack on Pearl Harbor, led the assault on Guadalcanal, and finally charged up the beaches for the climatic battle at Tarawa. Expert input and advice from the Congressional Medal of Honor Society and war veteran Capt. Dale Dye, U.S. Marine Corps, ensured historical accuracy, making for an authentic gaming experience.

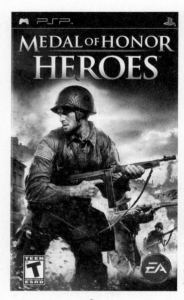

MEDAL OF HONOR: HEROES

Release: October 23, 2006
Platform: PSP

In *Medal of Honor: Heroes*, players fought their way through three campaigns as popular lead characters from past *Medal of Honor* games. This included a stint as Lieutenant Jimmy Patterson during his time in Holland during Operation Market Garden. Then gamers assumed control of Sergeant John Baker during a sabotage mission on German defenses positioned along the Italian coastline. Next, gamers tried on the officer's cap of Lieutenant William Holt in a OSS mission within the Ardennes Forest during the Battle of the Bulge.

2004   2005   2006   2007

MEDAL OF HONOR: EUROPEAN ASSAULT

Release: June 7, 2005
Platform: Playstation 2, Xbox, GameCube

In *Medal of Honor: European Assault*, the story was the star. The year 1942 was a desperate time for Allied forces as the Nazi war machine raged across a devastated European landscape. Players assumed the role of U.S. Army Lieutenant William Holt, hand-picked by William "Wild Bill" Donovan to be the first field agent of the newly formed Office of Strategic Services—the OSS. Players guided Holt through covert operations set in France, North Africa, and the Soviet Union. He even meets up with Manon, the heroine from *Medal of Honor: Underground*, in Belgium.

MEDAL OF HONOR: VANGUARD

Release: March 26, 2007
Platform: Playstation 2, Wii

Medal of Honor: Vanguard allowed players to join the ranks of the elite 82nd Airborne Division as Corporal Frank Keegan. From Operation Husky on the shores of Sicily to the Operation Varsity airdrop inside Nazi Germany, Keegan jumped behind enemy lines to fight the epic WWII battles that turned America's first paratroopers into heroes of WWII.

MEDAL OF HONOR: AIRBORNE

Release: September 7, 2007
Platform: Playstation 3, Xbox 360, PC

In *Medal Of Honor: Airborne*, players stepped into the boots of Boyd Travers, Private First Class of the 82nd Airborne Division, and engaged in battles throughout Europe, from rocky beginnings in Sicily to war-winning triumphs in Germany. Each mission began behind enemy lines, with an intense and fully interactive airdrop. The ability to determine your own starting point dramatically changed the way each mission played out, and earned the title high praise from gamers and critics alike.

MEDAL OF HONOR

Release: October 12, 2010
Platform: Playstation 3, Xbox 360, PC

This *Medal of Honor* reboot was inspired by and developed with Tier 1 Operators, bringing the series into the modern era. Players stepped into the boots of elite warriors and applied their unique skill sets to a new enemy in the most unforgiving and hostile battlefield conditions of present day Afghanistan. The intense story featured a diverse group of soldiers in a gritty campaign, showcasing the surgical tactics of Tier 1 Operators combined with the sledgehammer force of Army Rangers. The fast-paced campaign concluded with a dangerous rescue mission set in the unforgiving terrain of Takur Ghar as Voodoo, Preacher and a Ranger QRF scoured the enemy-infested mountains for their two captive SEAL comrades.

2007   2007   2010

MEDAL OF HONOR: HEROES 2

Release: November 13, 2007
Platform: PSP, Wii

Medal of Honor: Heroes 2 starts on June 6, 1944, when the war was far from over. Players took on the role of OSS Operative John Berg and were tasked with infiltrating Normandy from behind enemy lines to undermine the Nazi regime. As a special agent of the Office of Strategic Services, you used tactics of combat, infiltration, reconnaissance, and sabotage to carry out the covert operations that helped defeat the Nazi war machine once and for all.

MULTIPLAYER COMMUNITY EVENT

A group shot of the community members who made this event a smashing success.

Early in September of 2012, Danger Close held a community event at their offices in Los Angeles. This event gave community members a chance to mingle with the developers while previewing *Medal of Honor Warfighter's* multiplayer maps and game modes. Prima was lucky enough to attend the event, giving us our first in-depth experience with this game's multiplayer gameplay. Here's multiplayer author David Knight's first-hand account of what transpired over those fun-filled days in sunny Southern California—not that he saw the sun much.

DAY 1: MOUSE/KEYBOARD VS. GAMEPAD

I wasted no time making my way to EALA's office, where Danger Close is based. This wasn't my first visit to this studio, so I was able to navigate my cab driver from LAX to the office's somewhat obscured entrance in Playa Vista. Upon meeting with Daniel Chin (the event organizer) in the lobby, he guided me back to a large (and noticeably warm) room filled with twenty high-end PCs where the community members were just getting started. I stowed my luggage on the side of the room and hopped on the last vacant system, joining a game already in progress.

This is where the magic happened. And yes, twenty high-end PCs made the room temperature a bit toasty. But it added to the immersion when playing on Tungawan Jungle.

The game's branding was hard to miss. We even had Medal of Honor Warfighter branded gamepads and headsets.

The first hour of gameplay was a blur, as I tried to adjust to fast-paced gameplay and compact map design. It soon became clear that my fellow community members were more than just journalists—they were very competent gamers. I'm used to going to press events and rising to the top of the scoreboard, often because I have much more experience with the genre and game. But this time I had a hard time keeping up. After years of console gaming, my mouse and keyboard skills were extremely rusty. But as I looked around the room, I noticed most of the community members were playing with custom *Medal of Honor Warfighter* gamepads, complementing the high-end *Medal of Honor Warfighter* headsets attached to each system. Really? They were beating me with gamepads? I had a gamepad plugged into my system too, but I resisted the urge for several rounds. But when my kill/death ratio failed to improve, I finally grabbed the gamepad and never looked back. Suddenly I was holding my own, effortlessly staging ambushes and frontal assaults with my Fireteam Buddy. The frustration quickly melted away and I soon began unlocking more national units and weapons, giving me more options to customize my multiplayer persona.

This is the auditorium where we met frequently with the developers to provide feedback and debate different aspects of gameplay. The large projection screen came in handy when discussing specific areas on maps.

Following a full day of gameplay, interrupted only by a brief pizza break, all of us were ushered into a large auditorium. Here developer Thad Sasser moderated a lengthy discussion where the community members were urged to provide feedback on everything from the maps to the classes and to the weapons. The group didn't hold back, pointing out potential bugs while offering suggestions for improvements. On this particular day, there was a debate about the sniper class's secondary automatic G18 pistol being overpowered. The point man's 870 shotgun was the topic of a similar discussion, though I felt it worked perfectly. But one thing everyone agreed on was that the assault rifles just didn't have enough stopping power. Given the enthusiasm and broad FPS knowledge of the group, the discussion could have gone on for several more hours. However, Daniel had something else scheduled—a dinner at Medieval Times in Buena Park!

DAY 2: HARA DUNES FTW!

A late night of feasting, 11th-century-style entertainment, and even a mild earthquake didn't seem to phase the group as they took to their stations early in the morning for another long day of multiplayer action. And to my surprise, much of the feedback we provided the day before was implemented in the latest build. While the community members were busy eating and sleeping, the development team worked through the night to make improvements to the game. The first thing we all noticed was the improved effectiveness of the assault rifles. Suddenly these weapons felt just right. In fact, the day before I avoided using the assaulter class entirely due to this issue. But now the assaulter class quickly became my go-to soldier, particularly when trying out a new map or game mode, when I didn't quite know what to expect.

Between rounds and during breaks, the group had time to discuss tactics and take notes.

On this day, we were introduced to a mix of game modes on Basilan Aftermath, Hara Dunes, Sarajevo Stadium, and Tungawan Jungle. Playing Sector Control on Hara Dunes was the highlight of the day for me. This dusty desert-themed map offers great visibility in a compact urban setting, lending itself to intense close-quarters firefights. This is when I discovered the point man's heavy hitters class ability is most effective when firing the weapon on single shot, otherwise the recoil makes it difficult to control the weapon. I also had the chance to experiment with a variety of support actions, including the sniper's Switchblade. This cool weapon performs like a miniature cruise missile, ideal for dive bombing opponents grouped in narrow choke points.

The compact design and cramped alleys quickly made Hara Dunes my favorite map of the day. Sorry MOHW017, but I had to avenge the death of my Fireteam Buddy.

Realizing the benefits of the previous day's discussion, Thad conducted two feedback sessions in the auditorium: one before lunch and another at the end of the day. During these break-out discussions, we were introduced to more developers, including most of the map designers. In both sessions, the discussion focused mostly around the maps and support actions. Beyond providing the developers with feedback, I found these discussions to be extremely enlightening as various members of the group revealed unique tactics they found helpful on each map or when playing with a specific class. The final discussion lasted nearly two hours, after which we retired to the hotel for some much needed down time.

DAY 3: SHOGORE SHENANIGANS

Developers like Thad Sasser were never far away to offer technical assistance and answer our gameplay questions.

After two solid days of gameplay, everybody in the community was now familiar with the daily routine. We'd get into the "lab" early for a few warm-up rounds, have a quick bite to eat for breakfast, and then dive in for some more intense rounds of gameplay. While everyone played their best and tried to win, we were also focused on trying out the different classes and weapons. During the previous day's discussion, several people talked about the demolitions class and the powerful support actions associated with it. I decided to give this class a try, especially where I hadn't fully experimented with its tank stance ability. While I found the demolitions class to be a bit too slow for my taste, I could definitely understand the appeal, especially when I activated the M32 grenade launcher offensive support action during a Sector Control match on Novi Grad Warzone. This grants the class access to a semi-automatic grenade launcher capable of blasting opponents at various ranges. Combined with the tank stance class ability, which enforces the character with a layer of armor, the M32 support action makes the demolition class an absolute killing machine—slow, but very lethal.

A good Fireteam Buddy can make all the difference, as I found out during Team Deathmatch on Shogore Valley. Thanks MOHW002!

Apart from my experimentation with the different classes, we were also introduced to a few new maps, including Al Fara Cliffside and Shogore Valley. Shogore Valley quickly became a favorite of everyone as we played multiple rounds of Team Deathmatch and Hotspot among the ruins of a deserted hillside village. The stone buildings (including an ancient temple) and snow-capped peaks made this map really stand out from the rest. It soon became affectionately known as the *Skyrim* map before the group became familiar with its real name. I enjoyed several good rounds of Team Deathmatch here, working closely with my Fireteam Buddy and teammates to gain the upper hand. This is where I realized how important it is to stay close to your Fireteam Buddy so you can heal and resupply each other—if you run out of ammo, your Fireteam Buddy is the only one who can hand over fresh magazines. Later during Hotspot on Shogore Valley, I experimented with the sniper class's wicked proximity mines while testing the newly balanced G18 automatic pistol.

I admit it. I love the sniper's G18 automatic pistol. However, the weapon's performance was a frequent topic of debate.

As we did the previous day, we broke out of our gameplay sessions for a couple of feedback discussions with Thad and several developers. The information flowed freely once again as the group and developers talked about the day's maps and game modes. By now we each had printouts of all the maps so we could compile our notes and share them directly with the developers. The discussion was aided by the projection of these maps on a large screen, allowing all parties to easily identify potential problem areas. The evening's discussion lasted nearly two hours, after which Daniel rounded us up and took us out to Barney's Beanery is Santa Monica for an evening of drinks, food, and… shuffleboard!

Realizing the benefits of the previous day's discussion, Thad conducted two feedback sessions in the auditorium: one before lunch and another at the end of the day. During these break-out discussions, we were introduced to more developers, including most of the map designers. In both sessions, the discussion focused mostly around the maps and support actions. Beyond providing the developers with feedback, I found these discussions to be extremely enlightening as various members of the group revealed unique tactics they found helpful on each map or when playing with a specific class. The final discussion lasted nearly two hours, after which we retired to the hotel for some much needed down time.

DAY 4: TOURNAMENT FINALE

To my surprise, the late night revelry had little impact on the group, as everyone showed up on time to begin the final day of gameplay. The morning was spent going through some now familiar maps, such as Al Fara Cliffside and Basilan Aftermath. We even played a quick round of Sector Control on Somalia Stronghold, a map and mode most of us were familiar with from the game's multiplayer Alpha. Knowing this was my last day, I spent plenty of time taking notes on the various classes as well as the progression system.

Prior to the tournament, Fireteams were selected and squads were formed.

To my surprise, the late night revelry had little impact on the group, as everyone showed up on time to begin the final day of gameplay. The morning was spent going through some now familiar maps, such as Al Fara Cliffside and Basilan Aftermath. We even played a quick round of Sector Control on Somalia Stronghold, a map and mode most of us were familiar with from the game's multiplayer Alpha. Knowing this was my last day, I spent plenty of time taking notes on the various classes as well as the progression system.

The squads competed against each other in a round of Team Deathmatch to determine the finalists.

Since I had to leave early, I missed the tournament as well as a night out in Hollywood with the other community members, but in the time I spent with this group and the developers I came away with a greater appreciation of what it takes to fine-tune, tweak, and balance a complex game like this. The development team literally works night and day to try and get everything just right before the game ships. Sometimes things work and sometimes they don't. It's a constant back and forth between the developers and play testers, all with the common goal of making the best game possible. In the years I've been doing this I've been to many community and press events, but I've never attended one so lengthy and abundantly insightful as this one. I came away with nearly forty hours of gameplay under my belt as well as the opportunity to meet some very kind and passionate people who truly love what they do. I would like to extend my sincere gratitude to the Danger Close team as well as all the community members who made this event such a memorable one.

KEVIN HENDRICKSON
Director of Product Development

What are some highlights of your professional background?
I have worked at EA and on the *Medal of Honor* franchise for the last 7 years. In 2010, with the formation of Danger Close Games, I became the Director of Product Development. Prior to working at EA, when I was part of a small start-up company called Studio Mythos Inc., we got our first break helping out with some level art on *Medal of Honor: Frontline*, so you could say that my game career has been tied for a long time to EA and the *Medal of Honor* franchise.

What are your main responsibilities for *Medal of Honor Warfighter*? Which do you consider the most challenging and why?
My role of the team is to keep the trains moving on time. I am responsible for the overall schedule, timing, logistics, and execution of the product.
This was a challenging and exciting project as we switched over to the Frostbite 2 engine. It is extremely powerful, and it took some time to learn to harness all its strengths. Now the team is able to move at an extremely fast pace, which is gratifying to see. Another challenge on *Medal of Honor Warfighter* was working with lots of studios within EA. The level of coordination and support from all of them on *Medal of Honor* was impressive. The credits list is pretty epic.

What are your goals for the project and what were some of the challenges?
One of the goals was to add the additional element of real driving to the game in both the Karachi and Dubai levels. In order to achieve this real experience, we needed to use the Frostbite 2 engine that was set up for driving. This required us to switch between the two engines twice in the middle of the single-player campaign and make sure that the player didn't notice the switch. That was extremely challenging and thanks to all our world-class engineers, they pulled it off.

What do you want the player to experience as they play *Medal of Honor Warfighter*?
We really wanted players to be immersed in the wide variety locations, as in this version of *Medal of Honor* we move around the world and have some unique backdrops. Further, we wanted to take players on to the next chapter, carrying on the story of our main characters. The fight didn't end on the top of Takur Ghar after losing their fallen brother Rabbit. Mother, Preacher, and Voodoo continued the fight. With this game, the story is not just about the brotherhood story, but also goes deeper to show the special relationship that Preacher has with his family.

How involved were members of the Special Forces community in writing the missions in the campaign?
They were extremely involved with us through the whole process, not just story elements. It was great and we all felt honored to have them be a part of the *Medal of Honor Warfighter* product.

The campaign takes the player around the globe. How did you decide on which locations and mission types to include in the campaign?
The story of chasing the PETN helped to establish the locations and how Mother, Preacher, Voodoo, and Stump followed the trail around the world through the Cleric's distribution chain.

Was there a challenge in balancing realism and playability in the campaign?
It is a balancing act, but at the end of the day we want to make sure we are making a piece of entertainment that will keep the fans coming back for more.

MEDAL OF HONOR WARFIGHTER

What new features are included in *Medal of Honor Warfighter*?
There are a number of things we wanted to make sure that we brought back from the previous *Medal of Honor* games that fans like, for instance our Peak and Lean, Ammo Mechanic, and refined shooting controls. New to our single-player campaign is our door breach mechanic that unlocks new ways of breaching as the player progresses. Our multiplayer gameplay is an evolution of elements from the last *Medal of Honor*, coupled with new classes, units, gun customization, game modes, Fireteams, and Battlelog—and of course all driven by Frostbite 2.

Is there something in the game of which you are particularly proud?
The visuals, animations, and moments of micro destruction that all come together in a symphony of combat that captures the essence of *Warfighter*.

What do you hope that people will say about the campaign in *Medal of Honor Warfighter*?
Danger Close – Nicely Done.

BEN JONES
Senior Designer

What are some highlights of your professional background?

I was fortunate to be part of the *Day of Defeat* team many years ago, and learned a tremendous amount from that experience, but working on the PS3 game *MAG* from start to finish really pushed my professional career forward by working in Level, Systems, and UI Design.

What are your main responsibilities for *Medal of Honor Warfighter*? Which do you consider the most challenging and why?

Level and Game Type design, along with Systems Integration, were my primary focus on *Warfighter*. Among them, I'd say that integrating our gameplay systems into our environments was the greatest challenge because of their varied nature. On any given day I'd be looking at anything from MAARS Robot movement through the environment to how Blackhawks arrived at their destination.

What are your goals for the project and some of the challenges?

My goal as a senior member of the team was to remove roadblocks for less experienced co-workers so that we could focus on creating the best possible levels for *Warfighter*. The greatest challenge we faced as a team was making levels that catered to each class and their varied abilities.

What are the steps you go through when designing a new multiplayer level, from start to finish?

The first step is to work with the Art Director to create a theme for the level. Then, based off that direction, I'll draw a paper map to outline the gameplay space. Once that's approved, I take the design into FrostEd and transform the paper map into a 3D space, generally with simple block assets. We then test the space extensively and refine gameplay. Once we are satisfied and art resources become available we'll shift into production. A second design pass, and oversight throughout production, helps to push the level forward, and finally when lighting and effects are added the level comes into form.

Do you try to balance a map so that each side has some equality in cover and terrain?

Balance is a central component of our design process, but in order to give the player varied experiences and levels of challenge we must also consider the benefits of asymmetric gameplay. Though the *Team Fortress* classic 2Fort is an excellent design, I'm sure we'd all be quite bored by now if every level took such an approach.

Is there something in your levels of which you are particularly proud?

Combat Mission contains a series of progressive objectives that require a vast play space, and we've broken out each game mode into different sections of that larger map. Though this presented development challenges, the end result is that players get a fresh experience with each game mode, which greatly increases replay value!

What do you hope that people will say about the multiplayer levels in *Medal of Honor Warfighter* that you designed?

That they have long legs. Not in the physical sense, but that they're defined by rich and engaging gameplay opportunities that lead to longevity. You can make an environment that caters to all of your gameplay systems and be successful, but to create a classic you must open your environment to the unexpected and let players tell a different story each day.

Do you have any tips for players on how to get the most out of a multiplayer level? What should they do the first time they play on a new level/map?

Success in multiplayer depends on reducing unknown factors, and to best do this you must remove your environment from the equation. Time spent in any map breeds familiarity, but I'd urge every player to explore early and often. Seek out vantage points and hiding spots to gain an advantage and secure your team's victory.

Which level in *Medal of Honor Warfighter* is your favorite?

The levels in *Warfighter* are some of the best I've ever seen and, though I'm obviously biased, I'd have to say that Hara Dunes is my favorite. The setting is absolutely gorgeous and the Combat Mission objectives, dangerous cliffs, and engaging verticality make for a varied and enjoyable experience!

CHRIS SALAZAR
Art Director

What are some highlights of your professional background?
Developing the visual style of the *Ultimate Spider-Man* game (PS2), and working as Associate Art Director on *Call of Duty: Black Ops*. I hope my roller disco skills played a part in there as well.

What are your main responsibilities for *Medal of Honor Warfighter*? Which do you consider the most challenging and why?
I am responsible for the look and feel of the game as you see it when you play. This trickles down into every art department, from staffing it at the core, to finagling the levels at the end. The most challenging responsibility is the forever push for higher quality. As a studio, we are obsessed and fanatical about quality issues—everyone simply has amazing standards. It's a challenge because time and resources will always nip at that...but we never give up, we never back down. We will never rest.

What are your goals for the project and some of the challenges?
My goals were to bring to life the authenticity that Greg Goodrich impressed upon us, respect the real-world situations each country's people face with terrorism, and create a unique visual identity for *Warfighter*. In a competitive marketplace, I felt these goals would yield imagery and details that would set us apart. The challenge comes with marrying those ideals with gameplay, which has its own needs. The game has to be fun and entertaining throughout, so to retain high-minded ideals while having "fun" is a tough thing to do. I'm proud to say it's a line we kept intact.

Where does research come into play during the design of a game? Does it continue throughout the process?
Research is a cornerstone of the artistic design, and it's not just architecture and surface details. In order for research to have any validity, it must relate to the core fundamentals of the game, whether that is story or gameplay. For instance, a real world, Tier 1-based game requires an understanding of not just how the soldiers function, but the places they operate in, how the people who live there deal with adversity, how far back the roots of terrorism reach, and how we deal with it today. Learning the how and why of the world we live in provides all the visual inspiration ever needed...and it continues through the entire process, right up until the very end. Visuals need to have a strong understanding of the world they live in.

Do you feel the art helps set the tone for a mission?
Absolutely. The story or design might have a loose description handy, but in the end the visual is the only thing that will ever communicate what the mission was really like. Everyone knows the physical and environmental adversity Tier 1 Operators face—"man vs. nature"—but missions in *Warfighter* give us all the chance to experience it for ourselves. The tone for each mission is reflected in the weather, time of day, and architecture styles we chose.

Did you or the team travel to the actual locations for the missions? If so, where?
As the nature of *Warfighter* takes place in so many politically sensitive countries, it was difficult, but we did get the chance to travel to Manila, in the Philippine Islands. Experiencing with your own senses a country that faces so much adversity—natural, political, and economical—is overwhelming. It taught me what the Tier 1 Operators do is of the highest regard. To protect people over the world, and to pay homage to their homelands is an immense privilege. Travelling there gave me a sense of respect that brings tears to my eyes.

Did you also do research on the uniforms and clothing?
The uniforms and clothing in *Warfighter* are the absolute most accurate and highest quality I have ever seen. We were immensely fortunate—not only did we have actual Tier 1 gear at our fingertips, we had the Operators behind it to explain the nuances and features of it all. How it's worn, why, what the different roles one might play have different needs....no fantasy elements at all. We also worked with a fantastic costumer, who helped us physically outfit nearly all of the characters on live models, giving us all the realism and detail one could ask for.

What sources did you use for your information?
The Tier 1 Operators were the single most valuable source of accurate and surprising information we could ever get. They are immensely knowledgeable about the world in a practical way that surpasses expectation. From there we just had to follow their lead, to take the view they have on any research angle we needed.

Is there something in the game of which you are particularly proud?
The scene at the end of the Basilan level, when the boats are lifted by the helicopters. The boat fight was one of the first sequences we put together, and to watch it with the music and FX all playing at the right times, to witness the power and future of the team, was amazing. I could tell then we were capable of great things. I will always be proud of the team for pulling that off.

What do you hope that people will say about multiplayer in *Medal of Honor Warfighter*?
That is was fun! Really MP is all about fun... the visuals are there to help immerse you and carry the experience, and in the end, time spent with your Fireteam Buddy getting the best of everyone is a fantastic sense of satisfaction. We pushed hard to make the environments unique, the characters real, and the destruction tangible. I hope people love to talk about those things.

Any final thoughts?
Medal of Honor Warfighter has been a truly defining experience. It exists in a pantheon, a lineage reaching back to the core of military first-person shooters. To have been a part of that, and to have had it be a time of growth and coming together, will stay with me forever.

[CANADIAN]
JTF2

[SWEDISH]
SO

[BRITISH]
SAS

[US]
SEAL

[US]
OGA

[GERMAN]
KS

[US]
SFOD-D

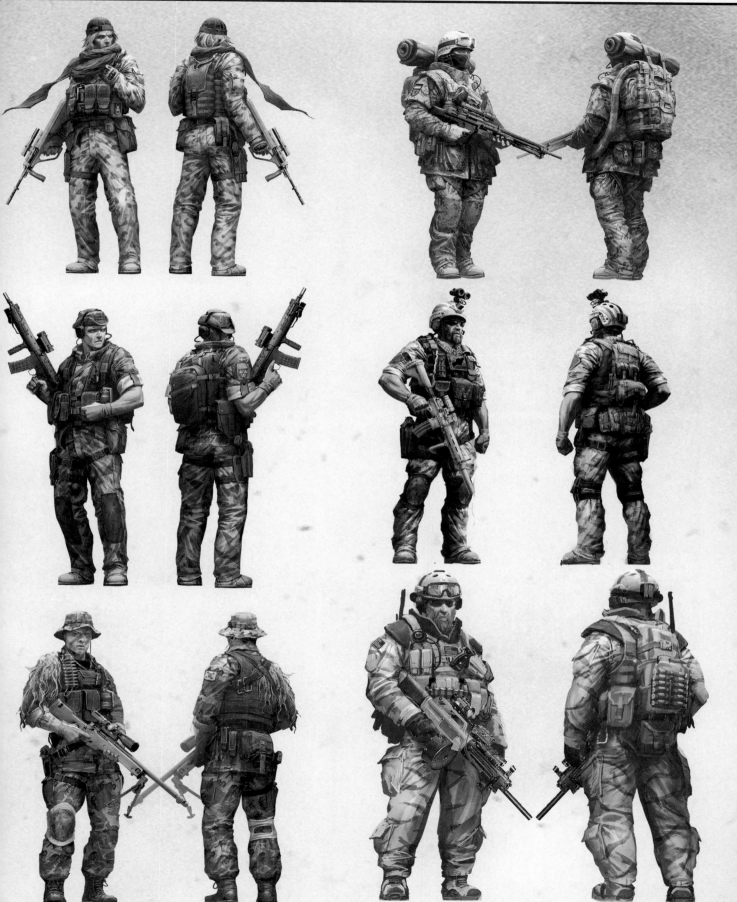

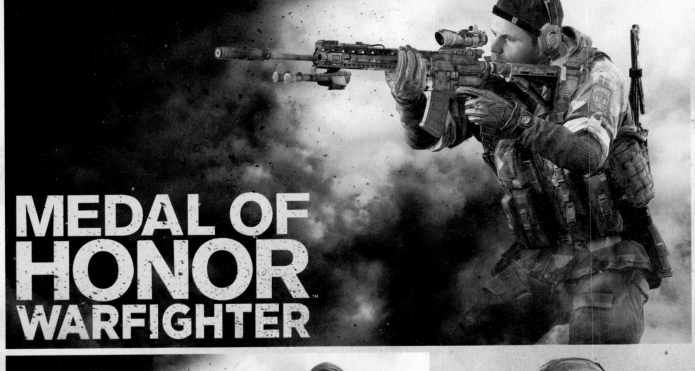

MEDAL OF
HONOR
WARFIGHTER

MEDAL OF
HONOR
WARFIGHTER

MEDAL OF
HONOR
WARFIGHTER

MEDAL OF
HONOR
WARFIGHTER

[N]
F

[SWEDISH]
SO

[CANADIAN]
JTF-2

[BRITISH]
SAS

[US]
SEAL

[US]
OGA

[US]
SFOD-D

"UNINTENDED CONSEQUENCES" 42

"THROUGH THE EYES OF EVIL" 48

"SHORE LEAVE" 53

"HOT PURSUIT" 61

"CHANGING TIDES" 67

"RIP CURRENT" 76

"HAT TRICK" 86

"FINDING FARAZ" 88

SINGLE PLAYER
CAMPAIGN WALKTHROUGH

"Eight Weeks Ago" Mako is on a mission to destroy a specific cargo container about to be loaded on a merchant vessel. Their goal is to enter by stealth plant and detonate the explosives and get out without ever being there. That's the plan. Plans rarely survive first contact with the enemy.

/HJK

[RUSSIAN]
SPETSNAZ
ALFA GROUP

[POLISH]
GROM

[AN]
SK

[SOUTH KOREAN]
UDT/SE

"CONNECT THE DOTS"   96

"HELLO AND DUBAI"   106

"OLD FRIENDS"   114

"BUMP IN THE NIGHT"   123

"SHUT IT DOWN"   134

[AUSTRALIAN]
SASR

UNINTENDED CONSEQUENCES

BRIEFING

**TASK FORCE MAKO
"PREACHER"**
*Karachi, Pakistan
24° 50' N 66° 58' E*

OBJECTIVES

You begin the mission teamed up with "Mother". The two of you must infiltrate a terrorist held port facility and destroy a shipping container with terrorist supplies and weapons inside. Once this is accomplished, advance to the extraction point and egress from the area.

LOADOUT

Primary – M4 with red dot scope/ironsights
Secondary – Silenced Pistol
Frag Grenades – x6

STORY

"Eight Weeks Ago" Mako is on a mission to destroy a specific cargo container about to be loaded on a merchant vessel. Their goal is to enter by stealth plant and detonate the explosives and get out without ever being there. That's the plan. Plans rarely survive first contact with the enemy.

PHONE CALL
PART 1

Our protagonist, Preacher talks with his wife on the phone. Things are not going well in the relationship. But we get a hint that things aren't going well professionally either. There is turmoil in and out of the relationship.

ACHIEVEMENTS

UNEXPECTED CARGO

Complete this first mission to earn this award.

BLOW UP TRUCK

"Mother" and you silently emerge from the water near the port facility. The first part of this mission requires absolute stealth. You are the lead for this first part of the mission with "Mother" there to provide support and help guide you along as needed. Since you don't want the terrorists to know you are in the area, you must use your pistol which has already been fitted with a silencer on the end of the barrel. This is perfect for now since all of your engagements are at very close range. Once you gain control of "Preacher", your character for this mission, move quietly up behind the terrorist sentry. Take aim at the back of the target's head and then squeeze the trigger to take him out with a single, suppressed round. He drops to the ground and no one is the wiser.

TIP

While you are taking aim at the first target, press the aim button. The targeting reticule will disappear and you will be able to aim over your pistol's ironsights. Using the aim button when firing increases the accuracy of your shots. Though it is not necessary to use at such close range, it is a good idea to get into the practice of taking aim before firing your weapon.

LOCATE TARGET VEHICLE

Move out from behind the van and slowly approach the next terrorist sentry. Don't get too close or you may alert him. Take aim at the back of the terrorist's head and pull the trigger. Another shot, another terrorist down—and still the enemy does not know you are in the port facility.

PLANT CHARGE

It is time to move out. A truck is approaching the checkpoint at the entrance to the port area. Move quickly, jumping over a short gate and get in behind the truck. You are carrying the explosives, so plant them on the back of the truck following the on-screen instructions. "Mother" continues to cover you while you complete this task.

ELIMINATE GATEHOUSE GUARD

Once the explosives are set, quickly move to the left and take cover behind the checkpoint structure. A single terrorist sentry is inside. However, don't kill him just yet. He has to open the gate to let the truck through. Wait until the truck is driving past the checkpoint, then take aim at the back of the terrorist's head and take him out with a single, silenced shot before he can turn around and notice "Mother" and you right next to his structure.

DETONATE CHARGE

Once the terrorist at the checkpoint is neutralized, move to the right of the gate and take cover behind a concrete barricade. Wait for the truck to drive farther into the port facility. "Mother" lets you know when it is far enough away for you to safely detonate the explosive. Press the button on the remote detonator in your hand and watch the action as the truck blows up. However, the resulting explosion is much, much larger than what should have resulted from the charge you placed on the truck. Not only is the truck vaporized, but the entire dock area looks like a war zone. Cranes are falling over and containers are falling all over. Your route out of the area is blocked, so you need another way to extract.

GET TO EXTRACTION POINT

After the explosions begin to subside, you automatically switch to your rifle which is equipped with a red dot sight which you can use by holding down the aim button. "Mother" and you now need to get out of dodge and make it to the end of the dock to the new extraction point. Begin to advance along the dock. Watch out for a terrorist who moves out from behind a shipping container. Take aim and drop him. Continue forward a bit and get ready to take down a second terrorist in this area.

TIP

After each engagement of one or two enemies, take the time to reload your rifle. You don't want to come upon a group of hostiles and only have a couple rounds in your magazine. Instead, be prepared for whatever might be around the next corner—or shipping container.

Follow "Mother" as he advances. Be ready to let loose with your rifle on enemies who run out in an effort to get away from the flames. As you advance, try to look for cover to the sides of your path—just in case you come under fire and need some protection.

As you come across a shipping container laying over your path, take caution. There is a terrorist inside a shipping container on the other side. Try to take him out with long range fire before going under the container. An other enemy, this one on fire, comes running out from the left side. Drop him as well. As soon as you advance under the container, you come under fire from an enemy on top of some containers to the left side of the dock. Take aim and kill him before he can hit you.

Once the hostiles in this area are neutralized, follow "Mother" into the open shipping container. He opens the door on the far end and leads you up a series of fallen containers as you make your way to the end of the dock.

ELIMINATE HOSTILE HELICOPTER

As you follow "Mother", the enemy helicopter appears overhead. It is armed with machine guns, so you need to move quickly across the tops of the containers. Stay on "Mother's" six while he advances and makes a series of left turns. As you get to the dock, a couple of terrorists are guarding the area. They are usually focused on "Mother", so take the opportunity to drop the closest one before he opens fire on you.

Once the hostiles are down, get behind cover near "Mother" as the helicopter makes a strafing run with its machine guns. After it moves past you, move out from behind cover and take out the second terrorist on the dock who is blocking your way to the extraction point.

As soon as he is down, follow "Mother" along the catwalk which leads below the dock. Move quickly since the helicopter is headed back for another strafing run. Pick up one of the SMAW (Shoulder-launched Multi-purpose Assault Weapon) lying on the catwalk near the pier. You need to use it to destroy the helicopter.

After grabbing the SMAW, rush under the pier and take cover among the concrete pier pilings. The helicopter makes strafing runs against you. Stay behind cover to avoid getting hit.

Make sure the SMAW is loaded and when the helicopter begins a strafing run, quickly move up the stairs from the catwalk and take a shot at the side of the chopper while it is trying to get "Mother." If you miss, rush back down to the pier and take cover while you reload. Then try the same tactic again. Once you get a hit, the helicopter loses control and begins to spin until it crashes.

As soon as the helicopter is destroyed, rush to the end of the catwalk where the rest of your team is waiting with a Zodiac to extract you. As you leave the scene of the destruction, you can't but wonder what the hell was in that container. What could have caused such a huge explosion?

THROUGH THE EYES OF EVIL

STORY

Somewhere in Yemen, terrorist recruits are being trained for battle. We play as one of the recruits and discover that something big is about to happen. Something global.

TOC X:

A familiar voice sits in front of a makeshift office with LCD screens, satellite phones and a laptop. One voice is clear, Mother. Seems that explosion in the first level has led them to something big. But whatever it is, Mother is no longer in charge of MAKO. And Mako is about to get their feet wet.

BRIEFING

OGA Asset "Argyrus"
Somewhere in Yemen

OBJECTIVES

For this training mission, you assume the role of an undercover OGA (Other Government Agency) assest who has infiltrated a terrorist training facility. Use this opportunity to learn how to control your character during battle as well as experiment with an enemy weapon. You can also learn what you are going to be up against as you fight against these terrorists around the globe.

ACHIEVEMENTS

KNOW THE ENEMY
Finish the terrorist training mission to earn this award.

ON THE CLOCK
Complete the airliner training section in under 18 seconds if you want this award.

LOADOUT
Primary – AKS-74U
Secondary – G23

COMPLETE THE TRAINING

In order to complete this mission, you must go through a terrorist training facility and complete all of the tasks. Here you learn how to use weapons and grenades, take cover and fire around cover, and move around the battlefield. After learning all these skills, you then practice a sample combat situation. Finally, the training ends with a breach against an enemy-occupied room. To get started, walk forward to the door after it opens and continue through a short hall to the next room.

TIP

Most of your rifles or submachine guns have two different firing modes. In semi-automatic, you fire one round for each pull of the trigger. In automatic fire mode, the weapon continues to fire as long as you hold the trigger down until you release the trigger or the weapon runs out of ammo in the currently loaded magazine. Semi-automatic fire is more accurate. However, if you do not get a headshot, you often need to hit an enemy more than once to take him down. When firing in semi-automatic mode, it is usually a good idea to get into the habit of firing two rounds quickly in what operators refer to as a "double tap."

There are three obstacles in this room. The first is a wooden beam with barbed wire wrapped around it. Since you are too tall to walk under it, press the change stance button to drop down into a crouch. Now you can move forward under this first obstacle.

The second obstacle is another wooden beam. However, this one is lower and does not have any wire around it. Hold down the change stance button until your character drops prone. Now crawl forward to get past this low beam.

The final obstacle is a short wall. Since you are prone, you need to get to a standing position. You can either press the jump button or press the change stance button to rise up to a crouch and then again a second time to stand up. In order to get over the wall, move forward towards the wall and as you reach it, press the jump button to hop over the wall. Continue on into the next room for some weapons training.

Advance towards the table next to the shooting range. You begin by learning to fire your rifle. Pull the trigger and try to hit the dummy at the front, center of the shooting range.

Now hold down the aim button. The targeting reticule disappears and you are now looking over the rifle's iron sights. This provides a slightly zoomed-in view of your target, making it easier to hit. You are also more accurate while in iron sights view than while firing from the hip or arm. Try shooting at the closest target again while looking over your iron sights. Press the fire mode button to switch to semi-automatic. Now your rifle shoots only one round each time you pull the trigger. This conserves ammunition and also provides greater accuracy.

While holding down the aim button, press the switch sights button to switch your view to your scope. This button toggles back and forth between iron sights and scope. Most of your rifles give you a choice of two different sight options. One is usually designed for close targets while the other is for targets at longer ranges. While peering through the scope, take aim at the target at the far right corner of the firing range and fire.

Sometimes you need to take out a group of enemies or hostiles who are hiding behind cover. Locate the three targets in the far left corner of the shooting range. Line up your targeting cursor and then hold down the throw grenade button. Aim just above the heads of the targets and release the button to throw the grenade. After it lands near the targets, it detonates and blows up the targets, completing your weapon training.

You can expect to do more training with your rifle, so reload it and then go over to the terrorist in the doorway to the right. Press the action button while next to him and he gives you more ammo to top off your supply.

TIP

During missions, you can always get more ammo by walking up to one of your team members and pressing the action button. It is a good idea to do this before your supply gets too low or you might end up in a firefight without ammo.

Continue into the next room. Here you learn how to fight from behind cover. This time you need to fire at targets on the sides of the room while a terrorist in the middle fires at you. Get behind the barricade in the middle of the room and crouch down by pressing the change stance button. Now move towards one of the sides.

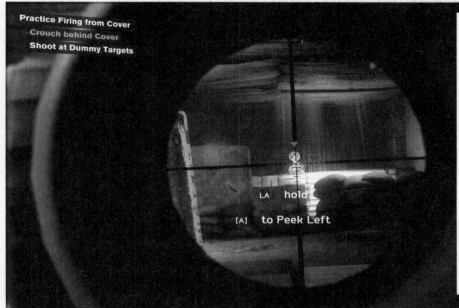

Practice Firing from Cover
Crouch behind Cover
Shoot at Dummy Targets

LA hold
[A] to Peek Left

Hold down the peek and lean button. When you now try to move, your feet stay put and your body leans to the left or right. By moving forward while the peek and lean button is being held down, you cause your character to peek up over an obstacle. (Note: PC players can lean by holding Left Alt plus W,A,S, and D)

While peeking or leaning, your view switches to iron sights or scope, depending what you have selected. You can toggle between the two. Now lean around the edge of the barricade and shoot the target on that side of the room. Move to the other side of the room and take out two targets by leaning in the opposite direction.

Finally return to the first side and shoot at the final target. If you are leaning carefully, the terrorist can't hit you while you are leaning. Once all four targets are hit, the terrorist stops firing and a door on the right side of the room opens. Reload your weapon and move through the doorway.

Continue through a short hall and another room until you come to a room with rows of chairs similar to what one would find in a passenger airliner. As you enter the room, three targets pop up. Quickly take aim with your iron sights mode and hit all three to clear this first area.

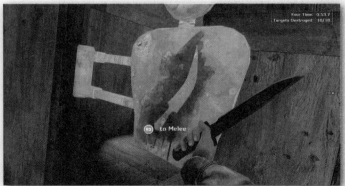

Reload as you advance to the end of the room and continue through a short passage to another room with rows of chairs. As you enter, take out the two targets that pop up on the right. As you advance further into the room, there are two friendly targets. Be careful not to hit them as you fire at the third target behind them, which pops up and then drops back down.

Head up the stairs at the far end of the room as you reload. When you get to the top, turn around and advance into another room. Shoot the four moving targets while avoiding the friendly targets, then jump over the boxes in the aisles between the seats to get through this area. Note: If you finish this section in less than 18 seconds you earn the On The Clock achievement.

As you approach the doorway to the next room, a metal target swings out in front of you. Quickly press the melee button to swing your knife at the target and knock it out of your way. During a mission, when an enemy gets in very close, it is quicker to use your melee weapon than to bring up your weapon to fire.

Continue on into the next area and fire at the three targets that pop as you enter. Again, watch out for friendly targets in this area.

After clearing out this last airline kill room, advance to the next room where a fellow terrorist is waiting for you.

It is now time to learn how to breach a locked door when there are enemies on the other side. Move up to the door and press the action button to begin the breaching process. You move to one side of the door while the terrorist moves to the other side. A breaching menu appears. Since most of the breaching methods are locked for now, select kick.

The terrorist kicks in the door and throws in a flashbang to stun the targets in the room. As soon as it detonates, move through the doorway.

Since the enemies inside a breached room are momentarily stunned, time seems to move slowly, allowing you to quickly get headshots on the two targets inside the room.

Once the room is cleared, the training is completed. You now have a choice. If you feel like you could use some additional practice before taking on real missions, head through the door on the left. Otherwise, go through the door on the right to continue to the next mission.

SHORE LEAVE
BRIEFING

**TASK FORCE MAKO
"STUMP"**
Mogadishu, Somalia
2° 1' N – 45° 21' E

OBJECTIVES

During this mission, you play as "Stump". You are part of a four-man team tasked with landing on the coast at the outskirts of Mogadishu and advancing into the city to the U.S. Marines of Task Force Grizzly. "Voodoo" is the other operator on your team and Sgt. Wright and Sgt. Xaysana round out the team. Together you are assaulting the camp of the heavily armed and highly trained Al-Shabaab pirates.

STORY

"One Week Ago" A splintered TF Mako is needed in "pirate town." Mako will be assisted by the US Marines' Task Force Grizzly to bring down the hammer with a full assault on the whole pirate stronghold to put them permanently out of business.

PHONE CALL PART 2

We cut back to Preacher and his wife, Lena on the phone. They are apart and agree to meet to talk. She is at her parents place in Madrid with Bella, their daughter.

MADRID TRAIN STATION

We fade out and next see Preacher walking through a Madrid train station. As he waits for his wife and daughter, he recognizes a face in the window of their arriving train. He races towards the train. A large explosion rocks the station, as we flash to white.

MISSION MAP

INSERTION

B – Breach

ACHIEVEMENTS

HIT THE BEACH
Complete this mission in Somalia to earn this award.

LEFTOVER LEAD
9 Complete the sniping section in this mission without missing a shot to get this achievement.

LOADOUT

Primary – HK416
Optics/Accessories – Aimpoint Micro T-1; Aimpoint 3x Magnifier; Magpul MBUS; HK Vertical Foregrip
Sidearm – HK45 Compact
Special – McMillan TAC-300
Optics/Accessories – Bi-pod; US Optics ST-10

CLEAR THE BEACH

FIND COVER AT THE SEA WALL

Your team is dropped off in shallow water a distance from the beach. While there are some rocks near your drop-off point, rush forward ahead of your team and take cover behind the first wooden crate. Drop down to a crouch so you have protection against fire coming from the building on the beach.

In addition to the red dot sight, your M4 is also equipped with a scope that magnifies the image of the red dot sight. Your first task is to provide covering fire for your team and clear out the enemy between you and the building. Hold down the aim button and then press the switch sights button to move the scope into position so you can engage enemies at long range.

Now either lean around the side of the crate or peek over it and begin engaging hostiles. There are some behind crates near the beach, so focus on them first. They often fire and then duck behind their crates. Wait for them to pop back up to fire and neutralize them. Clear out all of the hostiles on the beach. You can even begin firing at enemies up by the building.

After you have taken out most of the enemies from your first cover spot, it is time to advance. Sprint to the next wooden crate and crouch down behind it. Continue picking off enemies while leaning around or peeking over the crate. Watch for a machine gunner in the window above the door to the building. Neutralize him before he can inflict a lot of damage on you.

After you have cleared out most of the hostiles around the building, sprint forward to the concrete sea wall at the edge of the beach. Since you are closer to the enemy, you may want to switch your sights again so you are just using the red dot sight and not the scope as well. Be sure to stay low behind the sea wall and peek or lean to fire. Pull back behind cover when you need to reload or start taking enemy fire.

GET TO COVER INSIDE THE BUILDING

Neutralize as many hostiles as possible, then sprint up the stairs leading to the building and drop behind the concrete wall at the top of the stairs. Some terrorists charge you while others fire at you from the second floor of the building. Eliminate them all as your team catches up to you.

TIP

After each engagement of one or two enemies, take the time to reload your rifle. You don't want to come upon a group of hostiles and only have a couple rounds in your magazine. Instead, be prepared for whatever might be around the next corner—or shipping container.

As your team gets to the area in front of the building, you come under fire from a sniper in a building somewhere to your left. He is too far away to engage, so quickly clear out the remaining enemies between you and the building, and then rush into the building for cover from the sniper fire.

BREACH AND CLEAR

TIP

You can unlock new breaching methods by successfully killing enemies on the other side of the door with headshots during a breach.

Once inside the building, head up the stairs along with your team. This is a good time to get some ammo from a teammate so you are ready for the next series of engagements.

At the top of the stairs, stack up on the door with "Voodoo". Order him to breach the door using any of the techniques that you may have unlocked. Make sure your weapon is fully loaded and that the red dot sight is selected rather than the scope.

As soon as "Voodoo" throws in the flashbang and it detonates, rush into the room. There are four hostiles inside and you have a few seconds to take them all out while they are still stunned. The meter at the bottom of the screen keeps track of each enemy. Your goal is to kill as many of them as possible with headshots so you can unlock new breaching techniques. Take out the terrorist right in the middle as you enter, then the terrorist to his left. Two more enter the room—one at the center rear and one to the right. Quickly dispatch them to finish clearing the room.

USE THE LTLM

Don't hang out in this room or you'll get hit by the sniper who fires through the openings. Instead, follow "Voodoo" into the next room where there is some cover.

It is time to take out that sniper. Since he is in good cover, the best way to do the job is to take down the building in which he is hiding. Press the LTLM button to use your Laser Target Locator Module. This consists of a pair of high-tech binoculars with a laser designator built in. Aim at the sniper's position in the building and hold the trigger to lock on to the target. This lets your air support know where to attack. In a matter of seconds, the building is a big pile of rubble.

GET TO THE OP

As soon as the dust settles, move out along with your team. Move across the rubble towards the building the air support just attacked. Make your way up a ramp created by a fallen wall and enter the building.

EXPLORE THE BUILDING

As your team arrives at the building, drop down through a hole in the floor in order to continue exploring.

Due to the fact that the building is unstable following the air attack, your team is going to send a remotely operated vehicle through the rubble. You are tasked with controlling the vehicle. This "bot" has a flashlight as well as both a machine gun and grenade launcher. Not only can you use the bot to find the enemy, you can also engage and neutralize them as well. Drive through the hole in the wall and look for terrorists. They are all carrying flashlights so they can see in the dark. Keep your light off for now so they don't detect the bot. Zoom in the view and kill the first tango who walks by from left to right. Another appears from the right. Now that they know the bot is in the building, they try to destroy it by throwing grenades at it. Shoot first before they can attack.

Turn the bot to the right and continue driving through the rubble. Watch out for more hostiles moving in the area. Once they are cleared out, it appears that rubble blocks your path. Activate the flashlight and find a hole in the wall to the right. It is just large enough for you to drive the bot through to the other side.

Drive down a ramp of rubble into another area. Use the flashlight to find a way through the rubble and continue to a hole in the wall that leads outside of the building. Gun down the terrorist running ahead of you towards a group of American soldiers, then continue driving towards the soldiers.

TIP

Watch for the badges that appear over the heads of friendly troops. In the heat of battle, it can get quite confusing and you don't want to fire on friendlies.

The soldiers are coming under enemy fire from the building across the plaza from them. Switch to the grenade launcher and start firing at the enemy positions in the building. Your job is to provide fire support for the soldiers.

Drive around the vehicle that the soldiers are using for cover and start firing away. Eliminate any hostiles on the ground and then continue hammering the building. Not only are you providing fire support, you are also drawing the enemy fire away from the soldiers. Keep shooting until the bot is finally destroyed.

The bot has done its job, so now follow your team through the rubble of the building that the bot has already cleared. Keep an eye open for hostiles who might still be in the building. Continue to a locked door and stack up on it with your team. Select a breach tactic and then get ready. There are four enemies inside the room. Try for four headshots to unlock some more breaching tactics. Use the interface at the bottom of the screen to help you locate where the hostiles are located in the room. The icon for the currently selected target highlights, letting you know the position of that target in relation to the other three.

As you are clearing out the room, you begin taking fire from the building across the street. Some of the hostiles have RPGs, so don't stand too close to the wall. Instead, take cover behind wooden crates located away from the windows.

Use the scope on your rifle and start picking off terrorists as they appear and shoot at you. Try to prioritize your targets, focusing on RPG and machine gun enemies first since they present the biggest threat to you and your team. Keep up the firing until no more hostiles are firing at you.

"Voodoo" knocks open a door when the firefight is done. Head through the door and drop down to the ground level. Quickly take cover behind a wall inside the building. A terrorist technical, a pick-up truck with a machine gun mounted in the bed, drives by and opens fire. If you are not careful, it can easily kill you.

You can't take out the technical from your position without getting killed. Instead, you need to flank it while your team keeps it occupied. Start off by rushing across the street and taking cover behind a concrete block. Then jump over the rubble to get off of the street and into the building. Advance carefully through the building, neutralizing enemies as you go. If they are hiding behind cover, throw a grenade and then be ready to shoot at them as they move to avoid the grenade blast.

Advance through the building, killing hostiles as they pop out at you to attack. Also fire through the windows to pick off targets out in the street. If you don't they will fire at you from your flank—which can be a bad thing when you are fighting against enemies directly ahead of you.

Get to the end of the building and you have a perfect view of the technical machine gunner. While he is focused on part of your team down the street, you can take a flanking shot and kill him, allowing the rest of your team to advance up the street. Watch out for other enemies out in the street. Kill them as well.

Head up the nearby stairs to the top so you can provide fire support for your team. Take cover near the window and pick off enemies on the upper floors of the building across the street. Listen to your team. They call out targets to you. Listen for them to tell you about an RPG soldier. He appears on the rooftop above the stairs. Kill him quickly before he can fire his RPG at you or the team. Continue firing at the hostiles on the buildings until they move away from the fight.

Head back down the stairs and follow your team across the street. This is a great time to get some more ammo from a teammate. By now, you are probably getting low and still have more fighting ahead. Follow the team through a building and then up a flight of stairs up to a road.

When you reach the top of the stairs, another technical comes racing down the street. Don't waste time trying to shoot the gunner. He is protected by armor plating. Instead, rush forward and take cover behind the concrete barricade. Then throw a grenade at the technical to silence that machine gun.

Cross the street and stack up with your team on the door. Select a breach tactic and then rush inside as soon as the door is opened. Watch for a hostile to drop down right in front of you from an upper floor. Wait until his feet hit the ground to ensure you get a headshot rather than hitting his body. After all four enemies are dead, follow "Voodoo" up the stairs to the rooftop. Continue across to another room and then climb some more stairs to an upper room.

The buildings across the street from your position are crawling with hostiles. It is going to take air support to clear those buildings. However, several of the enemies are armed with RPGs or machine guns, which represent a threat to your helicopter gunships. It is up to you to clear the way for the choppers. "Voodoo" sets up a table and acts as a spotter while you get ready with your sniper rifle.

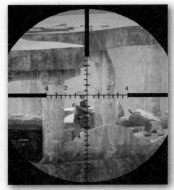

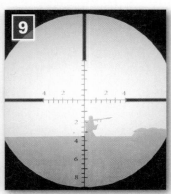

The hostiles you must neutralize have targeting arrows over them. Zoom in with the rifle's scope and start picking them off. Go for the RPG soldiers first. Since you are firing at long range, aim a notch or two above the target to take into account the drop of your bullet as it travels the distance from your rifle to the target.

Get all of the RPGs before they start shooting at you. Then, once you have all the assigned targets neutralized, start picking off any other hostiles on the buildings.

"Voodoo" gives the gunships the all clear after you kill the RPG soldiers. However, after the first choppers arrive on the scene, a couple more RPG soldiers appear on the tower on the right side of the building. Quickly target and neutralize both before they can shoot down your air support.

After the final RPG soldiers are eliminated, just sit back and watch the gunships come in and wipe out the rest of the hostiles for a satisfying end to the mission.

HOT PURSUIT

BRIEFING

TASK FORCE MAKO
"PREACHER"
Karachi, Pakistan
24° 49' 31" N 66° 58' 29" E

STORY

"Eight Weeks Ago" Preacher and Mother return to the scene of the explosion in the first level. The plan is simple: indentify whoever shows up to find out why their container failed to reach its destination and follow them. Unfortunately, when the contact shows up, he is shot on sight. Overhead surveillance shows a vehicle leaving the area, this shooter holds the key to what or who is behind that shipment. Preacher pursues the vehicle through the crowded streets and muddy slums of Karachi. But will he get back to Mother at the extraction point?

HOSPITAL PART 1

Back at the Hospital, we learn that Preacher survived the train station blast, and that Lena and Bella thankfully missed their train and were spared as well. Mother is there too and has something to tell him about these attacks.

MISSION MAP

OBJECTIVES

Shortly after the mission to destroy the shipping container at the port, Task Force Mako has returned to Karachi to find out who was shipping the explosives. During this mission, you play as "Preacher". "Mother" feeds you information from a UAV drone flying over the city. Instead of using rifles and grenades for this mission, you are driving a SUV. The target you are observing during the stakeout is killed by a member of a terrorist cell. Now you have to chase him down to find out why he killed your target and who is behind the hit—and the explosives.

ACHIEVEMENTS

PIT AND PIN

Crash into the enemy car in order to earn this achievement/trophy.

VENDER BENDER

Destroy 90 market stalls to earn this award.

CHASE THE TARGET

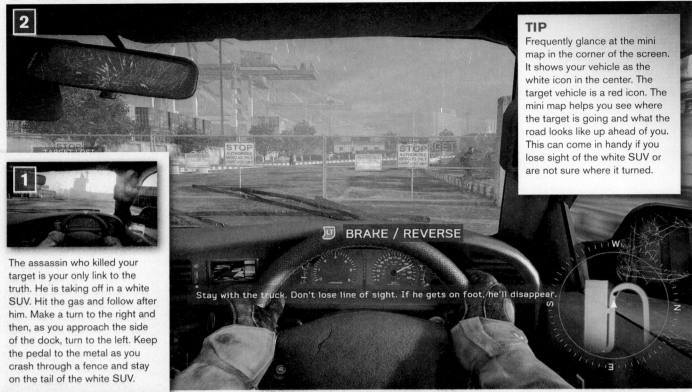

TIP

Frequently glance at the mini map in the corner of the screen. It shows your vehicle as the white icon in the center. The target vehicle is a red icon. The mini map helps you see where the target is going and what the road looks like up ahead of you. This can come in handy if you lose sight of the white SUV or are not sure where it turned.

LT BRAKE / REVERSE

Stay with the truck. Don't lose line of sight. If he gets on foot, he'll disappear.

1

The assassin who killed your target is your only link to the truth. He is taking off in a white SUV. Hit the gas and follow after him. Make a turn to the right and then, as you approach the side of the dock, turn to the left. Keep the pedal to the metal as you crash through a fence and stay on the tail of the white SUV.

The white SUV follows the road around in a 180-degree right turn. Keep the throttle down and you should have no trouble making this wide turn. At the first intersection, your target takes a left turn. If necessary, tap the brakes a bit to stay in the turn. However, don't let up on the gas.

The road up ahead is blocked by trucks, so follow your target on a side road leading through an oil refinery. This side road has a few easy turns before you need to make a tight right turn back onto the main road.

Shortly after driving along the main road, the white SUV takes a left turn into another refinery area. This has some right turns here, so be ready to tap the brakes right before entering the turn. Avoid running into something solid, such as a building. This brings your vehicle to a complete stop, forcing you to reverse the vehicle and allowing the target to get away.

After exiting the refinery area, you must drive through an urban area. Watch out for a locomotive coming from the left. Get across the tracks before this train blocks your path. Make a right turn after the tracks and then follow the white SUV through some narrow streets before making a left turn onto a main road.

Dodge the traffic on the main road. Remember that in Pakistan, traffic drives on the left instead of the right. This is a chance to make up some distance and get in closer to your target. Watch for a side street on the mini map off to the left and be ready to follow the SUV as it makes the left turn to try to lose you.

The side street is little more than an alley with some 90-degree turns in both directions. Tap the brakes as you go around some of these turns to avoid smacking into a building. Don't worry about crashing through objects in the middle of the alley. There is a tight spot in the alley after a bit of a straightaway. Be sure to line up your vehicle to make it through the gap in between buildings.

GET TO EXTRACTION POINT

As you get to the end of the alley, make a right onto another main street. There is a lot of traffic here, so you need to look for gaps and openings to drive through. You may even need to push other cars out of your way. As the road clears a bit, you can even drive on the sidewalk to get around vehicles so you don't get too far behind your target.

After driving a good stretch along the main road, the white SUV takes a left turn followed by another left turn. Keep your speed up and cut across the sidewalks so you can take the turns faster than if you stayed on the roads. Follow your target through a right turn and then along a road that curves to the left.

In an effort to try to lose you, the SUV makes a right turn and crashes through a street market. Follow him through the stalls and line up your vehicle to drive through narrow openings in a couple of buildings so you don't wreck. Continue through more of the market and then turn right onto another road.

Where the road comes to a fork, stay to the right and get ready for a tight turn to the right followed by an even tighter turn to the left. Slow down a bit as you drive through these alleys. This is one of the tougher spots of the mission since there are a lot of places you can crash into the corner of a building and let the target get away. This is where keeping one eye on the mini map can really help you prepare for upcoming turns.

The SUV leads you out of the alleys and across an open field before rejoining a main road. Watch out for oncoming traffic and cut corners by driving across sidewalks to save time and maintain your speed.

When the main road makes a turn to the left at an intersection, your way is blocked by trucks and busses. Drive past the truck and turn left down an alley that runs parallel to the road. Slow down a bit so you can make this tight turn and a couple more before returning to the main road.

CHASE THE TARGET

TIP

There are several spots where it is easy to lose the white SUV. If that happens, you start at the last checkpoint. Learn from your mistakes. Some of the turns are tough to see until you are right on them and it can be too late to alter your course. When you try again, you will have an easier time seeing where to turn and making the turn in time.

At the end of the alley and its tight turns, make a right onto a main road. At the first intersection, follow the SUV to the right, followed by an immediate left. Cut across a parking area rather than turning at the intersection to avoid traffic. Then make a left at the roundabout, careful not to run into the structure in the middle of the road.

After a short distance, the white SUV turns left off of the main road and then takes an immediate right into a narrow alley. This is a tough turn. You have a van on your right side making the turn as well and must avoid running into a parked truck blocking the road. If you overcorrect on either turn, you crash into either the truck or a building and end up losing your target. Keep your speed up right until you need to cut into the alley. Then tap the brakes to slow your vehicle down a bit so you can make the turns successfully.

Turn right at the next intersection and then be ready to follow the white SUV in a left turn into the slums. It is important to stay close to the SUV since it is easy to lose sight of it in the slums—even if it is not that far in front of you. However, don't try to gun it through these narrow alleys. Tap the brakes before entering turns so you don't slide into a building and crash.

The SUV crashes through a building and leaves a fireball in its path. Don't try to follow it through the rubble. Instead, steer to the right and drive across a bridge to a road that runs parallel to the SUV's road. Don't worry, he has to cross over to your side eventually. Use this straight stretch of road without any traffic to catch up to your target.

Once you get back behind the white SUV, you can stay in close since your vehicle can handle the turns in the slums a bit faster than the target. On the straightaways get right in behind the SUV and stay in tight.

Then when you come to a turn and the white SUV has to take it wide, cut inside the turn and crash into the side of the SUV to take it out.

Once the SUV slides to a stop, "Preacher" exits from his vehicle, walks over to the white SUV, and gets the driver's cell phone. This should provide some good intel and hopefully lead you to the terrorist leaders.

MISSION MAP

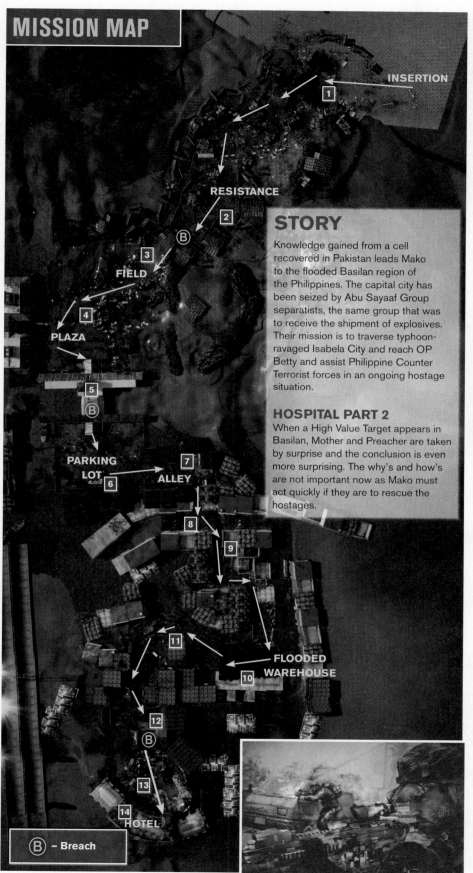

1

INSERTION

RESISTANCE

2

Ⓑ

3

FIELD

4

PLAZA

5

Ⓑ

PARKING
LOT

6

7

ALLEY

8

9

11

FLOODED
WAREHOUSE

10

12

Ⓑ

13

14

HOTEL

Ⓑ – Breach

STORY

Knowledge gained from a cell recovered in Pakistan leads Mako to the flooded Basilan region of the Philippines. The capital city has been seized by Abu Sayaaf Group separatists, the same group that was to receive the shipment of explosives. Their mission is to traverse typhoon-ravaged Isabela City and reach OP Betty and assist Philippine Counter Terrorist forces in an ongoing hostage situation.

HOSPITAL PART 2

When a High Value Target appears in Basilan, Mother and Preacher are taken by surprise and the conclusion is even more surprising. The why's and how's are not important now as Mako must act quickly if they are to rescue the hostages.

CHANGING TIDES
BRIEFING

**TASK FORCE MAKO
"PREACHER"**
*Near Isabela City, Philippines
6° 44' N 121° 58' E*

OBJECTIVES

While following the P.E.T.N. lead to the Philippines, Task Force Mako must now contend with ASG (Abu Sayyaf Group) terrorists who have taken hostages. This mission you play as "Preacher". You are teamed up with "Mother". The two of you must fight your way through the ASG and get to the Isabela Hotel where the terrorists are holding several people hostage. A monsoon has hit the area and the heavy rain has caused flooding. Use the storm to cover the noise of your attacks as you try to keep things stealthy for as long as possible.

LOADOUT

Primary – LaRue OBR 5.56
Secondary – HK MP7–Surefire suppressor
Frag Grenades – x6

ACHIEVEMENTS

RAIN OF TERROR
Complete this mission to earn this reward.

DOUBLE HEADER
To get this award, kill two enemies with a single bullet in this mission.

GET TO THE ISABELLA HOTEL

1

FOLLOW

Press to Melee

Clean work. Clear.

TF MAKO -"PREACHER"
NEAR ISABELA CITY, PHILIPPINES
6°42' N 121°58' E - INSPIRED BY ACTUAL EVENTS

≡ A 031/180

M67 **4**

ELIMINATE ANY RESISTANCE

Your two-man team has infiltrated an ASG-occupied village on the outskirts of Isabela City. It is important to maintain stealth for as long as possible. When the mission begins, you are directly behind an enemy. Press the melee button to silently kill the target with your tomahawk.

≡ A 000/180

Follow "Mother" to one of the shacks. While he hangs back to cover you, crouch down and move quietly through the shack towards the enemy standing in the doorway with his back to you. Come up behind him and kill him with a melee attack. If he sees you before you are close enough for a melee attack, quickly shoot him before he can raise an alarm.

Exit the shack and advance along with "Mother" towards another shack. You can't get in close enough to this hostile for a melee attack, so take careful aim and kill him with a headshot.

031/178

Take him out.

Now follow "Mother" as he rushes forward towards another shack. Drop prone and crawl beneath the shack's floor. "Mother" kills one of the hostiles inside the shack. However, one walks out of the shack. Use your rifle to kill the hostile before he can get to the cover of the next shack.

"Mother" leads you to another shack. Crouch down and enter it. There is a single enemy inside. Move in quietly and shoot him before he can open fire. Then exit the shack and move across a flooded open area.

After moving through a gap in a damaged wall, watch for a couple hostiles patrolling near a structure. Take aim and wait for them to move away from their cover. If you time it just right, you can kill both at the same time with a single shot. This is the best change to get the Double Header achievement/trophy.

Move through the structure and take cover behind a low wall. Three terrorists are talking out in the open. Take aim and make sure your rifle is set for automatic fire. Line up a shot so two of the enemies are one behind the other. This lets you kill both with a short burst. Then take out the third terrorist with a second burst. Once they are down, the resistance in the village is completely eliminated.

BREACH AND CLEAR

Move to a wooden door indicated by a target icon and select a type of breach you want to perform. Make sure your rifle is set for iron sights. The scope does not work well in this type of engagement. As soon as the door is breached, go after the four hostiles inside. Start on the left side and work your way to the right.

CLEAR THE FIELD

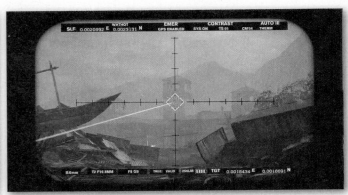

Exit the room and follow "Mother" through an area of destroyed shacks and rubble. Ahead is a single sentry standing on a beached boat. Take cover behind some rubble and kill him with a carefully aimed headshot.

Stay put for now. There are several more hostiles on the building up ahead. Take out your LTLM and target the building for an air strike to clear out the enemies that could cause a lot of trouble for your team as you advance.

TIP

Since you have enemies coming at you from more than one direction, it is important to listen to "Mother". He calls out the location of enemies in the area and often even the range from you. He uses a clock reference to help you know where the enemies are. For example, 12 o'clock is directly in front of you, 2 o'clock is ahead and to the right, and 6 o'clock is directly behind you. Pay attention to "Mother's" instructions. They can save your life.

The enemy knows you are here now, so no more need to stay quiet. Rush forward along with "Mother" towards the building that just got hit. Take cover before you get to the plaza with the planter boxes and open fire on enemies that come to attack you. There are a lot of enemies in this area, so it is vital that you stay behind cover and peek or lean to take shots at them.

Move forward and take cover behind the planters. In the twilight, it's difficult to see the enemies. However, several are using flashlights to find you. Therefore, locate the flashlights and fire at them to kill the terrorists holding the lights. It is important to stay behind or near cover. If you start taking hits, get low and behind cover.

After clearing out any enemies in the planter area, advance cautiously towards another area of planters at the far end of the plaza. As you move, more hostiles appear from between buildings up ahead and to the right. Get behind cover and then open fire. Next, turn to the left and watch for more hostiles coming from that direction. Move to cover that protects you from that direction. Also watch out for grenades. The terrorists throw them to try to flush you out. As you advance, always make sure you have a fall-back position to which you can return if a grenade gets lobbed in your direction.

Stay near "Mother" during the firefight in the plaza. You can get more ammo from him since you'll use quite a bit clearing out the enemies. As soon as all hostiles have been eliminated, follow "Mother" to a building.

Once inside the building, go to the double wooden doors and breach them. There are four hostiles inside. Start off by killing the enemies on the left side, because they are more likely to fire at you first. Then work your way to the right where the enemies dove away from the flashbang. Once the room is clear, follow "Mother" out the far door and back into the storm.

CLEAR A PATH TO THE HOTEL

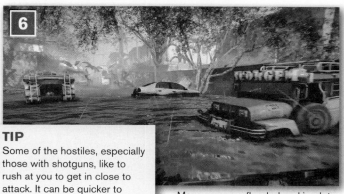

TIP

Some of the hostiles, especially those with shotguns, like to rush at you to get in close to attack. It can be quicker to move in for a melee attack than to aim your assault rifle and fire. This works well while an enemy is pumping a shotgun before he can fire again.

Move across a flooded parking lot with cars and jeepneys to an alley on the other side. There are no enemies in the parking lot, but use caution as you approach the alley.

As you get to the alley, kill the hostile patrolling the area before he sees you and can run away or return fire. Then quickly find some cover. There are lots of enemies in the alley or the small yards to either side. Some of the terrorists carry flashlights, so target the lights if you can't see the person. If necessary, back out of the alley and take cover by the gates.

In addition to the hostiles in the alley, watch for enemies up on the balconies overlooking the alley. Take them out because they can fire down on you while you are focused on the terrorists at ground level. One of the enemies on a balcony has an RPG, so be sure to take him out as soon as you see him or he can be deadly to your team.

The alley is a kill zone with terrorists around every corner waiting for you. Not only do you need to watch out for hostiles ahead of you, but also from the yards on the other side of the alley. Be sure to lean around cover before exposing your entire body and moving. The enemies also jump over gaps in the walls and are not afraid to charge you, so be ready with a melee attack if they get in too close.

Once all of the enemies in the alley are dead, follow "Mother" to the end and go through a gate. Continue towards a flooded street. An upside-down bus floats in front of you. Move inside via the front door, continue through the length of the bus, and emerge out the back door. Be ready to fire at a hostile on the other side of the street who is waiting to ambush you.

There are several hostiles down the street taking cover behind walls and cars. Fire at them, but be ready to move when they start throwing grenades. Advance down the right side of the road where you can find more cover and have a good chance of flanking the enemy. Once they are eliminated, leave the street and turn down a short alley leading to the right.

Take cover at the end of the short alley and wait for the enemy to appear. Target the machine gunner on the top deck directly ahead of you. Stay back and pick off enemies while "Mother" advances. Provide covering fire for your teammate. Don't rush into the fight yourself or you'll be rushed by enemies and overwhelmed. Thin out the opposition first.

TIP

Pay attention to your ammo. It is easy to run out in the close quarters combat in the alley. If you run out while still engaged, quickly switch to your pistol and open fire. You can draw your pistol a lot faster than reload your rifle.

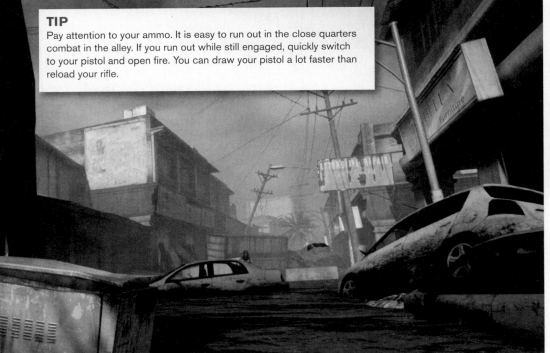

Once it seems clear, rush forward to some cover and get ready for more fighting. Hostiles seem to appear from nowhere. Shoot at them when they expose themselves. Don't forget you have frag grenades. When there are several enemies behind cover, a well-thrown grenade can do wonders. Just watch out for grenades thrown at you as well.

When "Mother" starts advancing to the end of the area, and then turns to the left, begin following him. Stay back so you can provide covering fire and engage hostiles trying to flank your teammate.

Once the area is finally clear, follow "Mother" through the flooded alleys until you see some more enemies up ahead. Stay back while your teammate begins the engagement and fire at those hostiles that charge "Mother" or yourself.

Advance into a flooded warehouse area and find cover. Several hostiles begin attacking from the other side of the area. Watch for flashlights and muzzle flashes as well as grenades. Lean around or peek over cover as you engage each of the enemies one at a time.

Clear the left side of the area and then rush across. Now you can begin advancing down the left side while "Mother" stays on the right. This allows your team to catch the enemy in a crossfire and forces them to attack one of you while allowing the other to get in shots. Use the concrete supports for cover and clear out all the enemies you can see before rushing forward to the next support.

Clear out the area at the end of the warehouse as well as any enemies on the buildings, then follow "Mother" out into the street. Keep going around to the right side so you have cover as you approach more hostiles.

As you get to the corner, be ready for a fight. Terrorists come at you from the street and fire at you from upper floors of the buildings on both sides of the street. If necessary, fall back so you are not taking fire from more than one direction, then work your way forward. Start off by getting those enemies up on the building to the right and then those on the left side. The key is to keep some type of cover between you and all of the enemies.

As you clear out the hostiles in the buildings, watch out for an RPG soldier on a rooftop. The first you know he is there is usually after his first shot. He is now your priority target. Kill him and then continue clearing out other enemies.

Now begin to cautiously advance down the flooded road between the buildings. Watch for enemies to rush towards you. Take shots and then duck behind cover. Clear out these enemies before continuing on.

Move forward towards the break in the brick wall. As you do, more enemies come down the stairs ahead of you. Try to gun them down as they are on the stairs and before they start attacking you. If necessary, pull back down the road and take cover behind buildings, since you can be quite exposed out in the road.

BREACH AND CLEAR

Voodoo, Mother.

Kill all the enemies, then head up the stairs along with "Mother". Stack up on the door and give the order to breach. However, as you rush into the room, there is nobody there. Instead, the ceiling collapses—just missing falling down on you.

The Hotel Isabela is directly ahead. Follow "Mother" down the ramp of rubble to the ground below.

GET TO THE ROOF

We just put down about three dozen ASG fighters. They're trained and know the area, so...

Advance across the area behind the Isabela Hotel. There are no hostiles in this area, so just stay with "Mother" as he contacts other members of your Task Force. Once you get to the hotel, move up several flights of stairs that lead to the roof.

Good kill. Let's get eyes on the capitol.

When you get to the top of the stairs, wait up for "Mother" and then move through the doors out onto the roof. Advance across the roof towards a high point behind the hotel's sign. Here the two of you can set up an observation post to put eyes on the capitol building where the terrorists are holding several people hostage. Observations from "Mother" and "Preacher" will be important in determining the next course of action.

RIP CURRENT

BRIEFING

TASK FORCE MAKO
"PREACHER"
Near Isabela City, Philippines
6° 42' N 121° 58' E

OBJECTIVES

This is the continuation of the previous mission. As "Preacher", you are still with "Mother" and watching the terrorists who are holding the hostages in the capitol building. After a bad call by the local authorities forces an emergency assault on the ASG-held capitol building, Task Force Mako must act quickly if the hostages are to be saved. The Philippine Army is sending in some troops to help you complete this objective.

ACHIEVEMENTS

MONSOON LAGOON

Finish this mission to earn this award.

RELEASE THE KRAKEN!

During the exfiltration in the boat, kill 25 enemies to earn this award.

LOADOUT

Primary – LaRue OBR 5.56
Secondary – HK MP7–Surefire suppressor
Frag Grenades – x6

MISSION MAP

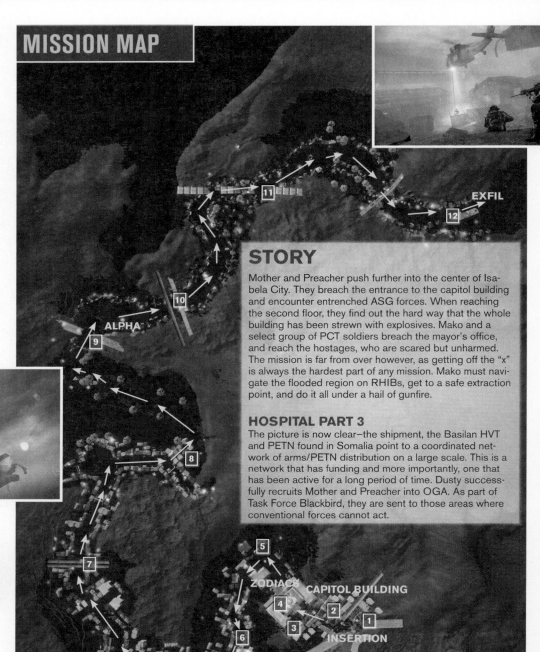

STORY

Mother and Preacher push further into the center of Isabela City. They breach the entrance to the capitol building and encounter entrenched ASG forces. When reaching the second floor, they find out the hard way that the whole building has been strewn with explosives. Mako and a select group of PCT soldiers breach the mayor's office, and reach the hostages, who are scared but unharmed. The mission is far from over however, as getting off the "x" is always the hardest part of any mission. Mako must navigate the flooded region on RHIBs, get to a safe extraction point, and do it all under a hail of gunfire.

HOSPITAL PART 3

The picture is now clear—the shipment, the Basilan HVT and PETN found in Somalia point to a coordinated network of arms/PETN distribution on a large scale. This is a network that has funding and more importantly, one that has been active for a long period of time. Dusty successfully recruits Mother and Preacher into OGA. As part of Task Force Blackbird, they are sent to those areas where conventional forces cannot act.

GET TO THE CAPITOL BUILDING

> **1** to the Capitol Building
> Clear the Street

Hoy! You are Mako, right?

CLEAR THE STREET

Your two-man team has infiltrated an ASG-occupied village on the outskirts of Isabela City. It is important to maintain stealth for as long as possible. When the mission begins, you are directly behind an enemy. Press the melee button to silently kill the target with your tomahawk.

Follow your allies to another damaged building and take cover. There are several hostiles inside. Stay outside of the building and engage the enemies as they pop up from behind cover and expose themselves to your line of fire. There is no reason to rush into the building until it is clear. When the Philippine commandos rush in, follow them.

Advance through the building and out the other side. Rush towards the low wall on the left and quickly take cover. There is a sniper on the roof ahead of you. Quickly take aim and kill him before he can harm you or your team.

The Philippine commander sends in a helicopter to help provide fire support. However, the terrorists are well armed. They fire an RPG and shoot down the chopper. As it is going down, get ready for some action. More hostiles rush into the area ahead of you and take cover. Watch where they drop down and then be ready to take them out when they pop up to fire at you. Your allies move forward, however stay put behind the wall and pick off enemies as they appear. Only move to avoid grenades that may be thrown at you.

TIP

During this mission, you can take a lot of fire from the enemy. If they start hitting you, duck behind cover and stay there for a bit until you recover. As red appears around the edge of the screen, you are taking hits. If you don't get behind cover and take more hits, you are likely to die. However, if you put something solid between you and your attacker, the red recedes and lets you know that you have recovered. Then get back into the fight.

When "Mother" moves forward, follow him. There are still some hostiles out in the flooded plaza. Rush from cover to cover and take them out. Watch for another sniper up on a lower roof of a building to the right. Take aim and drop him into the flood waters before he can get a hit on you.

Advance to a street that leads away from the plaza and quickly take cover behind a concrete barricade. There are lots of hostiles down the street from your position. Watch out for grenades and hug the concrete when you start taking fire. Use your iron sights to engage enemies up close and to find enemies at longer ranges. Then switch to your scope for engaging those enemies. The iron sights lets you maintain better situational awareness while peeking or leaning around your cover.

Once the street is clear, follow "Mother" and your allies down the street and into a building. After ensuring the building is clear, move up the stairs to a catwalk where there are windows looking out over the capitol building.

Pull out your LTLM and laze the entrance of the capitol building so you can call in air support. The rest of Task Force Mako is on a Blackhawk and fly in to gun down the opposition.

CAMPAIGN · RIP CURRENT

You now switch control to "Stump", who is manning the minigun on the Blackhawk. Press the aim button to zoom in your view and then begin clearing out the hostiles in the area outside of the capitol building.

Watch out for terrorists on balconies of the building. Some of them are armed with RPGs that can shoot down your helicopter. As soon as you see them, take them out. Also keep an eye on your gun barrels. As you fire, they heat up and turn red and then yellow. If they get yellow, the gun automatically shuts down while the barrels cool off. To avoid this, fire in bursts rather than holding down the trigger for extended periods of time.

Look for vehicles or other objects that explode when you shoot at them. A short burst at one of these objects can kill several nearby enemies rather than having to attack each target individually. Keep up your attacks until you have cleared out all of the enemies outside the building.

APPROACH THE CAPITOL BUILDING

Once the air support has done its job, you switch back to "Preacher". Follow "Mother" through a door to exit your building and rush across the road to get to the capitol building. There are no enemies left, so continue to the doors where the Philippine Army soldiers are preparing to enter. However, before you get there, one of them kicks in the door. Unfortunately, the terrorists have booby-trapped the door and the explosion takes down two of your allies—and knocks you to the ground as well.

As a result of the explosion, the Philippine commander orders his men to halt their attack and prepare for negotiations with the terrorists. However, "Mother" knows if you don't go in now to get the hostages, they are dead. Therefore, "Mother" takes charge and makes the call to go in after them. The Philippine leader on the ground agrees and places his unit under "Mother's" command.

ENTER THE CAPITOL BUILDING

Follow "Mother" and two of the soldiers to the left and through a gate that leads to a side entrance of the capitol building. The Philippine leader is taking some of his men around to the right side of the capitol building to hit the enemy from two sides.

Break out the window and climb through the opening to enter the capitol building.

RESCUE THE HOSTAGES

Follow "Mother" into a corridor on the right. Advance through this corridor carefully, looking for cover as you move. A couple hostiles move into the corridor directly in front of you from a doorway on the right. Use iron sights to aim and then take them out before they have a chance to return fire.

Near the end of the corridor, move through a door on the right. As "Mother" goes to the left, go to the right and be ready for enemies moving through this flooded room. Clear it out and then get ready to continue.

BREACH AND CLEAR

Your team has come to a dead end. However, there is no need to worry. You are carrying a breaching charge that can make an opening for your team. Wait until the team is in position, then place the charge on the wall and detonate it.

Quickly rush into the next room through the breach and kill the two hostiles who are stunned. This room opens into a much larger room where there are several more terrorists. Peek around your cover and begin engaging those closest to you while avoiding fire from those on the far side of the room.

Several enemies move in close to attack and throw grenades. Pull back through the breach if you need to avoid the grenades, then come back and finish off the hostiles.

CLEAR THE FIRST FLOOR

Move into the large room and take cover. Pick off hostiles at the far end of the room. Some throw grenades, so be sure to have a backup position behind cover to which you can quickly move if needed.

As "Mother" moves to the left side of the room, follow him. There is more cover along the left side and it provides a safer path to advance across to the opposite side of the room. Rush from cover to cover. As you get over halfway across the room, watch for an enemy on the stairs in the far left corner of the room. Peek around some cover and take him out.

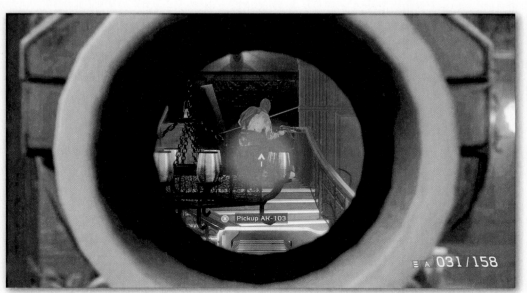

Clear the left side of the area and then rush across. Now you can begin advancing down the left side while "Mother" stays on the right. This allows your team to catch the enemy in a crossfire and forces them to attack one of you while allowing the other to get in shots. Use the concrete supports for cover and clear out all the enemies you can see before rushing forward to the next support.

CLEAR THE SECOND FLOOR

Head up the stairs on the right side of the room, since the stairs on the left side have collapsed. As you get to the top of the stairs, take cover and kill the enemies firing at you from the right side. They have taken cover behind sandbags, so wait for them to pop up or run so you can take your shot. Once the right side is clear, reload and begin advancing along the walkway to the left.

As you are heading along the second floor walkway, the terrorists detonate an explosive that throws you back. Once you get back up, seek some cover. There are several hostiles up ahead. Before you can advance, you need to clear them. They are good at using cover, so wait for them to pop up to fire and then take them out. It is easier to back away and then use the scope. The enemies can be tough to see through the smoke and debris, so watch for muzzle flashes.

After you have cleared out all of the enemies on the other side of the rubble, follow "Mother", jumping up and over the debris, and then turn to the right and take cover behind a wooden support or other object.

There are more hostiles at the end of the walkway. They appear as you begin advancing. Let "Mother" lead the way while you hang back and cover him. There are enemies behind sandbags at the end of this walkway as well as around the corner. A carefully thrown grenade can clear out these terrorists.

Once the enemies around the corner are defeated, move along the walkway, looking to the right and engaging more terrorists along the next walkway as you go. Other members of your team who have already reached the corner keep the hostiles occupied while you hit them from the flank.

FLANK THE MMG

Clear out the final walkway and then move towards the hallway through doors on the left side. As you approach, a medium machine gun opens fire.

While you could try to take cover and shoot the machine gunner, there are several hostiles near the machine gun and they take over when the gunner is killed. Instead, move past the door and turn left down another hallway that runs parallel to the first. This allows you to come in from the side and kill the enemy from a side on which they have no cover.

After the machine gun has been silenced once and for all, move with the rest of the team to a pair of locked doors located behind the machine gun. Select a breaching tactic and then get ready to rush in. There are four terrorists on the other side. Kill them all as quickly as possible and try to get each with a headshot. Be careful not to hit the hostages that are kneeling down on the floor.

EVACUATE THE HOSTAGES

After the hostages have been secured, the rest of your Task Force Mako is making their way to the capitol building in Zodiac boats. Your team evacuates the hostages out of the building and down to the boats so you can get them to safety.

As "Mother" takes the controls of the boat, you man the automatic grenade launcher. The terrorists are not going to allow you to take the hostages without a fight. Start firing at the hostiles along your route.

Since you are firing a grenade launcher, don't aim directly at the hostiles. Instead, aim for structures near them and as they blow up, they kill the nearby terrorists. Grenades are not as accurate as bullets, so it is harder to hit a person with a grenade launcher.

Listen to "Mother" call out targets to you. As a technical truck drives across an overpass, firing down on you, take aim and blow it up before it can damage your boat or hit the passengers. Also watch for enemies with RPGs that are deadlier than other enemies with just rifles.

When you reach a dead end, your boats have to backtrack and take a narrow passage between buildings.

Once you get out into open water again and approach Alpha, your destination point, it seems clear and you prepare to hook up with Paladin, your helicopter ride out of here. However, enemies arrive and start firing at you and the helicopter. An RPG blast is close to your position and knocks you to the floor of the boat.

DRIVE TO THE EXFIL

"Mother" takes over the grenade launcher. You are now driving the boat. One of the hostages is in critical condition. You have to get to the exfiltration point as quickly as possible before he dies. "Voodoo" is driving the other boat. Follow him along the flooded roads. Be careful not to run into objects such as overpass supports. This slows you down and makes it tough to get the hostage to the care he needs.

Enemies continue to attack. Let "Mother" worry about them. You need to concentrate on driving. There is lots of debris in the water that you have to avoid. Also try to dodge RPGs that fire at you. An RPG is easy to see because of its fiery trail.

12 When you get near the coast and the end of your boat ride, watch for a tanker ship that has run aground. Go around it on the left side so you don't get stuck.

Once you are past the tanker, Paladin hovers over your boats. After hooking up your boats, the helicopters take off and carry you to safety.

HAT TRICK
BRIEFING

TASK FORCE MAKO
"STUMP"
Near ???
6° 42' N 121° 58' E ???

OBJECTIVES
Somali pirates have captured an American ship captain and are holding him hostage in a lifeboat. The boat is located off the stern of the USS *Bainbridge*. You play as "Stump" and are one of the snipers who must put their sharpshooting skills to the test in order to rescue the captain safely.

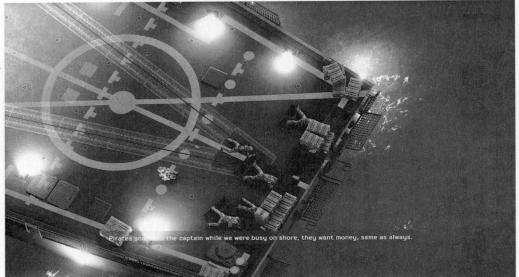

Pirates snatched the captain while we were busy on shore, they want money, same as always.

STORY
An escalating situation has TF Mako called back to the USS Bainbridge. Pirates have taken the captain of a merchant vessel hostage and are threatening his execution if a ransom isn't paid. Mako sets up a sniping position on the fantail and waits for the opportunity to take out the pirates with coordinated fire.

TOC 3
Preacher is now fully healed and along with Mother and a local asset named Ajab, they seek a Pakistani arms dealer known as Faraz Iqbal Khan. The mission: find him, find out what he knows and get out of the country.

LOADOUT
Primary – LaRue OBR 7.62
Secondary – None

ACHIEVEMENTS

ONE SHOT, THREE KILLS
Take your shot and complete this mission to earn this award.

RESCUE THE CAPTAIN

The mission begins with you lying prone on the deck of the USS *Bainbridge* watching the lifeboat. You are armed with a sniper rifle equipped with a scope. Look through the scope and take a look at your targets.

There are three pirates in the lifeboat along with the captain. This is a tough situation. If anyone fires on the pirates, they will kill the captain. Therefore, you and the other two snipers must all fire at the same time to simultaneously kill all the pirates in order to protect the captain.

One of the pirates is in the bow of the lifeboat and occasionally pops up to look out of a hatch on the lifeboat.

The second pirate stands guard at the rear of the lifeboat, looking out through the windows for trouble approaching the lifeboat. The third pirate is usually down out of view with the captain. Take time to study the actions of the pirates. However, don't fire. After a while, your shift is over and you are relieved by another team of snipers.

When you return to the deck of the USS *Bainbridge* 18 hours later, there is a new plan. A flare will be launched over the lifeboat. Then when the three pirates all look to see what is taking place, your team of snipers take their shots. You are assigned to target the pirate on the left behind the windows. The other two snipers will fire on your shot. Wait until you hear "Clear Shot" and then "Execute". Then press the button to hold your breath, line up your sights, and take the shot. Be careful not to hit the captain.

After each sniper has taken his shot and all pirates are down, two teams of operators rush across to the lifeboat in Zodiacs, secure the boat, and ensure the captain is safe before bringing him back to the USS *Bainbridge*.

Another successful mission. However, it won't be the last.

FINDING FARAZ

BRIEFING

TASK FORCE BLACKBIRD
"PREACHER"
Near ???
6° 42' N 121° 58' E

OBJECTIVES

The events of the Philippines now behind them, "Mother" and "Preacher" form Task Force Blackbird and pursue the P.E.T.N. threat under their own rules of engagement. Your task force is ordered to go after and capture Faraz Iqbal Khan, a gun runner who may have information about the P.E.T.N. Ajab, a local, is available to help out. This is a non-sanctioned mission. The Pakistani government and security force, ISI, does not know you are in country. Therefore, it is important that you are not caught.

ACHIEVEMENTS

NON-OFFICIAL COVER

Pursue Faraz and make your escape in order to earn this achievement/trophy.

TAG, YOU'RE IT

Catch Faraz within 15 minutes in order to earn this award.

LOADOUT

Primary – AKS-74U
Secondary – G23
Frag Grenades – x4

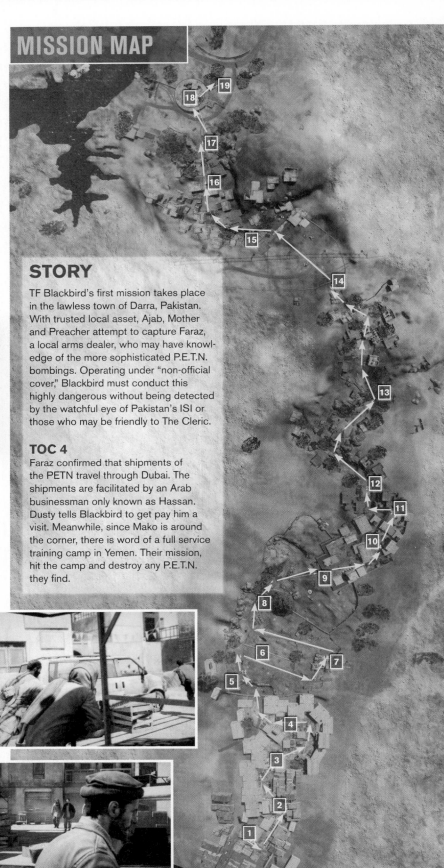

MISSION MAP

STORY

TF Blackbird's first mission takes place in the lawless town of Darra, Pakistan. With trusted local asset, Ajab, Mother and Preacher attempt to capture Faraz, a local arms dealer, who may have knowledge of the more sophisticated P.E.T.N. bombings. Operating under "non-official cover," Blackbird must conduct this highly dangerous without being detected by the watchful eye of Pakistan's ISI or those who may be friendly to The Cleric.

TOC 4

Faraz confirmed that shipments of the PETN travel through Dubai. The shipments are facilitated by an Arab businessman only known as Hassan. Dusty tells Blackbird to get pay him a visit. Meanwhile, since Mako is around the corner, there is word of a full service training camp in Yemen. Their mission, hit the camp and destroy any P.E.T.N. they find.

INTERROGATE FARAZ

CHASE FARAZ

1 As "Preacher" and Ajab begin to move in behind Faraz for the capture, the target takes off running. "Mother", who was waiting in the car, joins in the pursuit. While you are armed, do not fire at Faraz. You need him alive. Instead, you need to run after him and prevent him from getting away.

TIP

For the first part of this mission, all you need to do is focus on running, avoiding obstacles, and jumping across gaps or over things that get in your way. Be sure to not let him get too far ahead or you can lose him in the maze of buildings.

Follow Faraz up a flight of stairs and across a series of balconies and upper walkways. Watch for places where you need to jump from one building to the next. You may lose sight of him when he goes around a corner, so listen to "Dusty" on the comms. He is tracking Faraz using a UAV surveillance drone that is orbiting the area. "Dusty" lets you know to turn right or left.

After moving across several rooftops, Faraz drops back down to the ground and heads towards a junkyard. Stay on his tail so you don't lose him in the junk. Ajab and "Mother" are following behind you, but don't wait up for them. Keep running.

As Faraz takes a turn to the left while running away from you, "Dusty" calls in and tells you he sees men with weapons headed your way. The foot race has now become a firefight. Locate some cover and get behind it, then take shots at the several terrorists who are attacking you. Watch out for grenades that they throw to try to get you out from behind your cover.

After clearing an area, keep running after Faraz. "Mother" and Ajab catch up to you and help with the fighting. While you need to hurry so Faraz does not get away, it is important to take time to find cover—especially if you are taking hits. The enemy has a lot of firepower, so don't try to run and gun or you will end up dead in the dust.

Your rifle is equipped with a scope, so use it—especially against enemies at longer range. This gives you an advantage. Watch for the enemy to run at you or rush from cover to cover and hit them while they are exposed. If they get behind cover, wait from them to peek or lean and then get in a headshot.

There are a lot of things you can use for cover during the chase, from stacks of tires to lumber or wood crates—even vehicles. However, watch for enemies waiting to flank you. They sometimes hide until you run past them and then rush out to attack. Fire bursts from the hip. Even if you don't hit them, they will usually duck or try to seek cover instead of continuing their attack. This gives you a chance to follow up with aimed fire to kill them or to seek cover of your own. If it is only one or two, take them out. Any more and you need to find some cover.

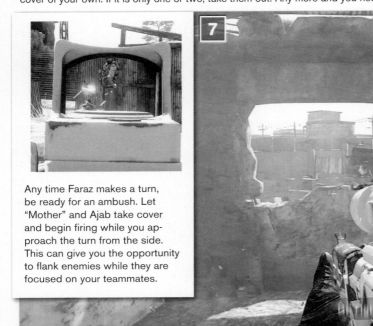

Any time Faraz makes a turn, be ready for an ambush. Let "Mother" and Ajab take cover and begin firing while you approach the turn from the side. This can give you the opportunity to flank enemies while they are focused on your teammates.

When Faraz leaps over a broken brick wall and moves through a small, ruined building, take caution. Fire through the window at a hostile behind some cover on the other side or he can seriously hurt you. Then take a right to exit the building. Hang next to the building and lean around the corner to engage the enemies as they attack or try to flee from you. Kill them, then advance to the cover they have vacated.

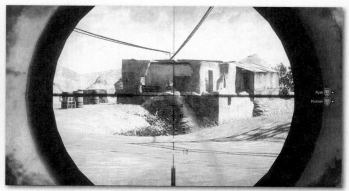

As Faraz is running along a series of power lines, right after you move away from the ruined building, find some good cover. There are several enemies up ahead. Use your scope and pick them off at long range. Some try to rush towards you and try to flank your position. Kill them as they move or when they peek out from behind cover. Just be careful not to shoot Faraz.

Look for the building where the power lines go down. There are some enemies inside that snipe at you. Get some cover and kill them before they kill you. By the time you take out these targets, the area should be clear. Reload as you continue the chase after Faraz.

Rush after Faraz as he crosses a bridge. He is headed towards his compound where he thinks he will be safe. Therefore, you can expect a lot more opposition up ahead.

As Faraz heads into the compound, rush after him. After dropping down from a broken bridge, take cover behind some rocks. Pick off some of the hostiles. Then, as it clears out, rush forward. Once you are in among the remaining enemies, engage them with close-range fire or rush them with a melee attack before they can respond.

TIP

During the chase, get in the habit of running from cover to cover, and if you don't come under fire, keep going. However, every second or third piece of cover, scan the area ahead using your scope. Sometimes you can see hostiles waiting for you and kill them before they know you are there. It is better to preempt an ambush instead of running right into one.

CLEAR FARAZ'S COMPOUND

By now, "Mother" and Ajab have caught up with you. While "Mother" takes cover to one side of the gate to Faraz's compound, take cover on the other side. Between the two of you, lean around the side of the gate and start picking off enemies inside. Watch for those hostiles that rush you. Be ready with a quick melee attack and then continue firing into the compound.

Clear the area near the gate, then rush into the compound and take cover. Engage more enemies in this first area. They come at you from the sides as well as from behind a building in the middle. Once they are all dead, Faraz runs farther into the compound.

CLEAR THE SECOND FLOOR

"Mother" orders you to go right around the building in the middle. Move through a small alley along the side of the building. Then stop and peek around the edge of the building to see a technical pick-up truck with a machine gun in the bed. Aim and take out the machine gunner before he can attack you or Ajab, who is going around the left side of the building. Continue firing at other hostiles in this area. From this spot, you can kill enemies on the ground as well as on the roofs of the buildings.

Faraz runs through the back gate of the compound as he continues fleeing from you. Find a position behind cover from where you have a good view of the gate. Hostiles come pouring out of that gate. Pick them off one at a time and also watch the roofs near the gate. Stay put until no more enemies come through the gate.

Once it is clear, Ajab and "Mother" rush through the gate. Follow them, take an immediate left, and drop down into a village area. The chase is on again.

As you run down a path between buildings, watch for enemies along the side and up ahead. Let your teammates lead and let them flush out enemies for you to take out with long-range fire.

When you come to a low wall, jump over it and continue to a turn to the left. Hold here and take cover. There are several hostiles up ahead. Pick them off. Watch out for one that tries to snipe at you from the rubble of a building. Kill them all, and then take up the chase again.

As you are running, a few enemies try to attack. They usually fire a bit and then run. Don't worry about cover—just take aim and kill them before they can get to cover. As you approach a small wooden bridge ahead, look for a terrorist crouched down on it. Locate and then neutralize this threat before continuing along the path.

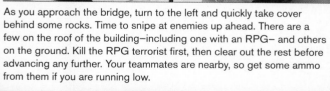

As you approach the bridge, turn to the left and quickly take cover behind some rocks. Time to snipe at enemies up ahead. There are a few on the roof of the building—including one with an RPG— and others on the ground. Kill the RPG terrorist first, then clear out the rest before advancing any further. Your teammates are nearby, so get some ammo from them if you are running low.

When the chase icon appears on the screen, you know Faraz is on the move again. Rush forward through a small building. The enemy is on the run. Try to kill any enemies as you see them. Continue up a short flight of stairs and then drop down into an alley and turn to the left.

Take cover behind a vehicle and engage more enemies up ahead who are covering Faraz's escape. Kill them and then advance. As you do, more enemies rush towards you. Gun them down or hit them with a melee attack if they get too close.

Now sprint up another short flight of stairs and continue along the path between buildings. "Mother" takes the lead, so follow him. Keep going until you see Faraz climbing over a low wall to try to get away.

Run after Faraz and as you get near, you tackle him. While you are holding him and waiting for Ajab to bring the van around, "Mother" begins interrogating him about where the P.E.T.N. came from. Faraz tells you he got it from a man named Hassan. However, before he can say more, he is killed by a sniper. You may be next, so the two of you take cover.

INTERROGATE FARAZ

GET TO THE EXFIL POINT

15 "Dusty" calls in and tells you there is a nearby building. Get to it and Ajab will pick you up you there. There are a lot of terrorists coming after you, so start running down a path between buildings. Don't even try to take cover and fight the hostiles behind you. Your best chance of survival is to run away—as fast as you can.

"Mother" leads the way. When it looks like you have hit a dead end, move through a door to the right and then drop down into a gully leading down to the building where Ajab is to pick you up.

As you begin to approach the building, several hostiles pour out and begin attacking. Quickly seek cover. You need to clear them out before Ajab can get to you. There are hostiles behind cover in front of the building as well as on the upper walkway and near the door. Peek or lean around your cover and pick them off one at a time. Move forward and take cover behind the vehicle and then begin engaging hostiles inside the building by firing through the doorway.

Rush forward towards the door and take cover to one side. "Mother" follows and moves to the other side of the door. Watch for hostiles coming down the stairs and fire at those inside.

After the stairs are clear, sprint up the stairs. Stay low as you get to the top and a low wall provides cover for you. There is a break in the wall. Move towards it and fire down on the enemy below from a flanking position. They are open targets for you.

Once the building is clear, rush back down the stairs and make your way to the front door where "Mother" is waiting. Breach the door and rush through it.

As you get out the door, you automatically take out a couple enemies and climb into the van as soon as Ajab brings it to a screeching and brief halt. He then drives away as fast as possible to get you away from a lot of terrorists who want you and your team dead. While you were not successful in capturing Faraz, you did get a name—Hassan.

CONNECT THE DOTS

BRIEFING

TASK FORCE MAKO "STUMP"
Haraz Mountains, Yemen
15° 23' – N 43° 43' E

OBJECTIVES

After gaining information from the gun runner Faraz and other intelligence, the picture is starting to come into focus. Task Force Mako is sent to raid a terrorist training facility deep in the mountains of Yemen. You play as "Stump" and are operating with "Voodoo" and other Tier 1 operatives as you take the fight to the enemy.

STORY

The discovery of P.E.T.N.in the Somali fort takes Task Force Mako deep into Yemen's hinterland to raid a supposed terrorist training facility. Hidden high in the Haraz mountains, they must infil via little bird helicopters, and secure the facility and report back to command on their findings.

TOC 5

With the Yemen training camp taken out of the picture, Blackbird has to "follow the money." They arrive in Dubai with one goal: "roll up" Hassan and get out of the country. The U.A.E. doesn't like spies carrying out operations in their country. So Dusty repeats this is a low signature operation. In and out.

LOADOUT

Primary – Mk17
Secondary – AA12
Special – HK MG4
Frag Grenades – x6

ACHIEVEMENTS

CLASS DISMISSED

Blow up the terrorist stash of P.E.T.N. and complete the mission to earn this award.

TARGET PRACTICE

Shoot down the targets in the training camp caves in order to get this achievement/trophy.

FIND THE TRAINING CAMP

DEFEND THE GROUND FORCES

1 This mission begins with your task force airborne. After circling a terrorist stronghold on a hill, part of your force is inserted and advances towards the objective on foot. Meanwhile, your chopper continues to orbit the area and watch for trouble.

All right guys, get your frogman on!

Shortly after your team lands, terrorists seem to come out of the woodwork—or brickwork. Use your machine gun to start taking them down. Look for hostiles armed with RPGs. They are often designated as a primary threat by icons over them. These are your main targets since they can cause a lot of harm to the boots on the ground as well as to the troops still in the air.

Use your scope to increase the accuracy of your shots. However, if you start taking fire, look up from the scope in order to increase your situational awareness. Locate new threats and then use the scope to take them out. By going in and out of scope view, you avoid the tunnel vision that is the disadvantage of trying to fight a battle only through the scope.

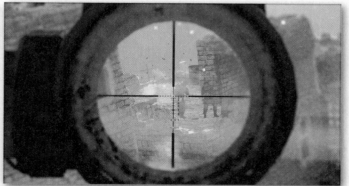

Once you clear out the hostiles covering the front of the stronghold, your helicopter begins to fly around the area as you look for more targets. Watch for enemies in an area with a damaged wall just after flying around the main tower. This is a dangerous spot, so be ready.

One of the terrorists is armed with an RPG. There are also more enemies located on the top floor of the tower just waiting for you to fly by so they can shoot at you. Keep firing at them until they are all neutralized.

Your helicopter begins to fly around the stronghold again. Look and listen for RPGs fired at you or other helicopters. Then quickly locate the terrorist as he is reloading and kill him before he can get off another shot.

While you are attacking enemies, look for barrels containing flammable material. Rather than trying to hit an individual, aim for the barrel. When it detonates, it kills any nearby hostiles—plus provides a nice explosion.

Watch for a technical pick-up truck to drive down a road and stop under an arch. The machine gunner in the bed is protected by an armored shield, so fire at the engine of the truck to try to blow it up and silence that gun. Then work over the hostiles in the central part of the stronghold.

Another technical drives up from the left and starts firing at your helicopter. Quickly make this your priority target and aim for the truck. Keep firing until the truck blows up. Then continue firing at other terrorists in the area. All of a sudden, an RPG round hits a nearby helicopter. As it starts to go down, the blast rocks your chopper as well.

ELIMINATE THE RPGS

You now have a new objective. Take out those RPGs. The terrorists armed with rocket-propelled grenade launchers are marked with icons. Take them out.

By this time, the hostiles are bugging out and escaping in technical pick-up trucks. Start firing at the trucks as they are fleeing. Aim for the barrels to get a big explosion.

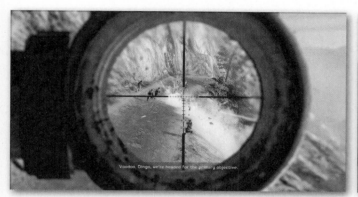

The helicopters now leave the stronghold and begin following the fleeing terrorists along a road. Engage any vehicles or hostiles on foot as you fly by. Watch for a technical parked across the road. Fire at it and eliminate that threat.

After passing by the enemies on the road, your helicopter approaches a building. There are more hostiles there and some are armed with RPGs. Use the scope on the machine gun to pick them off at long range before they can fire at your ride. Clear out as many terrorists at this building as possible as you fly by.

Your helicopter touches down briefly so you and "Voodoo" can dismount. It is good to be back on solid ground again where you are in control and can take cover. Follow your teammate into the village.

CLEAR THE VILLAGE

Get behind some cover and then start firing at the hostiles in the village. Look for a machine gunner on a rooftop. Kill him quickly and then focus on the remaining enemies. Several run out from the village, take cover behind crates, and then fire at you. Others fire from the windows. Stay put and clear them all out before moving on.

As you begin to advance, stay behind cover. There is a machine gunner down on the ground in front of the village. He is heavily armored, complete with a metal face mask. Don't try for a headshot. Instead, you have to put several rounds into his body to take him down. Try to do this while he is firing at others and then duck back behind cover when he turns to attack you.

Follow "Voodoo" and your team into the village. As you see enemies coming towards you, take cover and engage them. When a technical pulls up and adds its firepower, stay behind cover. You don't have to worry about taking it out. "Voodoo" will call in some close air support from "Buzzsaw". After it makes its attack run and clears the way for you, move out.

The terrorists have set up defenses in front of a large building complete with one of those armored machine gunners. If you have not picked up some ammo from a teammate, this is a good time to do so. While they take cover by the vehicle, you need to try to flank the enemies.

Turn to the right to see a road that leads up and around to the side of the battle. There is a lot of open ground, so sprint for the small building to the right of the road and take cover. Peek around the corner of the doorway and clear out any hostiles that can attack you while you make your next rush.

Once the fire dies down a bit, rush up the road. Be ready to engage any hostiles headed your way. When you get to the end, take cover. You now have a flanking position on the enemy. As they are focusing on your teammates, you can shoot at them from the side where they have no cover to protect them.

Continue along the upper walkway located at the front of the building as you keep hitting the enemy from the flank. If you get low on ammo, pick up a rifle from a fallen terrorist and use it against his brothers.

BREACH AND CLEAR

Now that the area outside the building is clear, it is time to enter. Stack up on the door along the walkway and then order a teammate to breach it. There are two hostiles inside. Quickly take them both out while they are stunned to clear the room.

Follow your team through the building. It is clear. Continue outside of the building and take cover behind a wall. The area between you and the next building in the distance is filled with hostiles. Your first target is the machine gunner on the technical. Then pick off the rest of the terrorists near the technical.

DEFEND WHILE AWAITING AIRSTRIKE

Once the area around the technical is clear, sprint around the cover, jump up onto the back of the technical, and man the machine gun. Engage the hostiles in the other building. Some fire at you from windows or the roof. Remember to fire in bursts to avoid overheating the barrel of the machine gun. Keep it up until "Buzzsaw" arrives to make a gun run against the building. This takes out some of the hostiles, but not all of them. Keep firing and watch for an RPG on the rooftop. "Buzzsaw" comes back around—this time with a rocket attack.

The rocket attack does the job. Leave the technical and follow your team to the building and head up the stairs. Go through the door and enter the building. There is no P.E.T.N., so continue out the back of the building.

Take cover and begin picking off enemies in the area behind the building. Let your teammates advance ahead of you and get behind some protection while you provide covering fire. Then, once they are in position, move up to join them. Take cover behind a stack of wood or other object and lean or peek around it to engage the enemies ahead of you. Don't rush ahead of your team or you risk getting flanked by the enemy. After you get the all clear, move forward with your team to the hidden entrance to the training camp.

CLEAR THE TRAINING CAMP

CLEAR THE HIDDEN SHOOT HOUSE

Move down into the underground shoot house. The first few rooms are empty. However, when you get to the larger room with shooting targets, there are hostiles inside as well. Take cover at the doorway or behind some crates inside and start engaging the enemy. If the enemy throws grenades at you, be ready to rush to another spot of cover.

Once the room is clear, advance with your team to a hallway and stack up at the doorway. After your team enters, follow them in. As you enter, a terrorist on a balcony throws a grenade right at you. After tipping a table to make cover from the grenade, begin taking out the hostiles in the room that attack you. They come at you from the balcony as well as at ground level.

Clear the room and then continue to the next room. Follow "Tick" up the stairs while the rest of your team stays low. Take cover at the top and fire down at the terrorists below as you carefully advance along the catwalks above the shooting rooms below. Be careful not to hit your teammates.

BREACH AND CLEAR

Once the shoot rooms are clear, head down another flight of stairs and move along a corridor to a door. Stack up and give a breach order. Once the door is open, rush in and kill the four enemies inside.

There are no more hostiles in this structure, so follow your team through a narrow passageway and through a door leading to the outside. Continue along a narrow path that leads to a cave. Stay quiet as you enter. It is unlikely the enemies in this cave heard your firefight in the underground shoot house.

CLEAR THE CAVES

After moving through the cave, you eventually come across a group of terrorists. Take cover behind a rock and wait for the order to go loud before opening fire and killing all of the hostiles. The cave is lit by electrical lights powered by a generator. Time to take out the lights. Shoot the generator while your team waits by a door that leads further into the cave.

Your team owns the night. After activating your NODS, you can see in the dark, but the enemy can't. As your team breaks up into pairs, stick with "Voodoo" and cover him as he advances. Once you get to a large area with training kill rooms, start firing on the enemies and eliminate them before they can tell from where the fire is coming.

Move into the training kill rooms. They are made to resemble a passenger airliner. Kill the hostiles inside as you advance through this area.

As you progress through the kill rooms, the terrorists have found some flashlights. This makes it difficult to see the enemies and they can now see and attack you. Fire at the lights and you are more than likely to hit the person holding it as well.

As you exit the kill rooms, the enemy has got another generator going to power several large lights. You no longer have the advantage. Quickly take cover and engage the hostiles waiting to attack you. Peek over the rocks to take your shots, then duck back down to avoid being hit yourself.

TIP

If the armored machine gunner sees you, he may come after you. Try to take cover. Don't try to shoot it out with him at close range. When he gets in close enough, rush out from your cover and hit him several times with melee attacks. Unlike other enemies, one hit of your tomahawk is not enough. Instead you need to keep hitting him until he goes down.

After clearing out this area, advance to an area built to look like a train station. Once again, take cover behind rocks and start picking off the enemies you can see. A good tactic is to move into the mock train on the right. Clear out any enemies inside and then use this position to hit the enemies on their flank. This is a good way to get in behind the armored machine gunner that begins advancing on your teammates.

Clear out the train station area, then follow your team to the opposite side and move through a door. On the other side is a room filled with the P.E.T.N. explosives. It feels uncomfortable to be in such a small room with so much destructive potential. However, while there are a lot of explosives here, it looks like a lot is missing.

"Dusty" tells you to take a sample and then get out of there so they can blow it up with an airstrike. Head out to the chopper and climb aboard. "Voodoo" places a smoke grenade at the entrance to the cave and as soon as your chopper flies away, the strike hits, with the resulting explosion taking out half of the mountain.

HELLO AND DUBAI

BRIEFING

TASK FORCE BLACKBIRD
"PREACHER"
Dubai, UAE
25° 13' 28" N – 55° 18' 60" E

OBJECTIVES

Following the money, "Mother" and "Preacher" head to the modern city of Dubai to find a banker with dirty connections. There are no weapons in this mission. Instead, you are the driver while "Mother" rides shotgun and "Dusty" provides support via your comms. Your job is to get Hassan out of the city without being caught.

STORY

Field intelligence gathered in Pakistan takes Blackbird to the modern city of Dubai, where supposed legitimate banker, Hassan, has been linked to payments connected to P.E.T.N. shipments. The mission is simple. Capture Hassan and bring him to the safe house for interrogation.

TOC 6

Although Blackbird has gone dark, Hassan's computer turned up a wealth of intel. The intel is solid enough for Mako to pay a visit to some old friends. One is an ally, the other, a new foe.

ACHIEVEMENTS

PEDAL TO THE MEDAL

Complete this mission to earn this award.

STORM WATCH

Get through the sandstorm without hitting any vehicles in this mission to get this achievement/trophy.

PARKADE

EXIT THE PARKADE AND ESTABLISH UPLINK

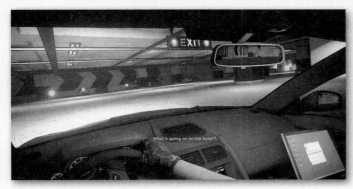

As "Preacher", you are the driver for this mission. As soon as "Mother" rolls Hassan to the car and deposits him in the trunk, start driving. You begin in a parking garage and need to get to the exit. Start driving around the corner to the right.

"Mother" has Hassan's laptop and cell phone and is attempting to establish an uplink to transfer the files to "Dusty" back at the headquarters. However, while you are in the parking garage, he won't get a signal. Follow the arrows on the wall in order to get to the exit. Once outside, you should be able to connect to the uplink.

You are able to get to the exit of the parkade without any problem. As you prepare to continue onto the main roads, it is important to remember that you are not in Pakistan anymore. In Dubai, you drive on the right side of the road. Continue out of the parking garage and through the gateway to complete your first objective.

As you come to the main street, take a left and avoid hitting cars or driving on the sidewalk. You don't want to raise anyone's attention. Instead, just blend in with the other cars on the road while driving as fast as you can. Use the mini map in the lower right corner to help guide you along the roads.

While approaching an intersection where you have the green light, a black car comes in from the right and cuts in front of you. It looks like this mission just got a lot more difficult. Hassan's security are after you and want to get him back.

OUTRUN HASSAN'S MEN

Drive right past the black car and get your foot on the gas. As you are weaving in and out of traffic, keep an eye on your two mirrors to see where the black car is behind you. Hostile vehicles show up on your mini map with red borders around them.

The black car is faster than you, so if you slow down or hit something, it will catch up. If this happens, try to crash into the black car to force it into a spin or a building. This will slow the black car down and give you a chance to increase the distance between you two. By this time, the uplink is connected and "Mother" starts uploading the files. Since it is a satellite connection, you need to stay out of tunnels or away from tall buildings.

"Dusty" keeps you informed of threats as you are driving. After leading the single black car on a chase, two more come at you head on. As you get near, they turn sideways and try to block the road to stop you. Drive right through the gap between the two cars and keep going.

The black cars continue to chase you. Their tactic is to get a car in front of you, then slide sideways to try to block the road. When you see one getting past you, be ready to dodge it to one side or the other.

Eventually the road you are following merges with the Sheik Zayed freeway. Here the road is relatively straight and you can get up to some high speeds.

ELIMINATE THE RPGS

Hassan's security keeps trying to stop you. Time to go on the offensive. When one pulls in front of you and tries to stop you, crash right into the front of it to cause it to spin around and hopefully hit the other black cars on your tail.

"Dusty" has a new plan. He wants you to take the exit to Old Dubai. Look for the orange cones in the road and get into the right lane. Try to maintain your high speed. However, this road has fewer lanes than the freeway, so you don't have as much room to maneuver.

The road you are now on also has some turns, so be ready to tap your brakes as you hit the turns to avoid running into barricades or other cars.

After taking several turns and briefly losing your pursuers, "Dusty" tells you to pull over and stop. Stay put while a couple black cars drive by looking for you. This mission has just gone from a high-speed chase to a game of cat and mouse.

"Dusty" routes feed to you of the area so you can see places to hide. Drive slow and the pull into hiding spots on the side of the road until the black cars drive by. These spots are marked on your map and have a bluish glowing overlay on them on the screen.

ESCAPE UNDETECTED

As soon as the two cars drive away, start driving slowly and take a right. Then maneuver the car into a construction area off to the right side of the road. Get in there before any black cars see you drive into the hiding spot.

Locate the exit from the neighborhood on the map and try to drive around to it. Use the hiding spots to avoid enemies. However, one of them will usually spot you. When this happens, the screen acquires a reddish glow.

SHAKE THE PURSUIT

Hit the gas and try to lose Hassan's security in the black cars. Take turns and as soon as you are no longer in their sights, slip into a hiding spot and hold there.

When you try to get to the exit, the enemy blocks it. "Dusty" finds another and marks it on your map. However, you need to approach it without being seen.

USE THE SERVICE ROAD TO ESCAPE

Lose the black cars by making several turns. When they are far enough back, hiding spots again appear on your map. Get into one and stay put. The screen loses its reddish glow, letting you know the black cars have lost sight of you and are now in patrol mode rather than pursuit.

Wait until Hassan's security have driven away and it looks like you have a clear shot towards the exit. Then pull out and hit the gas. If you see more black cars headed your way, look for a hiding place and get to it and lay low again until it is clear.

Get to the construction area at the western edge of the neighborhood and slip into this hiding spot.

Continue through the construction area, driving right through a chain-link fence. There is a black car headed your way, so quickly take a right and drive into another hiding spot until it passes by. This part of the mission is tricky since you have to watch the road as you are driving as well as the mini map to see where enemies and hiding spots are located.

As soon as this black car passes, hit the gas and follow a curving road that leads you back onto a main road.

As the main road takes you into a tunnel, you lose connection with the uplink. You need to get back onto the Sheik Zayed freeway where there are fewer obstructions to your uplink.

OUTRUN HASSAN'S MEN

The black cars appear again and use the same tactic they did earlier. They pass you and then try to block the road. Evade or crash into them, but keep moving.

As you enter a tunnel, there is construction ahead. While traffic is stalled as it moves to the left of the construction, go to the right through the closed portion of the tunnel. Weave left and right through piles of dirt, tractors, and trucks in order to lose your pursuers, then continue back onto the freeway.

HEAD TO CAR-SWAP LOCATION

Follow the road and dodge traffic. Hassan's men are no longer behind you, so there is no need to drive recklessly. You need to swap cars, so pull into the parkade off to the left side of the road.

The secondary car is on the first level of the parkade. However, as soon as you stop to make the swap, a couple black cars come up behind you. No time to swap now. Just get out of there.

ESCAPE THE PARKADE

Since you have lost contact with "Dusty" while you are inside the parkade, you no longer have access to the mini map. Keep driving and listen as "Mother" helps you navigate. You want to head up to the top of the parkade so you can regain contact with "Dusty". Once you get to level P3, get to a ramp on the outside edge of the parkade and follow it as it takes you back down. "Dusty" once again has eyes on you.

You finally reach the ground floor again. Be careful as you make a tight turn and then line up your vehicle for the exit. A black car tries to block your path. Go around it to the right and crash through the crossbar to exit the parkade.

Once out in the open again, take a left on the main road and get back into the city's traffic.

Just as you think you have made it, "Dusty" informs you that he has spotted Sad Al Din, Hassan's chief of security. He is driving an SUV and enters the road right in front of you, trying to block your path.

Steer around him. The tunnel up ahead is blocked, so swerve to the left and enter the other tunnel where traffic is going in the opposite direction. Dodge the traffic and try to avoid Al Din who is on your tail.

Once out of the tunnel, you are still driving against oncoming traffic. However, there is a sandstorm up ahead. Maybe you can lose him in that storm. Keep driving and avoiding black cars and Al Din's SUV.

COMPLETE THE UPLINK

Al Din stays on you. Try to force him to crash into other cars so you can push ahead and lose him in the sandstorm while trying not to crash into oncoming traffic yourself.

When you come across a pileup ahead, take the Hatta exit off to the left so you don't get stuck on the road where Al Din can get you. Keep driving while the uplink transmits the last files to "Dusty." Once it finishes, you have completed another objective.

As you are thinking you are in the clear, Al Din's SUV comes crashing into your car from the side. After your vehicle comes to a halt, lying on its roof, Al Din has his men drag you and "Mother" from the car before knocking you out with a blow to the head from his rifle. You are caught.

OLD FRIENDS

BRIEFING

TASK FORCE MAKO
"STUMP"
Sarajevo, Bosnia and Herzegovina
23° 2' N – 65° 12' E

OBJECTIVES

The P.E.T.N.'s source has been located and Task Force Mako is sent to Sarajevo to look up a few old friends who may be of help. You are playing as "Stump" in this mission and are paired up with "Voodoo" again. Upon arriving in Sarajevo, you meet up with Greko and his team of Polish soldiers that belong to one of their nation's special forces units, GROM.

STORY

The discovery of P.E.T.N.in the Somali fort takes Task Force Mako deep into Yemen's hinterland to raid a supposed terrorist training facility. Hidden high in the Haraz mountains, they must infil via little bird helicopters, and secure the facility and report back to command on their findings.

TOC 5

With the Yemen training camp taken out of the picture, Blackbird has to "follow the money." They arrive in Dubai with one goal: "roll up" Hassan and get out of the country. The U.A.E. doesn't like spies carrying out operations in their country. So Dusty repeats this is a low signature operation. In and out.

LOADOUT

Primary – Mk16 PDW
Secondary – HK45 Compact
Special – McMillan CS5
Frag Grenades – x6

ACHIEVEMENTS

CLOSING CEREMONY

Finish this mission and you earn this achievement/trophy.

GET TO THE ISABELLA HOTEL

1 Search the UN Building

ACCOMPANY THE GROM

Soon after meeting up with the GROM operatives, there is an explosion. Move out with "Voodoo" and your new allies to investigate.

Watch it! I.E.D.'s are hidden in rubble.

Get Kaska, Zuku, Szczuply, and Diabel to set up an assault.

You hear that? Stay away from the paint gents.

The area has lots of Improvised Explosive Devices (IEDs). The GROM have marked them with red spray paint. Stay away from them. If you step on one, it blows up and kills you: Mission over. After the GROM have disabled one of these, they spray a green "X" over the red paint.

2

Right away.

Follow your allies up the street, careful to avoid the IEDs along the way. When you get to the point where the street is blocked by rubble, move into a building on the right.

CLEAR COURTYARD OF ENEMIES

3 the UN Building
mpany the GROM

Head up the stairs along with "Voodoo" and continue through the door on the left. There are lots of hostiles down in the courtyard below and your new objective is to clear them out.

Take cover behind some of the rubble and crouch down. You now are armed with a sniper rifle. Peek up over your cover. The hostiles down below are marked with icons. Take aim, zoom in with your scope, place the crosshairs over the head of your target, hold your breath, and squeeze the trigger. You have to work the bolt after each shot to load another round. This slows down your shots and you temporarily lose sight of your target. Therefore, it is best to take careful aim and make sure each shot hits its target.

Keep firing at the many enemies in the courtyard. When you have to reload, duck back down behind cover. While you are sniping, listen for the sound of an RPG. When you hear it, move back away from the wall and wait for the rocket to hit. Then quickly take up your position and look for the terrorist with the RPG. Also be sure to duck down if you start taking hits from enemy fire and zoom the scope out to make it easier to locate targets.

After you have cleared out most of the enemies down in the courtyard, "Voodoo" orders you to begin neutralizing the enemy snipers in the top floors of the building on the other side of the courtyard. They are marked with icons.

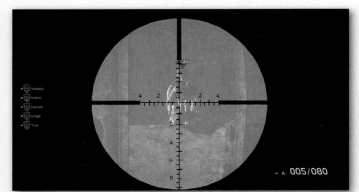

The snipers can be tough to hit. They often hide behind cover and move to the windows to fire—often at you. Aim at the window where they are located, and as soon as they appear, fire before they can shoot at you.

Once all the snipers are eliminated, you automatically switch back to your assault rifle. Now exit the room and head down the stairs to join up with your team. There are still hostiles in the courtyard, so now you have to move out into the courtyard and finish clearing them out.

Take cover immediately after you exit the building and before you descend down into the courtyard. Use your red dot sight to locate enemies, then switch to the scope to increase the accuracy of your shots. Clear out the hostiles in the area around the central fountain, since they are your main threat at first.

After clearing out several of the hostiles in the center, move down the stairs and then go left. Take cover behind the concrete planters and work your way around to the left side. From there you can engage enemies in the middle and far right from a flanking position. Just make sure you yourself are not flanked by enemies.

Advance towards the central fountain and use it for cover. From this position, you can attack enemies as they approach the fountain and catch them in a crossfire between you and your allies. Slowly work your way around to the other side of the fountain, clearing hostiles as you go.

Now sprint up the stairs to the right of the fountain and take up a position behind a short concrete wall on the far right side of the courtyard. This new perspective also provides a different field of fire and allows you to engage enemies as they try to make their way to the courtyard. Remain in this spot until the courtyard has been completely cleared.

BREACH AND CLEAR

Once your team begins moving, follow them to the UN building. The front door is locked, so you need to breach it.

Stack up on the door with your team and select a breach tactic. As soon as the door is breached, rush in and clear out the four hostiles inside. They are scattered throughout the room, so start on one side and work your way across the room.

CLEAR THE UN BUILDING

Now that all of your team is in the building, follow "Voodoo" up the stairs. As soon as you get to the top, terrorists drop down from the ceiling and pop up through holes in the walls. Take cover and then open fire.

TIP

The UN building is quite dangerous. Many of the walls have been blasted to rubble, so there is plenty of cover—and many spots where the enemy can set up ambushes. As you advance, be ready to run—especially if you start taking fire from your flanks. Some of the enemies are smart and wait for you to walk past before they open fire. As a general rule, never assume an area is clear until "Voodoo" gives the all clear.

After neutralizing the first few hostiles, advance into the room and then turn left and take cover before engaging more hostiles in this area. Work your way around this area, looking for cover as enemies pop up on your flanks.

Clear out this floor entirely, then follow your team up the stairs to the next floor. Be sure to get some ammo from a teammate if you are running low. There is still a lot of fighting ahead.

As soon as you get to the top, turn left and engage the terrorist waiting to ambush you. Kill him and then take cover. There are lots more hostiles in the rubble-filled area. Watch out for grenades that they throw towards you. If possible, try to shoot them before they release the grenade. As it falls near their body, it may kill nearby enemies as well.

Follow your team members as they advance away from the stairs after killing the first group of enemies. However, as you move further into this area, more hostiles drop down from an upper floor and begin their attack. As they all drop into one area, this is a good time to toss a grenade into their midst. You can kill two or three with a single blast.

Once you have finished clearing the hostiles away, your team completes their search and don't find what they're looking for. Follow them out of the UN building and onto a walkway leading to the next building.

SEARCH THE HOTEL

BREACH AND CLEAR

Move across the walkway and continue through a doorway. After climbing a flight of stairs, follow a path that leads to the hotel. There are no hostiles here, so sprint as you move with your team.

Half of your team is advancing down the street below your position when they come under sniper fire. The snipers are in the hotel. While the team in the street takes cover, your team is going to clear out the snipers. Move to the door and select a breach tactic.

PROVIDE OVERWATCH FOR GROM

Rush into the room and kill the two enemies inside with headshots to clear the area, then advance into the next room where a window allows you to look down on the street below.

As you approach the window, look for a hostile out on a balcony. Quickly neutralize him before he can throw a grenade at you. Then begin providing covering fire for your team below.

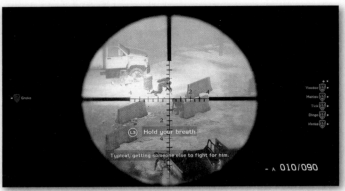

You switch to a sniper rifle once again. There are several hostiles in the street blocking the progress of your team. Start picking them off one at a time. Keep this up until all enemies in the street have been neutralized.

CLEAR THE HOTEL

Follow your team through a door and continue across a hallway to the hotel lobby. You are back to using your assault rifle again. Once in the lobby, hostiles enter through the other side. Quickly take cover and open fire.

In addition to the enemies on the other side of the lobby, several also attack you from the upper walkway along the left side of the area. They are a major threat, so begin firing at them before they can advance to your flank and start throwing grenades down on you.

Watch for a heavy gunner. As soon as you see him, engage him with long-range fire. If you can't take him down shortly after he arrives, he climbs up some stairs and advances along the upper walkway. Kill him as quickly as possible or he can decimate your team if he can flank them.

Since the upper walkway offers a major threat to your team, rush up the stairs to the left of where you entered the lobby. Take cover behind a billiards table and open fire on the enemy on the walkway. Since they are firing down on your team below, they often won't see you and you can attack from their flank.

After clearing off the walkway, turn the tables on the enemy and fire down on them from above. You have some great lines of fire that hit them from directions for which they do not have cover. Then head down the stairs at the far end of the walkway to come up behind the remaining hostiles in the lobby to finish them off.

Once the lobby is clear, follow "Voodoo" and the team through a smaller room at the far end of the lobby. Continue through a door and then down a long hallway and across an outdoor path that leads to the ice rink. That is probably where your target, Bosic, is located.

SEARCH THE ICE RINK
GET TO THE RINK

Once you enter the building where the ice rink is located, follow your team around through a series of corridors until you reach the rink. Bingo! You have found the P.E.T.N. In fact, the old Olympic ice rink looks like an arms warehouse.

SURVIVE

Bosic's men throw smoke grenades out onto the rink after your team moves in. Quickly take cover and watch for enemies trying to sneak up on you through the smoke. Pull back and be ready to engage enemies directly ahead as well as those trying to flank you from either the left or right. Some of the hostiles have flashlights, so fire at the lights to take them out.

When your team begins advancing down the middle of the rink, move along the right side to help cover them against flank attacks. Be ready with a melee attack if an enemy rushes in close to you.

After clearing the rink, advance to the end of it. Bosic and his men try to attack you from an upper level; however, when you return fire, they flee. Cover "Voodoo" while he opens up an exit from the rink so you can pursue Bosic.

CAPTURE THE ENGINEER

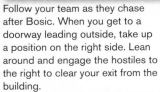

Follow your team as they chase after Bosic. When you get to a doorway leading outside, take up a position on the right side. Lean around and engage the hostiles to the right to clear your exit from the building.

Along with your team, advance along a path that follows the Olympic bobsled track, which is now in ruins as a result of the decades of war in this once great city. There are several hostiles that try to ambush you along the way. Drop behind cover, kill them, and then continue on. After passing some vehicles, walk inside a section of track that provides some cover from the sides. As you get to the spot where it is damaged, watch for hostiles in the section of track ahead who can fire down on your position. Neutralize them and any others that follow.

Fight your way through the bobsled area, then follow your team along a tree-lined path. Smoke fills the air, reducing your vision to tens of meters. Watch out for enemies that rush from the smoke to attack you. Fire from the hip or be ready with a melee attack. When you get to a fence, move forward and grab onto the fence, holding open some of the chain link so the rest of your team can pass through.

Once through the fence, sprint after Bosic to try to capture him. He gets into a car and begins to drive away. Fire at the car to disable it and bring it to a stop. Then rush forward to capture Bosic.

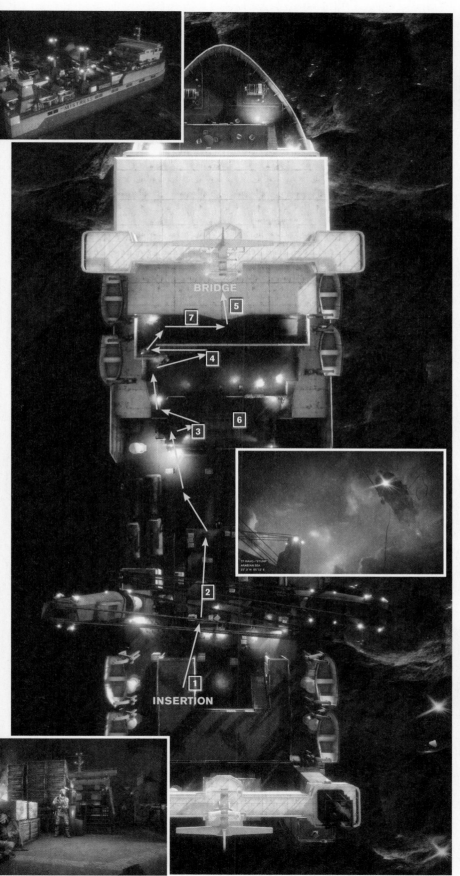

INSERTION

BRIDGE

BUMP IN THE NIGHT

BRIEFING

TASK FORCE MAKO
"STUMP"
Arabian Sea
23° 2' N – 65° 12' E

OBJECTIVES

One shipment of P.E.T.N. is currently en route to Pakistan. Task Force Mako must board, search, and seize the crew and cargo before the ship reaches port. You play as "Stump" and are working with other members of your team including "Mother". As your helicopters approach the ship, you notice that the ship seems to be adrift and not under power. That seems odd…

STORY

Mako fast ropes from SOAR Blackhawks onto the pitching deck of the MV Mistress. They encounter little resistance on board. What they do find is lots of bodies. Bodies of The Cleric's men. They fight to the bridge to gain command of the ship and this brings them to a startling discovery—one that leads them back to TF Blackbird.

TOC 9

The fate of Blackbird is now known; and now Preacher must team up with Mako and hit the Cleric's compound deep in the mountainous Chitral region of Pakistan. This is the last chance they will have, as actionable intel rarely lasts more than 24 hours.

LOADOUT

Primary – HK MP7
Secondary – HK45 Compact
Frag Grenades – x6

ACHIEVEMENTS

ONE MAN MUTINY

Complete the mission to earn this award.

DIRTY LAUNDRY

Find the grenades in the laundry room and earn this award.

STUMP'S NO CHUMP

Finish Stump's last mission to get this achievement/trophy.

GET TO THE BRIDGE

1 As soon as you rappel down to the deck of the ship near the bow, get your rifle up and ready for action.

2

Jump over the railing and rush forward onto the cargo platform where other members of your team are located. Take cover behind some of the crates and then start picking off enemies that appear along the railings near the bridge as well as in the doorways at deck level.

3

When your teammates move forward after all of the hostiles in this area have been neutralized, follow them and head through the doorway that leads from the deck into the superstructure.

Once through the doorway, head up the stairs. At the top, pause and watch the stairs directly in front of you that lead up to the next level. Wait to see if any hostiles come down to attack you and kill any that come down the stairs before they can shoot you. Then turn around and deal with any hostiles that come down the stairs on the right side.

Quickly rush up the stairs on the right and clear out any remaining hostiles on this deck. If you don't, these terrorists fire over the railing at you and your team on the lower level.

As you advance across the third level toward the stairs leading to the bridge level, you notice there are bodies on the stairs. These were some clean kills and your team did not make them. What is going on here?

Advance up the last flight of stairs and stack up with your team. As you go through the door, there are no hostiles on the bridge. However, you won't believe who you do find there.

GET TO THE BRIDGE

**1 HOUR EARLIER
"PREACHER"**
Arabian Sea
23° 2' N – 65° 12' E

FIND A WEAPON

This mission now switches perspective to "Preacher" an hour before Task Force Mako rappelled onto the ship. Sid Al Din executed "Mother" after capturing him and you (as "Preacher") in Dubai after "Mother" refused to talk and in order to threaten you into providing information. However, you are not going to give in—you are going to get revenge. Sid Al Din must pay for his actions. When your guard turns his back, you go into action and kill him. While you are no longer guarded, you are not free. You are still stuck on a ship filled with enemies somewhere in the Arabian Sea. They don't stand a chance. At the start, you are still a little dazed from the beatings. However, now that you can move about the ship, you need to find a weapon. Your guard did not have one on him.

Crouch down and move cautiously through the ship. Sneak up behind an enemy with his back to you and use a melee attack to kill him.

Unfortunately, he did not have a weapon on him either. Continue advancing through the ship and melee attack the next hostile. Once again, no luck on getting a weapon.

> **TIP**
> Pick up a shotgun dropped by one of the terrorists when you find one. This type of weapon is excellent in the narrow hallways and cramped spaces aboard the ship.

Keeping moving forward. Eventually you come across two hostiles. One has his pistol set down in front of him. Move in behind for a melee attack and you automatically kill him, grab the weapon, and kill the second enemy without alerting anyone else on board the ship. You now have a silenced pistol to help you get to Sad al Din.

Start moving towards the cargo bay. A terrorist is patrolling nearby. Aim for his flashlight to kill him before he sees you and opens fire. Then have your pistol ready as you begin walking up a ramp to the cargo bay. A hostile comes down the ramp and you need to try to kill him before he has a chance to see you and react. Be ready for a second hostile to jump out as you approach the top of the ramp. Pick up the shotgun dropped by one of these two. It only has a few shells in it, but it gives you greater firepower at close range than just your pistol.

> **TIP**
> While moving though the ship, try to get as many melee kills as you can. These will help you earn The Axeman achievement/trophy."

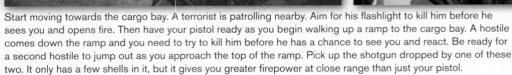

As you begin making your way towards the control room, move hostiles move into the area. Take cover behind some crates and then lean around the corner to shoot and kill them. Watch for more hostiles to show up. They are often armed with either shotguns or assault rifles, so shoot fast to take them out before they can get in a shot.

Advance cautiously and duck behind crates whenever you see enemies. A good tactic is to hide in ambush. As they walk past your crate while patrolling, shoot them as soon as they come into view and kill them before they even have a chance to react.

At times, it is better to rush an enemy before he can react and kill him with a melee attack—especially if that enemy has you outgunned. However, you need to wait until he is close before you leave your cover for the attack. Finish off all the hostiles in the area filled with crates and you can acquire an assault rifle. You may not have a lot of ammo for it to begin with, but you can get more ammo from other hostiles armed with assault rifles.

GET TO THE ENGINE ROOM

Head down the ramp that leads to an area with lots of parked cars. As you get near the bottom of the ramp, look out over the railing to the left and watch for a patrolling enemy. Kill him before he can kill you. Rush down the rest of way to the bottom and take cover behind a car. From there engage the other enemies in this area. Fire in short bursts to conserve ammo.

After they are dead, move over to their bodies and pick up any ammo they are carrying. Then begin moving through the area where a number of vehicles are parked. Use the vehicles for cover. The hostiles also use them for cover, so try shooting through the glass to kill enemies if they are not moving out into the open.

As you are clearing out enemies on your level, watch for others on upper levels as well who want to shoot down on you. Try to expose yourself to only one enemy at a time so that you are not overwhelmed. The steam leaking from the pipes in the cargo bay can make it difficult to see very far ahead of you, so look for flashlights, which give away the location of hostiles before you can actually see the silhouette of the person.

Advance from car to car, clearing as you go, and then neutralize any enemies near the door at the end of the cargo bay. Watch for one or two to try to ambush you as you move to the door. Once they are eliminated, move through the doorway.

Continue down a ramp leading to the engine room. There are terrorists that can be seen through the windows. However, the glass is bulletproof. Instead, watch for an enemy at the end of the corridor waiting to attack you.

Lean around the corner of the doorway leading into a control room and clear out the hostiles inside. Switch to an AKM assault rifle, since you will find more ammo for this in the next areas.

DISABLE THE SHIP

TIP

The floor of the upper level in the engine room is metal grating. This allows you to see and fire at enemies below. It also allows them to fire up at you. Therefore, you need to be aware of two different levels simultaneously.

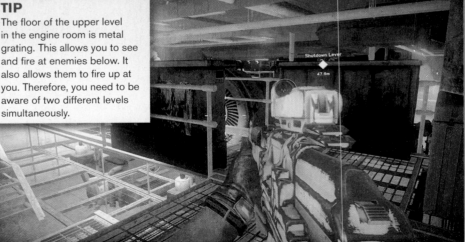

Since the ship is probably carrying P.E.T.N., you need to disable the ship so that it never reaches its destination. The engine room is a good place to do this. As you move through the doorway, watch for hostiles on your level as well as the level below. Clear as many as you can from the doorway before entering the room.

Advance along the top level and then descend a short flight of stairs to the lower level. Clear out hostiles here while taking cover behind the engines. There are lots of enemies down here, and be ready with a melee attack to deal with enemies as you turn a corner.

Keep moving towards the far end of the engine room. The hostiles like to hide and then pop out at you. Look for clues to their location, such as flashlight beams shining on the floor, and then aim in advance so you can kill them just as they pop out to attack.

Move across to the other side of the engine room and climb up the stairs to the upper level. Kill all of the hostiles on this level and watch for others in the level below. Fire right through the floor grates to kill the lower enemies. Then go down the stairs at the far end to return to the lower level.

Finish clearing out any remaining hostiles in the room on the lower level, then head up the stairs to the shutdown lever.

GET TO THE TOP DECK

Now that the ship is dead in the water, it is time to get to the top deck. However, while the engine room was all clear, as soon as you disabled the ship, alarms started going off and terrorists are rushing down to your location. You need to advance back across the engine room; however, there will be resistance. Find a good spot of cover and hold there while enemies come to you. Then, when it seems quiet, start advancing and clearing the room as you go.

Move across the center of the room, then head up the stairs, killing any enemies between you and the door on the side of the room. Continue through the door and then climb the stairs to the next area.

At the top of the stairs, walk through a doorway and along a corridor. Watch for a terrorist coming down another flight of stairs. Hug the left wall of the corridor and then lean to the right to pick off this threat, otherwise you are a sitting duck in the corridor. Now climb that flight of stairs to reach another corridor.

Walk to the end of the corridor and then take some stairs leading up to yet another level. Exit through a doorway out onto the deck of the ship. There is an enemy directly ahead of you with his back to you. Sneak up behind him and kill the hostile with a silent melee attack.

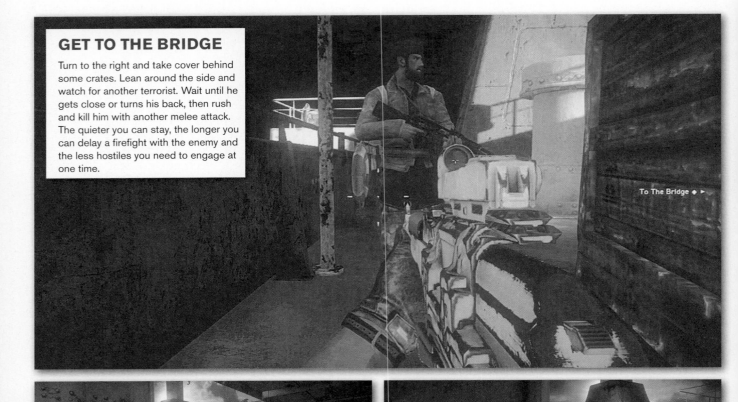

GET TO THE BRIDGE

Turn to the right and take cover behind some crates. Lean around the side and watch for another terrorist. Wait until he gets close or turns his back, then rush and kill him with another melee attack. The quieter you can stay, the longer you can delay a firefight with the enemy and the less hostiles you need to engage at one time.

Make your way towards the main part of the deck. If you have avoided making any noise, there should be a couple hostiles there. If not, they are already coming after you. Take careful aim and try to kill both of these enemies before they can turn and shoot at you or run away. Then duck behind the wall for cover. Lean around the corner of the wall and pick off other enemies in the cargo area of the deck. Kill as many as you can from this position.

Now move around to the left, using the wall for cover. Advance towards the bridge along the left side of the ship. Take out the terrorists on the upper walkways of the superstructure of the ship. It is important to clear out as many threats as possible before rushing across the deck.

Once you have done all you can, move towards the center of the deck where some cargo is stored. As you climb the stairs, be ready for hostiles to jump out at you. Kill them and then sprint to cover. Fire at the hostiles on the superstructure walkways.

After it looks clear, sprint the across the open space to the door in the superstructure that leads to the galley. If you get attacked, keep running and use the doorway for cover.

FIND SAD AL DIN

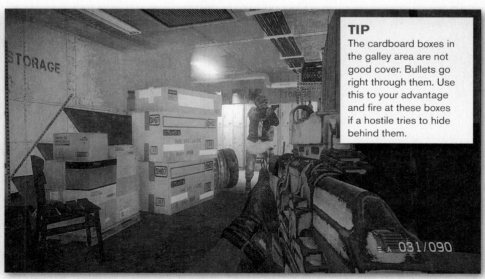

> **TIP**
> The cardboard boxes in the galley area are not good cover. Bullets go right through them. Use this to your advantage and fire at these boxes if a hostile tries to hide behind them.

As you enter the superstructure and walk along a corridor, watch the door at the end. A terrorist may burst through to stop you. Kill him and then move to the doorway.

Continue to the galley storage room. Watch for an enemy to charge you. Kill him with a melee attack, then lean around the corner of the wall at the edge of the storage room and kill the enemies inside. As you advance through this area, jumping over a fallen refrigerator that blocks your way, watch for enemies that tend to jump out and open fire at you. Keep a full clip in your rifle as you never know when you will need to let loose with a long burst from the hip.

As you approach the galley, be ready. There are several hostiles inside. Kill anyone near the entrance, then take cover behind the end of the long work counter. From here you can lean left or right to clear the two aisles in the galley. Eliminate as many hostiles as you can here, then move down an aisle and start clearing out the eating area. There are several more enemies here. One even throws grenades, so be ready to withdraw into the galley to avoid being hurt by the grenades. Once it is clear, exit through the door at the far side of the eating area.

Sad al Din is on the run. Follow him up a flight of stairs and into the crew quarters. Take cover and kill the hostile inside who thinks he can get the jump on you. Neutralize all of the other enemies that come in and take cover behind the furniture barricades. Next, go through the wooden door on the left, ready to kill another enemy on the other side.

As you move through one of the crew quarters, a door across the hall opens. Fire at the hostiles in another room of crew quarters before moving into the hallway between the rooms and turning left and engaging more enemies that rush into the hallway.

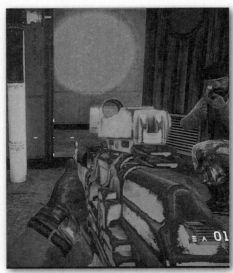

Continue around to the left and be ready to use a melee attack to kill a hostile hiding behind some crates who is waiting to ambush you. If you move fast, he won't be able to get off a shot.

When you get to the end of the corridor, lean around the corner of the doorway and engage more hostiles in the next room. There are several in hiding. As they pop up, shoot them. Slowly strafe to the left to enter the room and take cover so you can clear out the rest of the room.

Advance through the room and exit through the door on the left side. As you do, you see Task Force Mako rappelling down onto the deck. They can provide a distraction while you complete your own personal objective.

CHASE SAD AL DIN

As you turn to the right, you see Sad al Din running up the stairs towards the bridge. Rush after him before he can get away from you. Follow him all the way to the bridge.

Breach a wooden door and then enter the bridge to finish your business with the man who killed your best friend and partner. "Voodoo" and the rest of TF Mako burst into the bridge and capture Sal al Din. The team then evacuates you and the captive away from the ship.

SHUT IT DOWN

BRIEFING

JOINT TASK FORCE BLACKBIRD/MAKO "PREACHER"
Chitral Region, Pakistan
35° 50' N – 71° 47' E

OBJECTIVES

With all of the pieces of the puzzle in place, it's a race against the clock to raid the Cleric's compound deep in the Chitral region of Pakistan. This operation combines several task forces, and even "Dusty", the man who has been behind the scenes in supporting and organizing the task forces, is coming along. One of his men was executed and he is going to set it right.

ACHIEVEMENTS

LET HIM ROT

Finish this mission to earn this achievement/trophy.

PREACHER'S PATH

Complete the last mission as Preacher to get this award.

WARFIGHTER

You can earn this award the first time you complete the campaign on any difficulty level.

HARDCORE

Complete the mission on Hardcore difficulty level.

TIER 1

Complete the campaign on Tier 1 difficulty level to get this award.

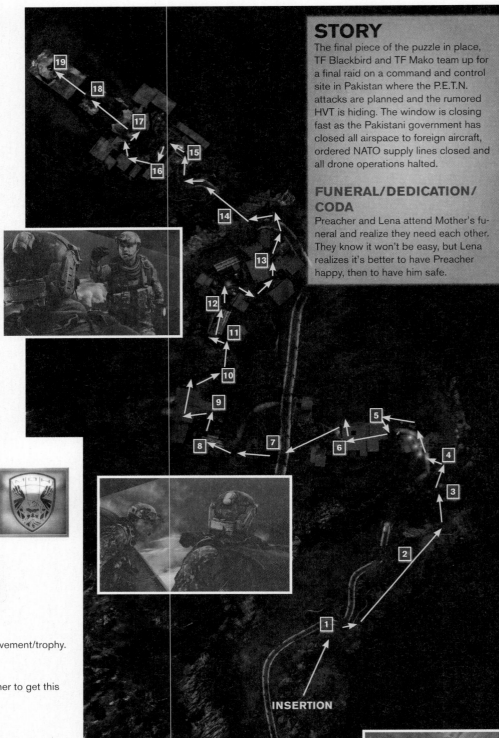
INSERTION

LOADOUT

Primary – Daniel Defense Mk18
Secondary – P226 with suppressor
Frag Grenades – x6

INFILTRATE COMPOUND

AVOID DETECTION

Your team makes an airborne insertion in the area around the Cleric's compound. The key to success for this mission is to stay stealthy. The closer you can get to the Cleric before he knows you are there, the better. Once on the ground, follow "Voodoo" as he takes the lead.

As your team approaches a road, crouch down and take cover behind a fallen tree as some vehicles and terrorists pass by. You don't want to alert them to your presence just yet.

As the column passes, two men stay behind to answer nature's call. "Voodoo" will take care of one while you kill the other. Pick the target on the right, take aim through your scope, and squeeze the trigger to eliminate the hostile.

Advance along with your team down a path to the side of the road. As you veer away from the road, you come across three enemies around a campfire. Wait until your team is set and open fire. As you shoot, so do other members of your team to ensure not one of the terrorists gets off a shout or a shot. Now that these sentries are neutralized, continue along with your team towards the wall surrounding the compound.

Make your way across a small stream and then take cover behind some rocks right next to the wall. The gates open and a truck drives out from the compound. A single hostile stands sentry by the gate. As soon as the truck drives away, kill the sentry before he goes back into the compound and closes the gates. You have completed the first objective and reached the compound without being detected by the enemy.

SHOOT THE FUSE BOX

Follow your team through the open gate and into the compound. Stay quiet for now. Move along the right side of the compound, hiding behind crates and vehicles to get to the right side of the building. Locate the fuse box on the side of the building and fire a couple of rounds into it to knock out the power and leave all of the enemies in the dark.

As the lights go out, you automatically activate your NODS so you can see in the dark. This gives you a major advantage over the enemy. Watch for a hostile that runs out the door to see why the lights went out. Kill him before he even realizes you are there, then advance into the building.

The rooms through which you move are empty, so continue to a locked door. Stack up and then select a breach tactic. After rushing into the room, quickly take out the four hostiles inside. Since it is still dark, this is an easier breach than you are used to. However, you can't waste time or they will start shooting at your muzzle flashes once they recover from the flashbang.

After you clear the room, a hostile runs down the stairs in the middle of the room. Kill him and then move up the stairs, eliminating any hostiles located near the top of the stairs. Continue to the top of the stairs and clear this room of any remaining enemies.

As the rest of your team follows you up the stairs, take aim at the open door on the right side of the room. There are more hostiles in the next room on the other side of the door. They have flashlights, so they can now see in the dark—though not as effectively as you. Kill as many of these enemies as possible as they appear near the doorway. Once you have cleared the room, your teammates enter to secure it.

Advance through the room and into the next room through a door on the right. Neutralize the hostile inside before he sees you in the dark. As you continue through this room and on into the next, the lights come back on. The enemy has restored power and now you have lost your night fighting advantage.

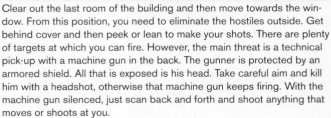

Clear out the last room of the building and then move towards the window. From this position, you need to eliminate the hostiles outside. Get behind cover and then peek or lean to make your shots. There are plenty of targets at which you can fire. However, the main threat is a technical pick-up with a machine gun in the back. The gunner is protected by an armored shield. All that is exposed is his head. Take careful aim and kill him with a headshot, otherwise that machine gun keeps firing. With the machine gun silenced, just scan back and forth and shoot anything that moves or shoots at you.

Once it quiets down outside, take a look at the terrain. You can also see another technical pull up and stop in the distance. It is too far away for you to engage and it is not shooting at you. Therefore, follow "Voodoo" through a door on the right side of the room, down some stairs, and then out of the building.

Head towards the left side of the area and take cover as enemies approach. Open fire and take them out before they can get behind cover of their own.

FLANK HOUSE THROUGH BARN

As you are engaging the enemies coming towards your position, you start taking RPG fire from a gunner on the roof of a building at the opposite end of the area. Locate him and take him out with a carefully aimed shot using your scope. Now get ready to move. If you stay put, more hostiles take the places of those you kill at the building. Therefore, you need to perform a flanking maneuver.

Follow "Voodoo" along the left wall of the compound, killing any enemies you encounter along the way. As you approach a barn, take cover and neutralize enemies inside that are firing at you. Once it looks clear, rush into the barn with your teammate. Be alert for any hostiles you might have missed.

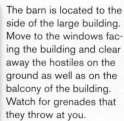

The barn is located to the side of the large building. Move to the windows facing the building and clear away the hostiles on the ground as well as on the balcony of the building. Watch for grenades that they throw at you.

SEARCH THE FARMHOUSE

After killing the hostiles by the building, follow "Voodoo" through the barn door and into the side door of the building. As you walk in, drop to a crouch and engage hostiles rushing down the stairs directly ahead of you.

Once enemies stop coming down the stairs, move to the foot of the staircase and kill any hostiles you can see at the top. Then rush to the top of the stairs.

As you get to the top of the stairs, don't stop until you are behind some crates near the wall. There are several hostiles to the right of the stairs. Lean around the crates and engage them. One of the enemies is an armored machine gunner. Take a few shots, then duck back behind cover. Repeat this a few times to finally kill him. If you stay exposed and try to kill him with sustained fire, he will more than likely kill you instead.

After this area is clear, move through the next few rooms along with your teammates until you come to a locked door along the side of a hallway. Stack up and give a breach order. As you enter the room, move quickly to take down the six hostiles inside.

Clear the room and then follow "Voodoo" and your team through a door that leads outside. Continue around the side of the farmhouse and across a yard to where the rest of the task force is waiting.

REACH CLERIC'S PALACE
CLEAR PATH WITH ROBOT

Move over to the combat robot and take control of it. Start off by switching to the grenade launcher and firing at enemies directly ahead who are shooting at your robot. Then fire at the door of the building where a targeting icon is positioned. Since the robot does not have a hand to open doors, you just blast your way in.

Drive the robot across the wooden foot bridge and then launch some grenades through the open doorway to kill some of the hostiles inside the building. Strafe past the door, using the machine gun to clear out any remaining enemies before driving into the building. As soon as you are inside, launch grenades through another doorway into the next room.

Keep driving through a doorway and along an outside corridor. Fire at enemies at the far end of the corridor with both machine gun and grenade fire as you drive forward. As you get to the end of the corridor, launch grenades at a technical to kill both the driver and the gunner. Then neutralize an armored machine gunner who appears and opens fire at the robot.

As you clear out the courtyard ahead, your teammates begin advancing on your left side. Start driving across the foot bridge and engage the terrorist with an RPG in an upstairs window to the right. Kill him before he can hurt your teammates. Keep providing covering fire until "Voodoo" declares the area clear. Then drive the robot over towards the gate where your team is waiting.

Now that the robot has done its job, it is time to get personal. Back on your feet, follow your team through the gate and along a walkway to another open space between buildings. Rush to take cover behind a stack of lumber and then start firing at enemies who arrive to try to stop you from reaching the Cleric's palace.

After this area is clear, advance around the buildings to the left and follow your team towards a bridge leading to the palace. Quickly take cover. A technical drives out onto the bridge. Take careful aim and hit the gunner with a headshot to kill him.

USE MMG TO CLEAR ENEMIES

After you kill the gunner on the technical, drop back behind cover and then engage the hostiles rushing across the bridge towards your position.

Sprint out onto the bridge, killing any hostiles in your way, and climb onto the technical to man the medium machine gun. Blast away at the wooden gate at the far side of the bridge and then mow down all enemies that try to rush across the bridge.

KILL THE CLERIC

Once the bridge is clear, hop down from the technical and follow your team across the bridge and through the driveway that leads to the palace. As you near the palace, you see flames and explosions coming from it. However, there is no resistance in this area at all. Keep moving.

After climbing some steps leading to the palace yard, turn to the left and be ready to engage some hostiles. Kill them both before they can get you. Then advance and be ready to kill more as you round a corner to the right. The terrorists can be difficult to see in the dark, so look for flashlights. Shoot at the light and you usually hit the person holding the weapon with the flashlight attached.

CAPTURE THE ENGINEER

As you approach the palace doors, they blow outward with an explosion. Wait for the smoke to clear and then enter the palace. As you do, there are flames up ahead and burning terrorists. Put them out of their misery and then follow a corridor to the left that is not yet on fire.

Follow "Voodoo" as he continues to advance through the burning palace. As the smoke gets thick, drop prone and crawl so you can stay low where there is still oxygen to breathe. Shoot any hostiles you come across—though they are not likely to put up much of a fight.

As "Voodoo" stands up, get up from prone and continue to a locked door. This is it. The Cleric is on the other side.

After kicking in the door, you enter the room. The Cleric is standing there, partially stunned. He has a bomb strapped to his back. As you look around the room, you see that the Cleric had planned terrorist attacks against many different targets.

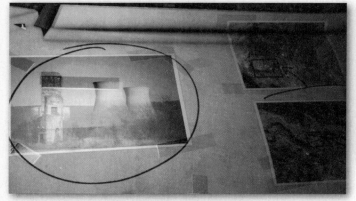

As the Cleric brings up his hand, you see a detonator in it. Quickly take aim with your pistol and kill him with a headshot before he can blow up "Voodoo" and you. "Mother" has been avenged.

MULTIPLAYER
BOOTCAMP

Medal of Honor Warfighter multiplayer puts two teams of ten players against each other within a variety of hostile environments scattered across the globe. As both teams clash, your skill and determination will help win the day. This chapter covers all aspects of multiplayer, helping familiarize you with the unique interface, features, and game modes. So whether or not you're new to Medal of Honor, take a few minutes to review the basics.

"BEGINNER'S GUIDE: GETTING STARTED" 144

"MOVEMENT" 148

"COMBAT" 148

"SCORING & STATS" 151

"SCORECHAIN & SUPPORT ACTIONS" 152

"GAME MODES" 153

"MULTIPLAYER TACTICS" 155

"COMMUNITY" 156

MULTIPLAYER BOOTCAMP

Medal of Honor Warfighter multiplayer puts two teams of ten players against each other within a variety of hostile environments scattered across the globe. As both teams clash, your skill and determination will help win the day. This chapter covers all aspects of multiplayer, helping familiarize you with the unique interface, features, and game modes. So whether or not you're new to *Medal of Honor*, take a few minutes to review the basics.

BEGINNER'S GUIDE: GETTING STARTED

You're only a few seconds away from starting your multiplayer career. So if you'd prefer to jump into the action immediately, follow these quick and easy steps to get started. However, you may want to browse through this entire chapter at least once before taking the fight online. The online action is fast-paced and can be a bit intimidating to a first-time player. But if you're experienced with online first-person shooters, you should have no problem picking up the gameplay.

1: CHOOSE MULTIPLAYER

When you first launch the game, you're prompted to chose between the single-player campaign and multiplayer. Each game mode is separate and loads independently of one another. At this point, select Multiplayer to load the online component of *Medal of Honor Warfighter*. Also, if playing on a console, make sure you're signed in with your Playstation Network or Xbox Live Gold account.

2: ACTIVATE ORIGIN ONLINE PASS

Before you can join a multiplayer match for the first time, you must first login with your Origin account profile and enter your online pass. If you already have an Origin account, simply enter your e-mail address and password to proceed. If you aren't registered with Origin yet, you can do it all from this screen. Simply enter your e-mail address and create a password. Agree with the terms and conditions to continue, then enter the online pass code included with your game to proceed.

3: SELECT NATION/UNIT

Your decision here determines which soldier in the assaulter class you unlock first. Carefully look at all options indicated by the flag icons to de-

termine which weapons and attachments are associated with each soldier. The assaulter soldier you choose here will be the first and only class made available to you at the start of your career. But you'll soon unlock other classes and soldiers as you make progress and rise through the ranks.

4: FIND GAME

After selecting your starting soldier, you are then dropped into the multiplayer lobby where you can choose from a variety of options. Feel free to browse through them, but since you're new, you haven't accrued any stats or unlocked any new weapons or soldiers. It's time to get busy. From the lobby screen it's possible to join a Quick Match already in progress—this is the quickest way to jump into battle. If you want to look for a more specific map or game mode, choose the Find Game option and open the Server Browser. This lists all available multiplayer servers showing the current map, game mode, and number of players. The Matchmaking feature allows you to make a more general selection, choosing from servers running a particular game mode.

5: SELECT CLASS AND PLAY!

You've most likely joined a match in progress and are automatically assigned to the team with the least players. But before you spawn on the map, you must choose the class you'd like to play. The assaulter class is the most versatile, making perfect sense why it's the only class made available to beginners. But don't worry, you'll unlock more classes, soldiers, and weapons soon enough as you rack up points and advance through the ranks. You can also customize your primary weapon from this screen, but if this is your first match, you have no customization options yet. Finally, you're ready to join a match. Press the deploy button shown at the bottom of the screen to enter the match. You're now ready to begin your online career.

INTERFACE

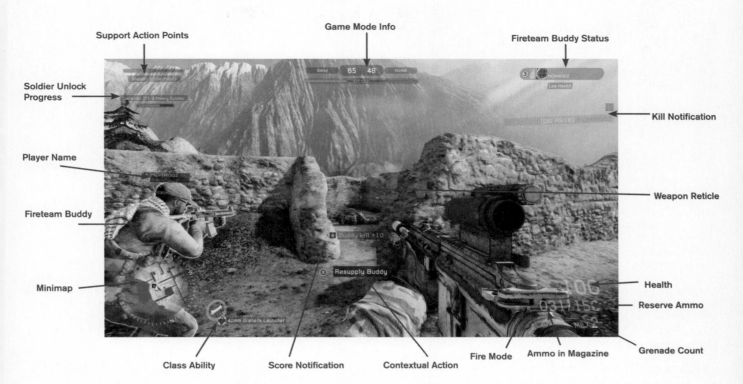

Support Action Points

Game Mode Info

Fireteam Buddy Status

Soldier Unlock Progress

Kill Notification

Player Name

Weapon Reticle

Fireteam Buddy

Minimap

Health

Reserve Ammo

Class Ability · **Score Notification** · **Contextual Action** · **Fire Mode** · **Ammo in Magazine** · **Grenade Count**

Fire Mode: This icon represents the selected fire mode of your primary weapon. Most weapons have different fire modes, allowing you to choose from automatic, semi-automatic, or burst.

Ammo in Magazine: This number represents how many rounds are remaining in your weapon's current magazine.

Reserve Ammo: This is how much extra ammo you're carrying, not including the bullets in your currently loaded magazine. You can receive more ammo from your Fireteam Buddy.

Grenade Count: The type and how many grenades you're currently carrying. All soldiers can carry a maximum of two grenades, but the type of grenade carried differs based on your chosen class. In this image the player has two M67 fragmentation grenades.

Health: This number, ranging from zero to 100, represents your health. If your health drops below 100, you'll slowly recover over time. Your Fireteam Buddy can also heal you, instantly restoring you to full health.

Weapon Reticle: Place this reticle over your target and fire to score a hit. Reticles expand and contract based on your movement and stance. A small reticle reflects improved accuracy, so always try to fire from a stable, crouched

or prone position. Using a weapon's iron sights or scope yields even better accuracy.

Kill Notification: Every time you kill an opponent, a string of text appears on the bottom of the screen identifying the name of your victim as well as the weapon used to score the kill. Similar kill notifications appear below the minimap when teammates kill or are killed by opponents.

Fireteam Buddy Status: Look here to see your fireteam's designation as well as your buddy's name, and overall status. If your Fireteam Buddy is injured or running low on ammo, you'll be notified here. Get to them fast to heal and resupply.

Game Mode Info: Each game mode features specific information at the top of the HUD. This may include items such as a timer, team health, team scores, available objectives, and other items specific to each game mode.

Support Action Points: This meter represents your progress toward achieving a support action. Support actions are awarded at 400-point intervals as long as you stay alive—if you die, the meter is reset. The available offensive and defensive support actions also appear here, differing based on your achieved scorechain level and selected class. You can only choose one

support action per level, offensive or defensive, so choose carefully. Support actions remain available until selected, even if you die.

Soldier Unlock Progress: This meter shows your progress toward unlocking the next soldier. There are a total of 72 different soldiers consisting of 12 units and six classes. Each soldier has a specific point threshold that must be met before it is unlocked. In this image the player is close to unlocking the Canadian JTF-2 heavy gunner.

Player Name: Every player's name appears directly above his or her character's head, making it easy to identify your Fireteam Buddy (green text), teammates (blue text), and opponents (red text).

Fireteam Buddy: Your Fireteam Buddy always appears on the HUD, outlined by a green silhouette, even when your buddy is outside your line of sight. This makes your buddy easy to spot, even if on the opposite side of the map. Make an effort to stay near your Fireteam Buddy so you can support, resupply, and heal each other.

Minimap: The circular minimap is your own personal satellite view of the battlefield, complete with compass readings on the outer rim. Teammates appear as blue dots while opponents appear as red dots—your

Fireteam Buddy appears as a green star. Opponents appear on the map whenever they fire their unsuppressed weapon or move nearby. Gunshots fired beyond the view of the minimap appear as white flashes on the perimeter, helping you easily locate firefights.

Class Ability: All six classes have a unique ability, indicated by this icon to the right of the minimap. This icon identifies the class ability as well as the key/button press required to activate it. In this image, the player's chosen assaulter class is equipped with a grenade launcher. The ring around the icon indicates how much of the ability the player has left.

Score Notification: Every point you earn appears here, just below the weapon reticle and in white text. Points are earned by killing opponents, capturing/destroying objectives, and completing a variety of other actions. You also earn points for actions performed by your Fireteam Buddy, assuming you stay within 20 meters. These point notifications appear in green text.

Contextual Action: A white line of text accompanied by a button/key icon appears here any time you're next to an interactive object. This is how you heal and resupply your Fireteam Buddy as well as arm/disarm charges in Combat Mission or Hotspot.

CONTEXTUAL ACTIONS

Press the button/key shown on screen to resupply and heal your Fireteam Buddy.

During gameplay, you have the opportunity to interact with a few objects as well as your Fireteam Buddy. At these times, instructions appear on the screen. For example, when you are near an interactive object, a note appears in the middle of the screen stating which button you need to press to place an explosive charge, pick up a flag, or resupply your Fireteam Buddy. Interacting with objectives (in Combat Mission and Hotspot) makes you initiate a timed explosive charge used to destroy them. In Home Run, you must interact with the flag before you can carry it back to your team's base. Resupplying or healing your Fireteam Buddy works the same way. Just make sure you're close enough to interact with them.

HEALTH

If this is what your screen looks like, find cover fast!

During multiplayer there is a health counter in the bottom right corner of the screen, starting at 100. As you take damage, the number decreases and the HUD's perimeter turns red with splotches of blood as your vision blurs. If the health counter reaches zero, you're dead and must respawn into the match after waiting a few seconds. Whenever you take damage, seek cover immediately before you die—dropping prone is a good way to avoid taking subsequent hits if cover isn't readily available. While in cover, you slowly heal over time and the HUD returns to its default pristine condition. But reaching cover before dying is easier said than done. The weapons in multiplayer inflict heavy damage, rarely giving you the chance to take evasive actions. If you do survive the first barrage, find cover immediately instead of trying to seek out your attacker.

MINIMAP

Activating the point man's UAV support action reveals the locations of enemies on your minimap.

The minimap is your best friend. Not only does it give you a top-down view of your surroundings, but it also relays vital real-time information including the positions of your teammates and enemies. The blue dots on the minimap represent your teammates—the green star icon is your Fireteam Buddy. Knowing where your friends are at all times is a vital tool in any combat situation. Try to stay in an area where there are several blue dots around you. If you see no blue dots on the minimap, find a good hiding spot as this indicates you're potentially deep in enemy territory—this is particularly important during Team Deathmatch. It's safe to assume areas that aren't occupied by friendly forces contain enemies. The minimap is a great way to gauge the distance between you and your teammates. While it's a good idea to stay within sight of your buddies, clustering too tightly together can make you vulnerable to explosive attacks such as mortar strikes. Keep an eye on the minimap to make sure you're not presenting the enemy with a tempting target for offensive support actions.

Red dots on the minimap represent enemies. These icons appear briefly whenever your opponents fire unsuppressed weapons. Watch for these red dot icons popping up on the minimap and use this information to hunt down nearby opponents. Activating the point man's UAV support action also reveals the locations of all enemies within a wide radius. This information is shared with all members of your team via their minimaps. If your team has a UAV in the air, there's nowhere for the enemies to hide. Take advantage of this intelligence while the UAV is still active. When a dot on the minimap becomes a ring icon it indicates a teammate or enemy is either above or below you. So look up or down to make visual contact.

TIP
If you have a suppressor attached to your weapon, your position is not shown on your opponents' minimaps while firing. However, a suppressor will not prevent you from being spotted by a UAV. Only the sniper can avoid UAV detection when their bipod is deployed.

FIRETEAMS

Stay close to your Fireteam Buddy at all times so you can support, resupply, and heal each other.

During multiplayer each team is made up of multiple fireteams comprised of two players. The other player on your fireteam is known as your Fireteam Buddy. Your Fireteam Buddy always appears on your HUD, represented by a green silhouette. Even if your Fireteam Buddy is out of sight, you can still see their green silhouette on the HUD. This helps you identify the location of your Fireteam Buddy at all times, allowing you to stay close and provide support to one another. In addition to watching each other's backs, you can also heal and resupply your Fireteam Buddy. Simply move next to your Fireteam Buddy until a contextual action box appears in the center of the HUD, then press the button/key shown on screen to hand over ammo or patch up your buddy. Your Fireteam Buddy is also a source for health and ammo, so never wander too far away. When you've been resupplied by your buddy, you gain ammo and health but are not replenished with new grenades.

If you die, you can also spawn directly on your Fireteam Buddy by choosing the Buddy Spawn option from the respawn screen. Spawning on your Fireteam Buddy is a great way to stay together, even following a death. However, you can only spawn on your Fireteam Buddy if he is in a safe location and hasn't been spotted by opponents. If your buddy is waiting to spawn on you, move to a safe location and wait, otherwise your buddy may be forced to wait or spawn at a different location.

RESPAWNING

The combat in multiplayer is brutal. You will die, and you'll probably die often. But no worries—your death is little more than a brief time-out during which time you can change your class, weapons, and even select your spawn location. By default there are usually two spawn options, Fall Back and Buddy Spawn. The Fall Back option puts you at a neutral location on the map, depending on the current game mode. Fall Back always puts you in a safe location, practically guaranteeing you won't encounter opponents nearby. But if you want to spawn closer to the action, choose the Buddy Spawn option. This spawns you into the match directly behind your Fireteam Buddy. If your Fireteam Buddy also is dead, the Buddy Spawn option is not available.

From the spawn screen it's possible to spawn directly at your Fireteam Buddy's location.

Spawning in the Blackhawk is risky. Consider spawning on your buddy or the Fall Back position instead.

If a teammate has activated the Blackhawk Transport support action, you can also choose to spawn from a hovering helicopter, automatically fast-roping to the ground. Spawning on the Blackhawk can be dangerous since it's such a highly visible target. You're invulnerable while sliding down the rope, but there's a good chance you may be ambushed when your feet hit the ground. Fortunately, the Blackhawk is equipped with a minigun operated by the player who initiated the support action. The gunner usually takes the brunt of all incoming fire, but don't be surprised if a few rounds zip past your head as you slide down the rope. When activating this support action during Combat Mission and Hotspot, the Blackhawk always hovers near the current objective, allowing for a steady supply of reinforcements at the most contentious point on the map.

MOVEMENT

Moving around the battlefield is fairly straightforward. On consoles, the left stick controls forward and backward movement as well as strafing to the left and right. Strafing is a lateral move where the direction you are facing does not change. It is useful for moving out from cover to fire, and then moving back behind cover for protection. The right stick controls where you look or aim—turning left and right as well as looking up and down. The peek and lean feature from single-player now carries over to multiplayer, allowing you to peek around objects without exposing your entire body.

It's possible to jump and vault over small objects like sandbags and low walls. This is a great way to continue forward movement when pushing toward an objective or other location. But use the jump action sparingly. Executing a series of jumps will slow you down, tiring your soldier until the soldier's movement is reduced significantly. Avoid bunny-hopping if you come under fire—you will only move slower and become an easier target for your opponents.

CROUCH, PRONE, AND SPRINTING

There is more to movement than just walking. Try crouching or dropping prone for greater stealth and stability. While crouched, you move slower. However, since you are lower, you make a smaller target for the enemy to hit and you can more easily duck behind cover. Dropping prone makes your soldier hit the dirt, lying belly-down. This makes you an even smaller target while providing you with the most stable firing position—the sniper and heavy gunner can deploy their bipod for increased stability while prone. When advancing against an enemy position, it is usually best to move crouched, as it is harder for the enemy to detect you. Crouching also causes the reticle to tighten up, indicating an increase in weapon accuracy. Make a habit of dropping to a knee (and aiming) before firing a shot. While it's possible to crawl around while prone, movement is sluggish, making you vulnerable to attack. Avoid crawling around unless you simply need to shift firing positions.

Your weapon is lowered while sprinting, preventing you from firing. However, you can reload your weapon while sprinting.

At times, it is better to move fast. Hold down the left stick while moving to sprint. You can't use weapons or equipment while sprinting, but you are much more difficult for the enemy to hit. Sprint when you have to cross a dangerously open piece of ground as you move from one position of cover to another, but sprint sparingly. If you suspect opponents are nearby, it's always best to keep your weapon raised and ready to fire. If you happen to sprint directly in front of an opponent, you won't have enough time to retaliate before the enemy empties a magazine into your body. If you crouch while sprinting, you'll initiate a slide. Although not ideal, sliding can save your life if you come face-to-face with an enemy while your weapon is lowered. Try sliding toward an enemy while firing the point man's 870 shotgun!

COMBAT

While moving about the battlefield is a major part of gameplay, the sole purpose of movement is to place you in a position where you can use your weapons to engage and eliminate the enemy. As a Tier 1 operator in training, you have access to different types of weapons. However, the controls for using these weapons are fairly common. For specifics on weapons, see the Classes and Weapons section, which covers this topic in greater detail.

FIREARMS

As mentioned earlier, the reticle in the center of the screen is your aiming point for using weapons. Most of the weapons you use are direct fire, meaning that the projectile you fire travels in a straight line from your weapon to the target. Using these weapons is simple. Place the reticle directly over the target and then press the fire button. For semi-automatic or single-shot weapons such as pistols, shotguns, and sniper rifles, each time you press the fire button, you fire a single round. However, for automatic weapons such as submachine guns, assault rifles, and light machine guns, they will continue to shoot as you hold down the fire button until they are empty. When firing automatic weapons, the longer the burst, the less accurate your fire. Therefore, to maintain greater accuracy and still put out a lot of lead, fire in short bursts. You are more likely to kill your target, especially at medium to long range, with a few accurate rounds rather than an entire clip spread all over. In addition, most weapons have fire select modes, allowing you to switch between automatic and semi-automatic. If recoil becomes a problem, switch to semi-automatic, particularly when engaging targets at long range.

Firing from the hip is not advised unless engaging targets at extreme close range... preferably with a shotgun.

IRON SIGHTS AND SCOPES

TIP

It's a good idea to get in the habit of pressing the zoom button to bring up your iron sights just before firing. This not only is more accurate, but it also provides a zoomed-in view of the target. To further increase accuracy, crouch or drop prone and remain stationary while firing. In the console versions, an aim assist function snaps your aim to a nearby target, making it much easier to score hits, even if your initial aim is slightly off.

Accuracy increases dramatically when taking aim through your weapon's iron sights or scope.

When you fire a weapon using the reticle to aim, you are essentially firing from the hip, with the butt of your weapon in the crook of your arm. This is not very accurate and should only be used at close range. To increase your accuracy, press the zoom button. This will bring up the scope or iron sights view, where you are actually looking through the weapon's sight to aim. The butt of the weapon is brought up to your shoulder, giving you greater stability and accuracy. Simply put the sight's front post over your target and squeeze the trigger to score a hit. If your weapon is equipped with a scope, the zoom button provides a view through the scope rather than iron sights. Scopes are often magnified, helping you get a closer view of the target before firing. Always aim for your opponent's head to maximize damage. Pressing down on the right stick or middle mouse button while in the iron sights view will toggle to a different optic if you've equipped a dual sight or a backup iron sight.

GRENADES

If you suspect an opponent is hiding in a building or other confined space, toss a grenade inside before entering.

Grenades require a bit more skill to use effectively since they are thrown. Unlike a bullet or rocket which travels in a straight line, grenades travel in a parabolic arc due to their lower speed and the effect of gravity. When throwing a grenade, the reticle on the screen turns into a tiny white dot—use this to adjust your aim before letting go of the grenade. When deploying a grenade, first take into account what kind of grenade you're throwing, depending on your chosen class. Snipers carry a proximity mine which is placed on the ground and explodes when enemies pass within a few feet—ideal for defending objectives or choke points. The assaulter and spec ops class carries a standard fragmentation grenade that explodes and scatters shrapnel across a wide radius. The demolitions class deploys a remote charge, a powerful explosive manually triggered by a remote control device. The heavy gunner is equipped with mini frags, three small fragmentation grenades that are thrown simultaneously and scatter before detonating. The point man carries flashbangs, non-lethal grenades that emit a bright flash and loud bang, temporarily blinding anyone nearby. Flashbangs will also spot enemies caught in the blast so your entire team will know where they are for a few seconds. Each grenade type has its own strengths and weaknesses, so take some time getting used to the characteristics of the grenade type carried by each class.

The frag grenades and mini frags can be cooked by holding down the grenade button. Cooking a grenade is a great way score kills as it gives your opponents less time to run away. As soon as you begin holding down the button, the grenade's fuse starts—if you hold the button down too long, it will explode in your face, leading to an embarrassing death. For best results, wait no longer than two seconds before releasing the grenade button. If you time it just right, grenades can explode in the air, just above your intended target. This is a great way to take out opponents hiding behind walls and other pieces of cover.

GRENADE AND ROCKET LAUNCHERS

The demolition class's M32 and SMAW offensive support actions are great for softening defensive positions.

Grenade and rocket launchers can only be equipped by the assaulter and demolitions classes. The assaulter class automatically has an under-barrel grenade launcher as their class ability, but the demolitions class must work to get their special weapons—both the M32 grenade launcher and SMAW rocket launcher are awarded as offensive support actions. Unlike the hand-tossed grenades, these weapons launch explosive munitions great distances. In the case of a grenade launcher, the farther away you are from the target, the higher you need to aim. That is why the reticle for a grenade launcher has several horizontal line aiming points. For a short-range shot, use the top line. The farther away your target, use the lower lines. By using a lower aiming point, you are essentially aiming the weapon up higher to lob the grenade toward the target. Unlike the assaulter class's single-shot grenade launcher, the demolition class's M32 is capable of firing up to six grenades in rapid succession. The M32 is also equipped with a scope for easier target acquisition. Still, even when using the M32's scope, you need to aim high to compensate for range.

The SMAW rocket launcher is carried exclusively by the demolitions class. While the SMAW is equipped there is a small reticle icon on the HUD, but to fire this weapon accurately, always aim through the weapon's iron sights. When properly aimed, the rockets have surprising range and accuracy, flying in a relatively straight line from the weapon to the point of impact. You don't need to compensate for drop, so aim directly at your target to increase the chances of scoring a hit. The SMAW is particularly effective against large groups of opponents gathered around flags and other objectives. Try to score more than one kill with each shot, because you only get two rockets per support action.

EXPLOSIVES

Remote charges and proximity mines are often placed near objectives—watch your step.

The demolitions class is the explosive expert in *Medal of Honor Warfighter*, each carrying a remote charge. Simply press the grenade button to throw one down. Pressing the grenade button a second time detonates the explosives, so make sure you're a safe distance away to avoid blowing yourself up. Explosives are great for staging ambushes at narrow choke points, such as bridges and alleyways, or you can use them to defend critical positions, like flags in Sector Control or objectives in Hotspot.

The sniper class's proximity mine is another nasty explosive device ideal for booby trapping objectives. Like the remote charge, press the grenade button to toss one of these devices down. Once placed, there is a slight delay before the proximity mine becomes active, indicated by a faint clicking sound. Proximity mines are only triggered by opponents—teammates and your Fireteam Buddy will not detonate these explosives if they walk over them. If you encounter an enemy remote charge or proximity mine, it will appear on the HUD as a red icon. The only way to clear out these explosives is with explosives of your own. Toss a grenade or deploy another explosive weapon to detonate the opposing team's booby traps—you'll get a 50-point EOD score for making the map safer for your teammates.

MELEE COMBAT

This isn't the way you want to die. Try using the tomahawk on opponents who are distracted, with their backs turned to you.

In *Medal of Honor Warfighter*, all classes and soldiers are equipped with a tomahawk, serving as a brutal (and lethal) melee weapon. However, never go charging at an opponent while swinging this small, bladed instrument unless you want to get shot in the face. For best results, always attack opponents from behind for a quick melee kill. If you attack an opponent from the front or side, it requires two swings to take them down. But don't get greedy. If you're busy trailing an enemy from behind, there's a good chance another opponent will shoot you in the back…or take you down with a tomahawk of their own. So if your target starts running away from you, settle for shooting the enemy in the back instead of chasing your foe halfway across the map like a crazed, axe-wielding lunatic.

SCORING & STATS

Almost every action you perform in multiplayer earns you points. The points you earn are tallied from round to round, accumulating over time, ultimately determining your overall rank and class progression. Players gain experience by performing actions that result in points on the field of battle. Points are gained by performing a wide range of actions and by completing certain game mode-specific goals, such as destroying or capturing objectives. You even gain points for actions performed by your Fireteam Buddy. Leveling up unlocks new soldiers along with weapons and attachments. The classes, including their progression and unlocks, are covered in detail in the Classes and Weapons section. For a complete scoring breakdown, flip to The Warfighter Compendium section at the back of the guide.

There's more ways to earn points than scoring kills. Each action performed (and points awarded) appears in white text below the reticle on the HUD.

NOTE

When you score enough points to level up, a badge appears on the top of the HUD, along with the name of your new rank. A similar notification appears every time you've unlocked a new soldier. Next time you're in the spawn screen, cycle through the weapon customization options to see what you've unlocked.

SCOREBOARD & LEADERBOARDS

The scoreboard can be viewed at any time during a match and is always displayed at the end of each round.

Want to see how you stack up against the competition? During a match you can access the Scoreboard at any time. This shows your ranking within your team based on your points earned. It also shows your kill/death ratio. The Leaderboard offers a much broader view of the competition, ranking every player on each respective platform. Select the Stats and Leaderboards option in the Main menu to sort through this dynamic collection of data. By default, the player with the highest points appears atop the Top Players leaderboard. But these rankings are fluid and can also be sorted to show the player with the highest score, kills, or play time—recorded in days, hours, and minutes.

SERVICE RECORD

Check out the Service Record screen to learn exactly what you must do to earn new equipment and awards.

For greater detail on personal performance during your multiplayer career choose the Service Record option under Stats & Leaderboards from the Main menu. The Service Record screen shows you more specifics about your profile pertaining to unlocks and progression. Here you can browse through all available unlocks, ranging from units, ribbons, and medals. In all, there are 154 unlocks, each with their own specific criteria. From the Service Record screen you can browse through all available unlocks and check your progress toward attaining each.

SCORECHAIN & SUPPORT ACTIONS

The scorechain system rewards skilled players with an increasing powerful array of offensive and defensive support actions. You earn points by shooting other players or by performing certain in-game actions, as described in the previous section. Once you begin accruing points, the scorechain begins. The scorechain builds as long as you remain alive, but is reset to zero when you die. However, if you die before using a support action, the earned support actions can still be used upon respawn. At regular intervals, players are awarded support actions, which can be activated to provide an offensive or defensive boost to the team. There are a variety of support actions to choose from based on your selected class—all classes have different offensive support actions but the defensive support actions are the same. Here's a quick breakdown of the support actions available to each class.

All points earned apply to your scorechain. Each scorechain level allows you to choose an offensive or defensive support action. If you die, the scorechain resets to zero.

SUPPORT ACTIONS

ASSAULTER

LEVEL	POINTS REQ.	OFFENSIVE	DEFENSIVE
1	400	60mm Mortar	Smoke Screen
2	900	Guided Missile	Fireteam Replenish
3	1,500	Cluster Bomb	RQ-7 Shadow
4	2,300	Apache Pilot	Apache Pilot

POINT MAN

LEVEL	POINTS REQ.	OFFENSIVE	DEFENSIVE
1	400	RQ-11 Raven	Smoke Screen
2	900	Airburst Mortar	Fireteam Replenish
3	1,500	AH-6J Little Bird	RQ-7 Shadow
4	2,300	Apache Pilot	Apache Pilot

DEMOLITIONS

LEVEL	POINTS REQ.	OFFENSIVE	DEFENSIVE
1	400	M32	Smoke Screen
2	900	SMAW	Fireteam Replenish
3	1,500	MUSA Robot	RQ-7 Shadow
4	2,300	Apache Pilot	Apache Pilot

SNIPER

LEVEL	POINTS REQ.	OFFENSIVE	DEFENSIVE
1	400	Switchblade	Smoke Screen
2	900	81mm Mortar	Fireteam Replenish
3	1,500	Rocket Artillery	RQ-7 Shadow
4	2,300	Apache Pilot	Apache Pilot

HEAVY GUNNER

LEVEL	POINTS REQ.	OFFENSIVE	DEFENSIVE
1	400	Blackhawk Transport	Smoke Screen
2	900	Mk19	Fireteam Replenish
3	1,500	MH-60L DAP Blackhawk	RQ-7 Shadow
4	2,300	Apache Pilot	Apache Pilot

SPEC OPS

LEVEL	POINTS REQ.	OFFENSIVE	DEFENSIVE
1	400	Radar Jammer	Smoke Screen
2	900	120mm Dragon Fire	Fireteam Replenish
3	1,500	A-10 Warthog	RQ-7 Shadow
4	2,300	Apache Pilot	Apache Pilot

Support actions are extra military assets that can be used against the opposition, such as artillery or air strikes. If you die while you have a support action that has not yet been activated, you may use it when you respawn. If you want to gain a different support action, you must rebuild your scorechain to the necessary level. A meter in the top left corner of the HUD displays the current level of your scorechain and the requirement for the next level. Using a granted support action will not cancel your scorechain, and you will keep getting better ones as long as you manage to stay alive. Make a habit of using your support actions as soon as they're awarded. The points earned through activating these support actions can help build up the points required to achieve the next scorechain level.

There are two types of support actions, offensive and defensive. Offensive support actions are usually different forms of artillery, like mortars or close air support, provided by fighter aircraft. Defensive support actions help you and your entire team by supplying intel and ammo. Most offensive support actions require you to designate a target area with a set of binoculars—just aim where you want the incoming munitions to hit and press the fire button. In addition to designating a target area, some offensive support actions require to mark and approach vector, indicating the direction of incoming strafing runs. Defensive support actions are called in using your radio or cell phone—equip it and press fire. The defensive support actions influence all members of your team, but they don't stack. Offensive support actions give you extra points if you manage to kill enemies with it but defensive actions guarantee you a specific amount of extra points with each deployment. For specifics on each class's support actions, flip ahead to the Classes and Weapons section.

Offensive support actions like the sniper's Switchblade or assaulter's Guided Missile allow you to manually guide airborne weapons toward your opponents on the ground.

GAME MODES

Medal of Honor Warfighter offers five multiplayer gameplay modes that support up to twenty players for ten-on-ten combat. Each mode is accessible via pre-set playlists residing on a dedicated server. Playlists are set by the server's host and can be composed of several gameplay modes, which are cycled during online matches.

If there are not enough players present on a server, the match begins with a preround. During this period, all players are frozen and cannot move around the map. This is a good time to make adjustments to your class by selecting weapons, attachments, and camo patterns. After the preround is complete, or if no preround was needed, players proceed to the warmup. While warming up, players can still select their load-out and get ready to go into combat. Players remain frozen in place until the match is ready to begin. After a brief countdown, the players unfreeze and are able to begin the battle. While playing, if the number of players drops below the minimum threshold, the match will return to the preround to give other players a chance to join and repopulate the match. This ensures that every server is appropriately populated for combat.

COMBAT MISSION

The area around objectives is extremely dangerous, so be ready to cover your buddy or teammate as they set or defuse a charge.

In Combat Mission, the away team are the attackers and the home team are the defenders. The attackers must destroy three consecutive objectives to win. The defenders are tasked with stopping the attackers at any cost. As the away team clears objectives, new areas of the map are unlocked, which then reveals the next objective of the attackers. After each round, the sides switch, allowing both teams to have a chance to be on the offensive. The counter at the top of the HUD represents the remaining reinforcements for the away team. If this counter reaches zero, the match ends and the attackers are stopped in their tracks. However, if the attackers destroy all three objectives before the counter reaches zero, they claim victory. The counter resets after each objective is destroyed, giving the attackers more reinforcements with each objective they destroy.

SECTOR CONTROL

Capturing flags is a quick way to earn a lot of points. But don't forget to defend them as well.

Sector Control forces two sides to fight for possession of three sectors: North Base, South Base, and Center Base. These sectors are represented by flags. Holding an objective causes your team to accrue control points, tracked within the blue and red meters at the top of the HUD. The first team to fill their meter wins. If time expires before either meter is completely full, the team the fullest meter wins. Stand close to flags to capture them. The more friendly soldiers nearby, the faster the capturing process goes—and the more flags your team holds, the faster your team's meter fills. Sectors can be lost and recaptured as the match goes on. During the match, study the team meters at the top of the HUD—the blue meter represents your team's score and the red meter shows the opposing team's score. If your team is trailing behind, capture and hold more flags. Once a flag is captured, take efforts to defend it. Leaving a flag undefended just makes it easier for the opposing team to capture it.

HOTSPOT

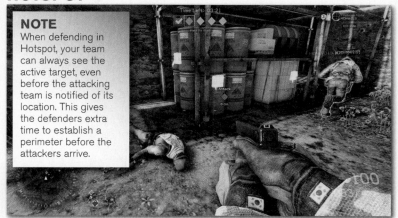

> **NOTE**
> When defending in Hotspot, your team can always see the active target, even before the attacking team is notified of its location. This gives the defenders extra time to establish a perimeter before the attackers arrive.

In Hotspot, there are multiple spots where you can plant a charge at the target location as indicated by the yellow charge markers.

Hotspot plays similar to Combat Mission, but with a twist. There are a total of five potential targets on the map, and the defending team always knows which target will be selected. Soon after the match begins, one of five targets is chosen at random, prompting both teams to race to the location—the attacking team must plant a charge and the defending team must prevent the destruction of the target. Once the attackers have planted a charge, they must then defend the target, preventing the opposing team from defusing the charge. Each target must be destroyed within three minutes, or else the defenders gain a point. If the attackers destroy three targets, they win the round. If the defenders stop the attackers three times, they win the round. After each target is destroyed or successfully defended, there's a brief cool-down period before the next target is randomly selected, prompting another race to the new location. Since all potential target locations are known (and shown on the HUD as gray icons) it's a good idea to position your team somewhere near the center of the map so they can quickly react when the next target location is identified. When playing as the attackers, monitor the defending team's movement to get a hint on what site will be activated next.

HOME RUN

You can't respawn in Home Run. But if you die, you can still watch your teammates from a tracking camera view—and let them know if an opponent is chasing them!

Home Run is a six-on-six capture-the-flag-style game mode with the away team playing as the attacker and the home team as the defender. There are two flags on the map that must be defended by the home team. Each player only gets one life per round, with no respawns. This makes the game mode rather intense, particularly as the number of players dwindles. It's the job of the away team to sneak in, grab a flag, and rush it back to their team's initial spawn point. Only one of the two flags must be captured to win each round, but since there are two flags, the defenders must keep an eye on both of them. The defenders can win the round by killing all the attackers or preventing a flag capture within the round's timed duration. Once a flag is captured, the other flag disappears, making the captured flag the sole target of the defenders—they must kill the flag carrier before the flag carrier can escape. If the flag carrier is killed, the flag is dropped and remains stationary unless picked up by another attacker. Each team plays five rounds as the attacker and five rounds as the defender. The team who wins the most number of rounds is declared the winner of the match. Support actions are not available during Home Run matches.

TEAM DEATHMATCH

Safety in numbers definitely applies to Team Deathmatch, so move around with a small group of teammates and support each other.

Team Deathmatch is a ten-on-ten no-holds-barred battle in a confined area where you fight for kills and points. The two teams struggle to score 75 kills to win the match. Each kill earns your team a point, so take down your enemies to increase your team's points, represented by the kill count number at the top of the HUD. If time runs out before either team scores 75 kills, the team with the most kills wins the match. It's your choice whether to stick with your team or to go on a solo hunt. But be warned, the tempo is high and enemies can pop up from behind almost any corner. At the very least, stick close to your Fireteam Buddy so you can heal and resupply each other.

HOME RUN SCORING

Event	Points
Eliminate Attackers	1
Eliminate Defenders (Attackers do not have flag)	1
Eliminate Defenders (Attackers have flag)	2
Capture flag	2

REAL OPS

When playing with the Real Ops setting, nearly all HUD elements are removed, including the minimap and weapon reticle.

Tired of the easy-to-use interface and minimap showing you exactly where to go? Then try the Real Ops setting. This allows you to play any of the game modes with hyper-realistic parameters. This setting removes most of the HUD elements, including weapon reticle. Therefore, you must aim using only your weapon's iron sights or scope. Even more notable, protection from friendly fire is turned off. You can injure and kill your teammates and vice versa, something that impacts poorly on your score. To up the realism even more, weapons inflict much more damage. If you get hit only once or twice, it's back to the spawn screen. This mode is intended solely for experts, so make sure you have plenty of experience before tackling Real Ops.

MULTIPLAYER TACTICS

Tactics is the combining of maneuvers and firepower to achieve an objective. Both movement and weapons have already been covered, so this section focuses on using the two together.

PLAN AHEAD

Before a round begins, take a few seconds to discuss tactics with your teammates. Any game plan is better than none.

There is an old saying that those who fail to plan, plan to fail. You need to come up with a plan before the bullets start flying. The best place to start is to look at your game mode's objectives, since those determine victory or defeat. While killing the enemy is always a goal, it is often a means to an end. Instead, focus on the objectives. Do you have to destroy a target, defend a position, or just get to a certain point on the map?

Once you know what you must do, look at the map and examine the terrain. Where are you located? Where is the objective? How will you get there? These are all questions you need to ask yourself. Once you have determined how to get to the target, you must then consider how to accomplish your orders. Will you need to get in close to plant an explosive charge on the target? If so, how will you secure the perimeter? Finally, you need to take into account your opposition. What does the enemy have and where are they located? Usually you will not know that type of information until you get in close to the target and can see the enemy with your own eyes. Therefore, planning continues on the fly as you learn new information about enemy positions and actions. Stay in close contact with your Fireteam Buddy and teammates over headsets. The team that communicates is most likely to come out on top.

LONG-RANGE COMBAT

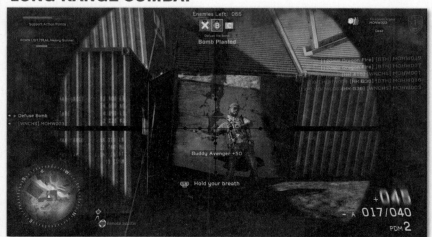

When sniping, try to focus your fire down narrow choke points. Also, be sure to hold your breath to steady your aim—you can hold your breath for approximately seven seconds.

COVER

Objects made from metal, concrete, and rock provide the best protection against small arms fire. These metal shipping containers on Basilan Aftermath are ideal for absorbing incoming bullets.

Combat is very dangerous. Bullets and other deadly projectiles fly through the air and can kill you outright if they make contact. The concept of cover is to place something solid between you and the enemy that will stop those projectiles and keep you safe. The multiplayer maps are filled with objects that you can use as cover—buildings, walls, trees, rocks, earthen mounds, and so on. Some types of cover will stop small arms fire such as rifle bullets, but not stop the heavier machine gun fire. Walls of buildings will stop machine gun fire, but not rockets or grenade launchers. Therefore, pick cover that will protect you from the current threat—objects constructed from wood or flimsy sheet metal won't stop a bullet.

Cover should become ingrained in your combat thinking. In addition to looking for enemies, you also need to be looking for cover. During a firefight, always stay behind cover. The only reason you leave cover is to move to another position with cover. If the cover is low, you may need to crouch down or drop prone behind it, standing only to fire over it. When moving from cover to cover, sprint to get there quicker. While you want to stay behind cover, you also want to try to deny the benefit of cover to your enemies. Destroying their cover is a way to do that. Another way is to reduce the effect of their cover by moving to hit them from a direction for which they have no cover. This is called flanking. For example, if an enemy is taking cover behind a wall, move around to the side of the wall so that the wall is no longer between you and your target. In the single-player campaign, your squad is great at holding an enemy's attention, giving you the chance to flank, surprising threats from the side or rear. Try the same tactics in multiplayer, using teammates to provide support fire while you flank or vice versa.

If possible, it is best to try to attack the enemy at long range before they're even aware of your presence. While sniper rifles work great for this type of combat, you can even use assault rifles, light machine guns, or rocket launchers to hit targets at long range. The key to winning at long range is to take your time. Drop prone, stay still, and use iron sights or scopes to increase your magnification and accuracy. As always, make sure you have some good cover in case the enemy decides to shoot back—if you can see them, they can see you. Also remember to fire in short bursts to ensure that more of your bullets hit the target.

CLOSE-QUARTERS COMBAT

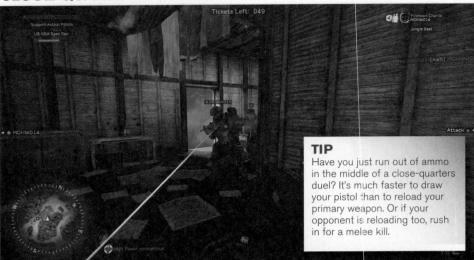

TIP

Have you just run out of ammo in the middle of a close-quarters duel? It's much faster to draw your pistol than to reload your primary weapon. Or if your opponent is reloading too, rush in for a melee kill.

Activating the point man's UAV support action reveals the locations of enemies on your minimap.

This type of combat is the exact opposite of long-range combat. In close quarters, such as in a town or even within a building, you don't have a lot of time to aim before shooting. However, at such short ranges, accuracy is not really a factor. Instead, you need a weapon that puts out a lot of firepower with some spread so you are more likely to get a hit while moving. Shotguns and submachine guns are great for close-quarters combat. Your minimap is also an important tool, especially if a friendly UAV is in the air. Since you can see where enemies are located, use this info to set up shots while strafing around a corners. Your weapon will already be aimed at the target as it appears on the minimap, which saves you just enough time to have the advantage and make the kill rather than be killed. Don't forget to use grenades, which can be thrown around corners or over walls to hit enemies who think they are safe behind cover.

COMMUNITY

Everything about *Medal of Honor Warfighter's* multiplayer is designed to be played and enjoyed with friends. Even if your current friend list is nonexistent, there's always the opportunity to make new friends while playing the game. Thanks to the Social Hub, platoons, and Battlelog, finding friends and starting games is fast and easy.

SOCIAL HUB

The Social Hub is the one-stop interface for managing friends and all invites.

The Social Hub overlay is available at any point during multiplayer, even during matches. Through this interface it's possible to set up a party and invite friends. You can also change your VOIP channel, interact with the Battlelog feed, manage friends, and even set up platoons.

FRIENDS

Need some friends to play with? Can't seem to find a good server to play on? Select the Friends tab. Here you can find all your online friends or platoon mates connected to your Origin, Xbox Live, or PSN accounts. By selecting a friend from the list you can invite that friend to a party, game, or even a platoon. If a friend is already in a match, you can even join the server your friend is playing on.

PARTY MANAGEMENT

When opened, the party widget will let you set up your fireteams before even joining the game. Do you have the ultimate fireteam pairings already figured out? In here you can manage all of that. Are you the natural leader? Invite your friends and you get to be the party leader—which means you are the one selecting where and what mode to play. Once satisfied

with your fireteam slot, both you and your Fireteam Buddy have the ability to lock yourself in. If you do this, nobody can swap fireteam slots with you.

PLATOON VS. PLATOON

Once you join a platoon, you need to represent them. To get playing all you need is four to six platoon mates online. Invite them to your party or join others. Once formed, you enter the Platoon vs. Platoon Matchmaking screen where you can find opponents.

VOIP CHANNELS

During multiplayer there are a couple of VOIP channels to choose from. By default the auto channel option is selected. The auto channel allows you to speak with your party members when not in a game. While playing, the auto channel only allows you to speak with your Fireteam Buddy. This default option is often preferred, allowing clear and concise communication between yourself and your Fireteam Buddy. If you want to keep talking to everyone in your party during a match, you can override the auto channel and select the party channel. This allows you to speak with everyone in your party, regardless of whether you're in a game or not.

BATTLELOG FEED

Did you earn that hard-to-get medal? Did you beat your friend to get the first sniper unlock? The Battlelog feed is your way to keep tabs on your friends—and show them who's boss. Share your achievements or show your appreciation by liking your friends' achievements. The game is highly connected to the Battlelog website—this feed is just the tip of the iceberg. Go to the Battlelog website for much more content.

INVITES

Got invited to that awesome platoon? Did that latest round with your best kill/death ratio pay off? Maybe one of your friends just invited you to his or her party? This is where you take action on those kind of things. Keep in mind that joining another platoon will have you leave your current one, so make your choice carefully.

PLATOONS

Creating a platoon is easy. But you'll need to leave your current platoon before creating one of your own.

If you prefer playing with a tight group of friends who are serious about winning, you should always join a platoon or form one of your own. But when joining a platoon, choose carefully, because you can only be the member of one platoon at a time. You can find the Platoon Directory under the Platoon Browser, accessible from main Multiplayer menu. This interface allows you to open each platoon's card for more detail. If you can't find a suitable platoon to join, why don't you create one? Use the Create Platoon option to start a new platoon. When creating a platoon, you must first select a name as well as a platoon tag—the platoon tag will appear next to your name on leaderboards and during the game. Next, choose your platoon's soldier—all 12 soldiers can be selected. Finally, choose a platoon patch. You can choose from a variety of stock images for your platoon's patch or you can create your own on the Battlelog website: battlelog.medalofhonor.com/platoonpatch

BATTLELOG

battlelog.medalofhonor.com

The Battlelog website offers a detailed breakdown of your multiplayer performance as well as the performance of your friends and platoon mates.

Battlelog is the center of your online experience, tracking nearly every action performed during multiplayer matches. Here you can find out exactly how accurate you are as well as boast or lament over your kill/death ratio. Awards and unlocks are also available to browse here, keeping you informed of how much work you need to do to unlock that next weapon or medal. If you're familiar with Battlelog introduced by *Battlefield 3*, you'll be pleasantly surprised by all the new features offered by *Medal of Honor Warfighter*. Most notable is the new Warfigher Nations meta game, allowing players to show their national pride by competing against other gamers around the globe. To access Battlelog, log in to the website using your Origin account. If playing on a console, you will need to link your Xbox Live or PSN account to your Origin account before you can access Battlelog.

OTHER RESOURCES

MEDAL OF HONOR WEBSITE

URL: www.medalofhonor.com
This is the official *Medal of Honor* website. The forums here are a great way to connect with other players as well as get information directly from the developers.

MEDAL OF HONOR BLOG

URL: www.medalofhonor.com/blog
The *Medal of Honor* blog is updated regularly, and maintained by EA/Danger Close employees. This is your go-to stop for all news for everything related to *Medal of Honor*.

OFF DUTY GAMERS

URL: www.offdutygamers.com
This site is for all the active duty military and prior service veterans who enjoy video games and the associated hardware. This site is about delivering all the same news, reviews, and sense of community coupled with a collective bond of service and unique point of view.

MP1ST

URL: mp1st.com
This is what MP1st is all about: community and the games that bring us together. MP1st strives to create a place where online gamers can view some of the best gaming content on the web, as well as get the latest news about the games they love.

EVIL SOURCE GAMING

URL: www.evilsourcegaming.com
Tune into ESG for the best gaming news, reviews, gameplay, giveaways, and more! From indie games to major publishers, the team at ESG will keep you informed on the things you want to know about.

WARFIGHTER NATIONS META-GAME

Tokens are earned while playing multiplayer matches, giving you the chance to represent your real-world country in an online battle for supremacy and national pride. Tokens give players additional XP and are spent in the Warfighter Nations meta-game on Battlelog. When redeeming a total of ten tokens for their given nation, players earn a ribbon and XP—all 10 tokens don't need to be handed in on the same day, or at the same time. The number of tokens each nation receives in a given time period are tracked on Battlelog. At regular intervals, Battlelog will declare a winning nation based on how many tokens were handed in for that nation during the time period. The winner is strictly for bragging rights/national pride. Players who hand in tokens on multiple days in a row will earn extra tokens. You don't have to affiliate with the nation you live in—you can switch your affiliation at any point.

WARFIGHTER NATIONS SCORING SYSTEM

ACTION	TOKENS AWARDED
Finish a Round	1
Win a Round	2
Featured Fireteam	2
Win Streak (3+ wins)	1
Win Streak (5+ wins)	3
Win Streak (10+ wins)	5

[N

[SWEDISH]
SO

[CANADIAN]
JTF-2

[BRITISH]
SAS

[US]
SEAL

[US]
OGA

[US]
SFOD-D

"SUPPORT ACTIONS" 160

"MY GUN: WEAPON CUSTOMIZATION" 162

HJK

[RUSSIAN]
SPETSNAZ
ALFA GROUP

[POLISH]
GROM

AN]

SK

SOUTH KOREAN
UDT/SE

"ASSAULTER"   164

"DEMOLITIONS"   171

"HEAVY GUNNER"   178

"POINT MAN"   185

"SNIPER"   192

"SPEC OPS"   199

CLASSES AND WEAPONS

In *Medal of Honor Warfighter*, you select one of six classes to play, each with its own unique characteristics, weapons, and appearance. Pick from assaulter, heavy gunner, sniper, point man, special ops, or demolitions to find the class that best suits your style of play. In addition to this, as you progress through your multiplayer career you can unlock new national units, allowing you to play as a wide mix of special operators from around the globe, such as the U.S. Navy SEALs, Polish GROM, British SAS, or German KSK. With each new unit you gain access to new weapons and attachments for each class, adding more customization options to your online experience. Experiment to find the best combinations for different game modes and maps. Play to the strength of each class to lead your team to victory.

CLASS ABILITIES

Each of the six classes has a unique ability designed to give them an edge over the competition. Your character's class ability is shown on the HUD, represented by a small icon to the right of the minimap. The icon also shows the button press required to activate the ability. Some class abilities can only be used one time, such as the point man's heavy hitters, a special magazine loaded with high-damage-output ammunition. But other abilities can be used multiple times, like the spec ops' signal scan, or the heavy gunner and sniper's bipod. During the heat of combat, it's common to forget about these special abilities. But if used in the right situations, you can gain a significant advantage over your opponents.

The spec ops' signal scan ability is great for identifying the heat signatures of opponents, particularly during Home Run matches.

ABILITIES

Class	Ability	Description
Assaulter	40mm Grenade Launcher	Fires a high-explosive grenade round, capable of killing multiple enemies.
Demolitions	Ballistic Armor	Imbues soldier with a heavy layer of armor. Offers protection but impedes movement.
Heavy Gunner	Bipod Setup	Can be deployed on the ground or low cover to stabilize light machine gun for improved accuracy and reduced recoil.
Point Man	High Power Ammunition	Loads a magazine of high-damage-output ammunition at the cost of heavy recoil.
Sniper	Remote Spotter	Can be deployed on the ground or low cover to stabilize sniper rifle. Sniper can also spot targets while bipod is deployed.
Spec Ops	Signal Scan	An x-ray vision-like ability allowing soldier to glimpse the heat signatures of nearby opponents, even through solid walls.

SUPPORT ACTIONS

Available support actions are prominently displayed on the HUD when they are earned. Stay alive to maintain your scorechain.

Each class has access to a total of eight different support actions—four offensive and four defensive. Support actions are earned by scoring points without dying, essentially awarding kill streaks. The available support actions vary based on your class. Offensive support actions usually give you access to a special weapon or vehicle that you can target or even control to score more kills. Defensive support actions don't result in kills, but can help your team in other ways, such as identifying the locations of opponents or resupplying your Fireteam. Support actions are awarded at regular intervals. When awarded, two large icons appear at the top of the HUD, notifying you of the two support actions currently available. These icons are then moved to the upper-left corner of the HUD, acting as reminders that you have support actions available. All earned support actions are still available after dying and respawning into the game. However, when you die, the scorechain is broken and your support action points are reset to zero, requiring you to start your chain over. If you're nearing the third or fourth tier, avoid any risky actions that may result in your death.

TIP

If you've earned a support action and die, you can switch classes and come back into the game with the same level of support action options under the new class. For example, if you die as an assaulter with first tier support actions available, you can spawn back into the game as a sniper and take advantage of the sniper class first tier support actions.

FREE MEDAL OF HONOR WARFIGHTER™ EGUIDE WITH UPDATES!

Login with the voucher code below to get:

- **Updated weapon strategies keeping you prepared for battle.**
- **Interactive maps for both single and multiplayer maps.**
- **Zoom in and out and toggle map markers on and off to reveal only the information you want to see.**
- **Access strategy anywhere you have an internet connection.**
- **Enlarge screenshots, search tables, bookmark pages and so much more.**

1. Go to www.primagames.com. Select "Redeem Code" located at the top of the page.

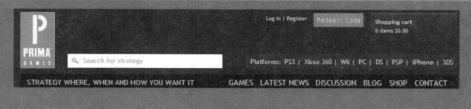

2. Enter the voucher code in the text field and click the "Submit" button.

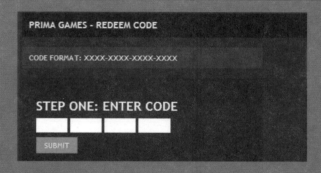

3. You will be redirected to your content now.

VOUCHER CODE

twa5-zq2e-9h9v-rf3w

 **Follow us on Twitter**

 **Like us on Facebook**

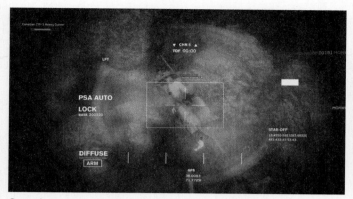

Sometimes support actions can be used to counter others. For instance, use a Guided Missile to target an enemy Blackhawk Transport.

Make an effort to use a support action soon after it becomes available. While support actions remain available if you die and respawn, if you manage to score another 400 points without using a support action, the previous support actions are lost and replaced by those from the next tier. For example, if playing as the assaulter class, you earn the 60mm Mortar offensive support action and the Smoke Screen defensive support action at the first 400 points. But if you earn another 400 points, those first tier support actions are replaced by the Guided Missile offensive and Fireteam Replenish defensive support actions. Keep an eye on the support action points meter in the top left corner of the HUD. If you're close to earning a new set of support actions, be sure to use the previous ones.

COMMON SUPPORT ACTIONS

All classes share the same defensive support actions as well as the final offensive support action, allowing you and your Fireteam Buddy to temporarily take the controls of a devastating Apache attack helicopter. The unique support actions available to each class are covered in the following class profiles. But here we take a look at the common support actions available to every class.

SMOKE SCREEN
Support Action Points: 400

When this defensive support action is selected, your soldier brings up a pair of binoculars, allowing you to pinpoint the target area for the incoming smoke barrage. Within seconds of initiating the support action, the target area is saturated with thick white smoke, greatly impeding visibility. This action can come in handy for concealing your team's movements, particularly when moving toward a flag in Sector Control or an objective in Hotspot or Combat Mission.

FIRETEAM REPLENISH
Support Action Points: 900

Compared to its offensive counterpart (depending on class), Fireteam Replenish is a tough sell. When activated, this support action instantly replenishes you and your Fireteam Buddy with health, ammo, and grenades. The support action also replenishes your fireteam's class abilities. You can already heal and resupply your Fireteam Buddy without activating this support action, but this is the only way you can get a new pair of grenades. In rare instances, this support action has some serious benefits, instantly replenishing the Fireteam's class abilities. So if you're playing as an assaulter and need more grenades for your grenade launcher, this support action may be worthwhile.

RQ-7 SHADOW
Support Action Points: 1,500

The RQ-7 Shadow is a small unmanned aerial vehicle (UAV) that orbits around the map, revealing the locations of all opponents. This is an extremely powerful support action, allowing your teammates to see all enemy contacts, appearing as red dots on the minimap. The RQ-7 only remains airborne for approximately a minute. But in that time, your team can effectively hunt down and eliminate the opposing team no matter where they're hiding. In a tight match, knowing exactly where the enemy is can make all the difference.

APACHE PILOT
Support Action Points: 2,300

This support action puts you directly in the pilot seat of an Apache helicopter, giving you access to the chopper's high-explosive rockets. Flying the chopper is as easy as regular movement, only you're suspended above the battlefield in a stable hover. Use the Apache's rockets to target opponents scurrying about the map. Although impressive, the rockets are less effective than the chopper's chin-mounted chain gun, operated by your Fireteam Buddy. So instead of looking for targets to take out with the rockets, spend your time maneuvering the chopper around the map so your gunner can unleash the full potential of the chain gun. The Apache can be struck by incoming small arms fire as well as rocket and grenade launchers. If the Apache sustains heavy damage, your ride will be cut short. Keep moving to make the Apache a more difficult target to hit.

When this support action is activated, your Fireteam Buddy automatically takes control of the helicopter's chin-mounted turret. The HUD changes to a camera view on the front of the chopper, allowing you to pan and tilt while lining up targets within the 30mm chain gun's reticle. The chain gun is absolutely devastating against opponents, rapidly firing explosive rounds with significant splash damage. However, you will need to coordinate with your Fireteam Buddy to effectively line up targets. Communicate and work together to make the most of this powerful support action.

MY GUN: WEAPON CUSTOMIZATION

You can customize almost every aspect of your weapon, including the paint scheme.

With every new unit you unlock, you also unlock a new weapon along with several attachments. Weapons can be customized from the Multiplayer main menu, choosing the My Gun option. But you can also enter the customization interface during a match, from the Deployment screen where you choose your class—select the Change Weapon option to enter the My Gun interface. Here you can change your weapon, choosing from all unlocked weapons within your selected class—there are twelve different weapons per class. Once you've selected a weapon, you can customize it by adding different attachments. There are five different modification points on each weapon: muzzle, barrel assembly, magazine style, optics, and receiver group. As you apply different attachments, make note of the fluctuating weapon stats in the top right corner of the screen. Each attachment can alter a weapon's performance, affecting its effective range, magazine size, agility, magnification, and stealth, so pay close attention when customizing your weapon. Ultimately weapon customization comes down to personal preference. Create the build that best fits your style of play. This is much more important than trying to build out the weapon with the best stats. In addition to selecting different attachments, you can also paint your weapon with a variety of unique camouflage pattens. Painting your weapon has no impact on the weapon's performance, but choosing a bright color may make you easier to spot. Take into account the map you're playing on and try to choose a camo pattern that blends in with the surroundings.

SELECTING A NATION/UNIT

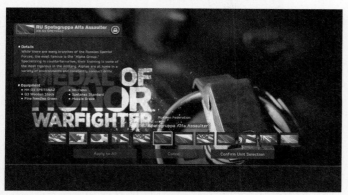

There are twelve units to choose from. Your choice here determines which assaulter unit is unlocked first as well as the unique unlock progression of your multiplayer career.

When you begin multiplayer you are prompted to choose a nation and unit to represent. Don't make this decision lightly. The nation and unit you choose to represent will determine which assaulter unit you unlock first. For example, if you choose to represent the Swedish SOG, you'll start with the Swedish SOG assaulter—usually this unit isn't available until you reach higher ranks. In this sense, selecting a unit like the Norway FSK/HJK or Russian Spetsgruppa Alfa allows you to unlock assaulter units (and the G3 assault rifle) that are off-limits to new players who select other nations/units at the beginning. Make your decision carefully based largely on the type of assault rifle and attachments you'd like to unlock first. All other differences between the units are purely cosmetic.

> **TIP**
>
> Your unlock progression will differ based on which nationality/unit you choose to represent at the start of your multiplayer career. For a complete rundown of the unlock progression of all twelve units, reference the tables in the Warfighter Compendium at the back of the guide. These tables show the rank at which each class/unit is unlocked based on your starting unit.

DANGER CLOSE EXPLAINS WEAPON STATS

A weapon's stats are displayed as a horizontal bar graph in the My Gun interface. Here's a brief breakdown of what each stat category means, as well as how each affects a weapon's performance.

EFFECTIVE RANGE

Effective Range is the ability to deal damage at longer ranges. A player that is cautious, precise, defensive, and likes to shoot in controlled bursts will be successful with this stat line. Effective range is affected by the following factors:

- **Weapon Range:** How much more effective a weapon's damage is at longer ranges. More effective range means more damage at medium to long ranges.
- **Accuracy Movement Penalty:** A penalty is applied to the accuracy of a weapon (with bullet spread), if the player is moving (strafing) while firing the weapon. More effective range means more accuracy movement penalty.

MAGAZINE

Magazine pertains to the amount of bullets each magazine can hold. Magazine is affected by the following factors:

- **Reload Time:** Pertains to how long it takes to reload a fresh mag from an empty one. More magazine means a longer reload time.
- **Magazine Size:** Pertains to how many bullets each magazine can hold. More magazine means larger magazine size.

AGILITY

Agility is the ability to play as a "run and gun" player—a player that is in constant movement, is light on his or her feet, and likes to close in on opponents to shoot them. Agility is affected by the following factors:

- **Aim Down Sight Speed:** The speed at which a player can raise a weapon down the particular sight to shoot at the enemy. More agility means more speed.
- **"Spray and Pray" Penalty:** This pertains to the player that holds down the trigger for long periods of time while firing at a player. A penalty is applied to the accuracy of a weapon (with bullet spread), if the player is holding down the trigger for long periods of time and not using short, controlled bursts. More agility means more penalty.
- **Recoil:** This pertains to the weapon's jump from center screen every time a bullet is fired. More agility means less recoil.

MAGNIFICATION

Magnification pertains to the type of views each scope can provide. Magnification is affected by the following factors:

- **Zoom:** How much zoom distance does the scope give you? More magnification means more zoom.
- **Dual Sights:** The ability to have more than one zoom level per optic. This could mean that one particular optic has two variable zooms or that there are two different optics with different zoom levels mounted on the weapon.

STEALTH

Stealth is the signature of the weapon. How noticeable is it that you're firing the weapon? Stealth is affected by the following factors:

- **Report:** This pertains to the audible volume of the weapon when fired. At what range can the weapon be heard? At what range can the weapon be pinged on the minimap while being fired?
- **Suppression:** Lowers the sound of the weapon being fired. Decreases at what distance the weapon can be heard while being fired. Decreases the distance at which the weapon can be pinged on the minimap while being fired. Also decreases the effective range (damage over distance) of the weapon by 15%.

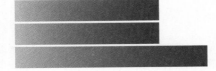

ASSAULTER

A medium-speed operator who holds a secondary grenade launcher. Useful for multiple kills when enemies are clustered together.

Sidearm: SIG Sauer P226
Grenade: M67 Frag

SUPPORT ACTIONS

Level	Points Req.	Offensive	Defensive
1	400	60mm Mortar	Smoke Screen
2	900	Guided Missile	Fireteam Replenish
3	1,500	Cluster Bomb	RQ-7 Shadow
4	2,300	Apache Pilot	Apache Pilot

The assaulter is the most versatile of the classes, offering a great balance of speed, durability, and firepower. This is the first and only class available when starting your multiplayer career, meaning you'll need to master the assaulter before trying the other five classes. The assault rifles associated with this class are all lethal instruments, capable of dropping opponents with only a few hits. But these are long rifles, best suited for deployment in environments where there are long sight lines. While assault rifles are capable of operating in close quarters, they are rather cumbersome when compared to the smaller SMGs carried by the spec ops class. Consider switching to your pistol when operating in tight quarters for greater mobility and faster target acquisition. By default, all assault rifles are set to automatic fire, but they can be switched to semi-automatic when precision shooting takes priority over rate of fire.

CLASS ABILITY: 40MM GRENADE LAUNCHER

The grenade launcher ability is not immediately available to the assaulter—it is unlocked at the Private 2 rank, earned early on. Just play multiplayer for a few minutes and you'll have a grenade launcher to play around with. Once unlocked, the assaulter can be equipped with two different types of grenade launchers. One is the M79 grenade launcher, which is an entirely separate weapons system. But some of the assault rifles can also be fitted with an under-barrel grenade launcher like the M320. In any case, the grenade launchers function the same way. Grenades fired from these launchers explode on impact and can destroy light cover including wood fences, trees, and some stone walls. By raising the barrel you can launch these munitions impressive distances, especially if you're standing on a hill. Use the horizontal lines on the HUD to adjust your aim, raising the barrel to engage distant targets or lowering the barrel to for a more direct firing arc. Grenades have a high splash damage and can kill or injure opponents within a modest blast radius.

TIP

Grenades fired from launchers must travel a minimum distance before they can detonate. This prevents the shooter from injuring themselves by engaging targets at close range. However, it's possible to score kills with a grenade at close range even if the round doesn't explode. It appears getting hit dead-on with a 40mm round is just lethal enough. So if you have the launcher equipped and an opponent appears around a nearby corner, go ahead and take the shot.

PERFORMANCE

	1	2	3	4	5
SPEED					
ARMOR					
FIREPOWER					

UNIQUE SUPPORT ACTIONS

60MM MORTAR
Support Action Points: 400

This is the first of four offensive support actions available to the assaulter, and it's always a good choice, particularly if you've spotted a large cluster of enemy troops. Before you activate the support action, find a relatively safe area with a clear view of your intended target area. Once activated, your soldier raises a pair of binoculars that you must use to call in the mortar strike. Place the aiming reticle directly over the target area, preferably targeting the ground instead of a wall or rooftop. Within seconds highly explosive mortar rounds rain down on the target area, killing any opponents within the wide blast radius. These strikes are best focused on choke points, such as narrow areas like alleys and stairways where opponents tend to bunch up.

GUIDED MISSILE
Support Action Points: 900

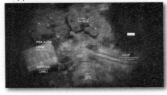

Of all the support actions, this is one of the most fun to activate, giving you direct control of an incoming missile. Before you can take control of the missile, you must first laser designate a target area. As with the 60mm Mortar, try to identify large groups of opponents before taking aim. Once you've designated your target, the HUD changes to a camera fitted onto the tip of the missile. At this point you can aim the missile by steering it toward opponents scurrying about on the ground. But the missile moves fast, plummeting to the earth at high speed, giving you little time to make minor adjustments. This is why it's so important to mark your target area carefully with the laser designator. If you score a direct hit on a cluster of enemies, you can expect to rack up multiple kills, putting you well on the way toward your next support action.

CLUSTER BOMB
Support Action Points: 1,500

In critical situations, assaulter soldiers can call in A-10s loaded with Cluster Bomb munitions. The ordinance can quickly cover large areas with devastating results. Initiating a Cluster Bomb strike is much like calling in the 60mm Mortar support action. Upon activation, you're prompted to select a target area using a binocular-like laser designator. Once you've set the target area, you must choose the approach vector for the incoming air strike as indicated by the green conical icon in the center of the sight. Setting the approach vector can help spread the incoming munitions over a wide area. While Cluster Bombs are spread over a wide target area, still try to focus these attacks on narrow choke points where multiple opponents are gathered. Also, don't bother targeting buildings with these bombs. Unfortunately, the air strike will have no impact on opponents hiding in buildings with solid rooftops.

AUSTRALIAN SAS-R ASSAULTER

Quick and deadly, their motto is "Who Dares Wins." Formed in 1957 with just one company, and now boasting three Sabre Squadrons, OZ SAS-R are experts in reconnaissance missions, surveillance, and counterterrorism.

BRITISH SAS ASSAULTER

"What color is the boathouse in Hereford?" These guys would know. Their tactics, training, and equipment have been the model for the Special Forces in many other countries including the U.S. Army's Delta Force. Their motto is "Who Dares Wins." These guys dare.

EBR SAS-R

STOCK WEAPON STATS

- EFFECTIVE RANGE (ER)
- MAGAZINE SIZE (MS)
- AGILITY (A)
- MAGNIFICATION (M)
- STEALTH (S)

WEAPON ATTACHMENTS

ATTACHMENT	TYPE	ER	MS	A	M	S
Muzzle Brake	Standard Muzzle	—	—	—	—	—
EBR Stock (Collapsed)	Standard Receiver	—	—	—	—	—
20-Round 7.62mm Magazine	Standard Magazine	—	—	—	—	—
SAS-R Precision Barrel + Handguard	Precision Barrel	+20%	—	–10%	—	—
Aimpoint Micro T-1	Reflex Sight	—	—	–5%	—	—
White Honeycomb	Paint	—	—	—	—	—

DANIEL DEFENSE M4V1 SAS

STOCK WEAPON STATS

- EFFECTIVE RANGE (ER)
- MAGAZINE SIZE (MS)
- AGILITY (A)
- MAGNIFICATION (M)
- STEALTH (S)

WEAPON ATTACHMENTS

ATTACHMENT	TYPE	ER	MS	A	M	S
Maqpul UBR Stock	Standard Receiver	—	—	—	—	—
Compensator	Standard Muzzle	—	—	—	—	—
SpecterDR	Reflex Sight	—	—	–5%	—	—
30-Round 5.56mm PMAG	Standard Magazine	—	—	—	—	—
SAS Standard Barrel + 40mm Grenade Launcher	Standard Barrel	—	—	—	—	—
SAS Fatigue	Paint	—	—	—	—	—

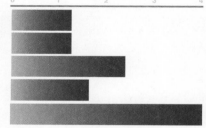
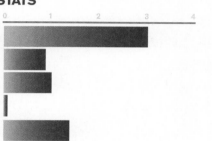

CANADIAN JTF-2 ASSAULTER

JTF-2 is an elite special operations force of the Canadian military specializing in counterterrorism. Although small in number, they make up for their size with relentless and aggressive suppressive firepower. These guys have your six.

GERMAN KSK ASSAULTER

This highly specialized, elite unit consists of the best of the best of Germany's special operations soldiers. Their small numbers are testament to a rigorous selection process. The KSK's five platoons can take the fight anywhere in the world—mountain to sea, pole to pole.

EBR JTF-2

HECKLER & KOCH G3KA4

STOCK WEAPON STATS

	0	1	2	3	4
EFFECTIVE RANGE (ER)					
MAGAZINE SIZE (MS)					
AGILITY (A)					
MAGNIFICATION (M)					
STEALTH (S)					

STOCK WEAPON STATS

	0	1	2	3	4
EFFECTIVE RANGE (ER)					
MAGAZINE SIZE (MS)					
AGILITY (A)					
MAGNIFICATION (M)					
STEALTH (S)					

WEAPON ATTACHMENTS

ATTACHMENT	TYPE	ER	MS	A	M	S
SpecterDR	Low-Power Dual Sights	—	—	−12%	+50%	—
20-Round 7.62mm Magazine	Standard Magazine	—	—	—	—	—
Lightweight Barrel	Close-Quarters Barrel	−15%	—	+15%	—	—
Surefire Suppressor	Silenced Muzzle	—	—	—	—	—
JTF-2 EBR Stock	Precision Receiver	+15%	—	−15%	—	—
CADPAT	Paint	—	—	—	—	—

WEAPON ATTACHMENTS

ATTACHMENT	TYPE	ER	MS	A	M	S
Heavy Barrel + Surefire M720v Light	Precision Barrel	+20%	—	−10%	—	—
30-Round 7.62mm Bakelite Magazine	Standard Magazine	—	—	—	—	—
AK Triangular Folding Stock	Close-Quarters Receiver	−10%	—	+20%	—	—
Compensator	Standard Muzzle	—	—	—	—	—
M145 (M4 Reticle)	Low-Power Sight	—	—	−8%	+40%	—
Sand Dune	Paint	—	—	—	—	—

NORWAY FSK/HJK ASSAULTER

Although relatively new, these two units of Norway's Special Forces were born to counter terrorist threats to their nation. Since inception, they have been active in campaigns around the world, including Bosnia, Kosovo, and Afghanistan.

POLISH GROM ASSAULTER

GROM is Polish for "thunder." And that is what this SF unit brings to the table: they hit hard. Formed in 1990, they have earned the respect of every operator around the world for their tenacity.

HECKLER & KOCH AG3

HECKLER & KOCH 416 GREKO'S

STOCK WEAPON STATS

	0 1 2 3 4
EFFECTIVE RANGE (ER)	
MAGAZINE SIZE (MS)	
AGILITY (A)	
MAGNIFICATION (M)	
STEALTH (S)	

STOCK WEAPON STATS

	0 1 2 3 4
EFFECTIVE RANGE (ER)	
MAGAZINE SIZE (MS)	
AGILITY (A)	
MAGNIFICATION (M)	
STEALTH (S)	

WEAPON ATTACHMENTS

ATTACHMENT	TYPE	ER	MS	A	M	S
Surefire Suppressor	Silenced Muzzle	–15%	—	—	—	+60%
Lightweight Stock	Close-Quarters Receiver	–10%	—	+20%	—	—
Aimpoint Micro T-1	Reflex Sights	—	—	–5%	—	—
20-Round 7.62mm Magazine	Standard Magazine	—	—	—	—	—
Lightweight Barrel + Tactical Rail	Close-Quarters Barrel	–15%	—	+15%	—	—
Winter Stick	Paint	—	—	—	—	—

WEAPON ATTACHMENTS

ATTACHMENT	TYPE	ER	MS	A	M	S
Heavy Barrel + M952V Light & PEQ-14	Precision Barrel	+20%	—	–10%	—	—
Maqpul CTR Stock	Standard Receiver	—	—	—	—	—
Aimpoint CompM4	Reflex Sight	—	—	–5%	—	—
GROM 30-Round 5.56mm Green PMAG	Standard Magazine	—	—	—	—	—
Surefire Mini Monster Suppressor	Silenced Muzzle	–15%	—	—	—	+60%
Grecko's	Paint	—	—	—	—	—

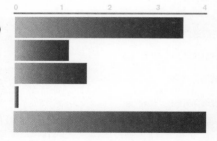

ROKN UDT/SEAL ASSAULTER

This Special Forces unit is part of the Republic of Korea Naval Special Warfare Flotilla. This unit is heavily modeled after the U.S. Navy's SEALs in training and tactics. They have already proved their skill in a number of successful maritime hostage rescues.

RU SPETSGRUPPA ALFA ASSAULTER

While there are many branches of the Russian Special Forces, the most famous is the Alpha Group. Specializing in counterterrorism, their training is some of the most rigorous in the military. Alphas are at home in a variety of environments and constantly conduct drills to hone their skills.

DANIEL DEFENSE M4V1 ROKN

HECKLER & KOCH G3 SPETSNAZ

STOCK WEAPON STATS

EFFECTIVE RANGE (ER)
MAGAZINE SIZE (MS)
AGILITY (A)
MAGNIFICATION (M)
STEALTH (S)

STOCK WEAPON STATS

EFFECTIVE RANGE (ER)
MAGAZINE SIZE (MS)
AGILITY (A)
MAGNIFICATION (M)
STEALTH (S)

WEAPON ATTACHMENTS

ATTACHMENT	TYPE	ER	MS	A	M	S
Aimpoint CompM4	Reflex Sights	—	—	–5%	—	—
30-Round 5.56mm Magazine	Standard Magazine	—	—	—	—	—
Heavy Barrel + 40mm Grenade Launcher	Precision Barrel	+20%	—	–10%	—	—
Surefire Suppressor	Silenced Muzzle	–15%	—	—	—	+60%
Maqpul PRS Stock	Precision Receiver	+15%	—	–15%	—	—
UDT	Paint	—	—	—	—	—

WEAPON ATTACHMENTS

ATTACHMENT	TYPE	ER	MS	A	M	S
G3 Wooden Stock	Standard Receiver	—	—	—	—	—
Spetsnaz Standard Barrel	Standard Barrel	—	—	—	—	—
Flash Hider	Standard Muzzle	—	—	—	—	—
SpecterDR	Low-Power Dual Sights	—	—	–12%	+50%	—
20-Round 7.62mm Magazine	Standard Magazine	—	—	—	—	—
Pine Needles Green	Paint	—	—	—	—	—

SWEDISH SOG ASSAULTER

Formed by the merging of the SSG (Special Protection Group) and SIG (Special Reconnaissance Group) in 2011 to provide a variety of strategic applications across many disciplines. In addition to conducting small-scale, low-profile ops, SOG operators can also be inserted as a component of large-scale conventional warfare operations.

U.S. ARMY SFOD-D ASSAULTER

SFOD-D is one of the United States' secretive Tier 1 counter-terrorism and Special Mission Units. Commonly known as The Unit, it was formed under the designation 1st SFOD-D, and has been involved in every U.S. ground operation since its inception.

HECKLER & KOCH AK4

STOCK WEAPON STATS

	0	1	2	3	4
EFFECTIVE RANGE (ER)					
MAGAZINE SIZE (MS)					
AGILITY (A)					
MAGNIFICATION (M)					
STEALTH (S)					

WEAPON ATTACHMENTS

ATTACHMENT	TYPE	ER	MS	A	M	S
SOG Standard Barrel	Standard Barrel	—	—	—	—	—
Aimpoint CompCS	Reflex Sight	—	—	–5%	—	—
Flash Hider	Standard Muzzle	—	—	—	—	—
G3 Stock + Recoil Pad	Standard Receiver	—	—	—	—	—
20-Round 7.62mm Magazine	Standard Magazine	—	—	—v	—	—
Swedish Flat	Paint	—	—	—	—	—

HECKLER & KOCH 416 SFOD-D

STOCK WEAPON STATS

	0	1	2	3	4
EFFECTIVE RANGE (ER)					
MAGAZINE SIZE (MS)					
AGILITY (A)					
MAGNIFICATION (M)					
STEALTH (S)					

WEAPON ATTACHMENTS

ATTACHMENT	TYPE	ER	MS	A	M	S
Muzzle Brake	Standard Muzzle	—	—	—	—	—
Standard Stock (Extended)	Precision Receiver	+15%	—	-15%	—	—
Lightweight Barrel + Contour Camera	Close Quarters Barrel	-15%	—	+15%	—	—
Aimpoint Micro T-1 +3x Magnifier	Low-Power Sight	—	—	-8%	+40%	—
SFOD 30-Round 5.56mm PMAG	Standard Magazine	—	—	—	—	—
Brown String	Paint	—	—	—	—	—

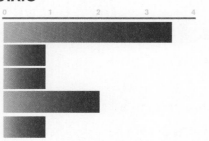

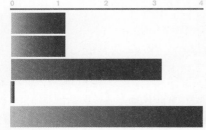

U.S. NAVY SEAL ASSAULTER

Frogmen have the most grueling selection process in the military. Those who make it through become highly trained experts in assaults, hostage rescue, and counterterrorism. And expert snipers—just ask a pirate.

U.S. OGA ASSAULTER

Other Government Agency (OGA) Operators are recruited from the military's special operations community. They're nimble and use technology to their advantage in direct action and intelligence gathering.

HECKLER & KOCH 416 DEVGRU

DANIEL DEFENSE M4V1 OGA

STOCK WEAPON STATS

	0	1	2	3	4
EFFECTIVE RANGE (ER)					
MAGAZINE SIZE (MS)					
AGILITY (A)					
MAGNIFICATION (M)					
STEALTH (S)					

STOCK WEAPON STATS

	0	1	2	3	4
EFFECTIVE RANGE (ER)					
MAGAZINE SIZE (MS)					
AGILITY (A)					
MAGNIFICATION (M)					
STEALTH (S)					

WEAPON ATTACHMENTS

ATTACHMENT	TYPE	ER	MS	A	M	S
Standard Stock (Collapsed)	Close-Quarters Receiver	−10%	—	+20%	—	—
SEAL 30-Round 5.56mm Magazine	Standard Magazine	—	—	—	—	—
Surefire Suppressor	Silenced Muzzle	−15%	—	—	—	+60%
Trijicon TA31H + BUIS	Low-Power Dual Sights	—	—	−12%	+50%	—
Standard Barrel + 40mm Grenade Launcher	Standard Barrel	—	—	—	—	—
AOR1	Paint	—	—	—	—	—

WEAPON ATTACHMENTS

ATTACHMENT	TYPE	ER	MS	A	M	S
Lightweight Barrel + VFG & M952V Light	Close-Quarters Barrel	−15%	—	+15%	—	—
Maqpul CTR Stock	Standard Receiver	—	—	—	—	—
Aimpoint Micro T-1 + 3x Magnifier	Low-Power Sight	—	—	−8%	+40%	—
30-Round 5.56mm PMAG	Standard Magazine	—	—	—	—	—
Surefire Suppressor	Silenced Muzzle	−15%	—	—	—	+60%
Gray Digital	Paint	—	—	—	—	—

DEMOLITIONS

While being the slowest operator, the demolitions class is heavily armored and can resist blasts that would kill weaker classes. This class can arm and disarm charges faster than any other class. Plus the ballistic armor ability helps shield the demolitions soldier from salvos fired by enemies.

Sidearm: Vickers 1911

Grenade: Remote Charge

PERFORMANCE

	1	2	3	4	5
SPEED					
ARMOR					
FIREPOWER					

SUPPORT ACTIONS

Level	Points Req.	Offensive	Defensive
1	400	M32	Smoke Screen
2	900	SMAW	Fireteam Replenish
3	1,500	MUSA Robot	RQ-7 Shadow
4	2,300	Apache Pilot	Apache Pilot

If you can tolerate the sluggish speed of this class, you're in for a real treat, particularly if you like watching things blow up. The demolitions class is not only decked-out in heavy armor, but once the support actions start rolling in, this class can hit hard, armed with weapons like the M32 grenade launcher and SMAW rocket launcher. But before you can score enough points to acquire support actions, you must first master the stock weapons of this class, including the submachine guns, shotguns, and remote charge. While the SMGs offer a high rate of fire, they exhibit heavy recoil, making it difficult to hit targets at intermediate and long ranges. Consider switching the weapon to semi-automatic if you're having trouble managing the recoil. Shotguns are only effective at extremely close range, so avoid open areas if carrying one. Instead of standard grenades, the demolitions class is equipped with a remote charge, ideal for booby trapping objectives and high-traffic choke points. In addition to carrying a variety of lethal weapons, the demolitions class is your go-to soldier when it comes to arming and disarming charges in Combat Mission and Hotspot. When interacting with a charge, this class can accomplish the arming or disarming process much faster than the other classes. But when focusing on a charge, always deploy the ballistic armor ability for greater durability.

CLASS ABILITY: BALLISTIC ARMOR

If you thought the demolitions class was slow before, just wait until you deploy the ballistic armor ability. This causes the demolitions class soldier to pull down a ballistics visor over the soldier's face, limiting visibility and further restricting movement. But the ballistic armor has a big payoff when it comes to absorbing damage. When deployed, the ballistic armor greatly increases the survivability of the soldier, effectively blocking incoming bullets and shrapnel. When under fire, the armor takes the brunt of the damage, while health remains intact. However, the armor does deteriorate with each hit, eventually canceling the ability. When the armor reaches its breaking point, the soldier's helmet falls to pieces. Once the armor is destroyed, the ability cannot be deployed again. But as long as the armor is intact, the ballistic armor can be activated and deactivated multiple times. For best results, activate the ability when you're about to engage opponents in a firefight. Otherwise, avoid leaving the ability active as it greatly inhibits vision and mobility.

> **TIP**
> If engaging a demolitions soldier using the ballistic armor ability aim for the head to quickly chip away at the armor. Better yet, try to flank the soldier, hitting the enemy from behind and preventing the soldier from retaliating.

UNIQUE SUPPORT ACTIONS

M32
Support Action Points: 400

The M32 grenade launcher is easily one of the most deadly weapons available to any class—and it's relatively easy to acquire, offered in the first tier of support actions for the class. This semi-automatic grenade launcher is pre-loaded with six high-explosive 40mm rounds.
The weapon functions similarly to the grenade launchers of the assaulter class, but the M32 fires rounds with a higher velocity, requiring less compensation for range. This is helped by the weapon's scope, allowing for quicker and more direct target acquisition. However, when engaging hostiles at long range, you will still need to aim high to compensate for gravity. Once the support action is activated, you can stow the weapon and return to your SMG, but any remaining rounds left in the M32 will be lost, so make sure you expend all six grenades before you stow this weapon. Focus your fire on narrow choke points and other areas where opponents are likely positioned, such as objectives or flags.

SMAW
Support Action Points: 900

The Shoulder-Launched Multipurpose Assault Weapon (SMAW) is a shoulder-fired missile designed to attack fixed positions, such as bunkers. This variant as been fitted with a high-explosive warhead, ideal for engaging infantry. When you activate this support action, the weapon is raised onto the demolitions soldier's shoulder and prepared to fire. While you can use the reticle on the screen to aim the weapon, it's better to zoom in, using the weapon's iron sights. Given the close quarters in which the weapon is most likely deployed, there is no need to aim high with this weapon. Once fired, the rocket travels in a straight line, detonating upon impact with the target. The SMAW has a very large blast radius, ideal for taking out multiple opponents. Instead of aiming directly at an opponent, aim at the ground beneath their feet to help guarantee a kill. The SMAW is also ideal for taking out opponents hiding in buildings. Send a rocket through a window to silence snipers and other opponents posted in overwatch positions. You only get two shots with the SMAW, so make them count.

MUSA ROBOT

Support Action Points: 1,500

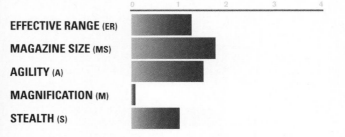

The MUSA Robot is a tracked remote-controlled drone fitted with a coaxial machine gun. Be careful when deploying this support action because you're extremely vulnerable while controlling the robot. Find a remote area of the map, preferably near your team's spawn area and hunker down before sending your robot out to do the dirty work. Once activated, the robot deploys from your position and the HUD changes to the drone's camera view. The robot can be operated using the standard move and fire controls. The MUSA isn't much faster than a demolitions soldier, so it may take some driving around before you find your first target. For best results, keep the drone near teammates or your Fireteam Buddy. This robot can take a serious beating, but it isn't invincible, so avoid driving into a large groups of opponents. If flanked, the MUSA has a tough time rotating to defend itself. Therefore, make an effort to keep the enemy in front of you at all times so you can engage them with the mounted machine gun—fire the machine gun in short bursts to prevent overheating. Otherwise the machine gun can fire with little interruption as it has unlimited ammo. The MUSA's camera lens becomes cracked as the robot takes heavy damage. Do your best to eliminate the threat or retreat to a safer position to prolong the robot's life as long as possible. If it can't be saved, drive the drone directly toward your opponents to inflict as much damage as possible when the robot eventually explodes.

TIP

If you disengage from the MUSA robot before it's destroyed, it serves as a stationary turret, automatically engaging opponents from a fixed position. Try parking it near high-traffic areas and let it do the dirty work for you. But once you disengage from the MUSA, you can't take control of it again.

UNIT PROFILES

AUSTRALIAN SAS-R DEMOLITIONS

Quick and deadly, their motto is "Who Dares Wins." Formed in 1957 with just one company, and now boasting three Sabre Squadrons, OZ SAS-R are experts in reconnaissance missions, surveillance, and counterterrorism.

AA-12 SAS-R

BRITISH SAS DEMOLITIONS

"What color is the boathouse in Hereford?" These guys would know. Their tactics, training, and equipment have been the model for many other country's Special Forces including the U.S. Army's Delta Force. Their motto is "Who Dares Wins." These guys dare.

HECKLER & KOCH 416C SAS

STOCK WEAPON STATS

- EFFECTIVE RANGE (ER)
- MAGAZINE SIZE (MS)
- AGILITY (A)
- MAGNIFICATION (M)
- STEALTH (S)

WEAPON ATTACHMENTS

ATTACHMENT	TYPE	ER	MS	A	M	S
12-Round 12 Ga. Drum Magazine	Extended Magazine	−15%	+30%	—	—	—
AA12 Iron Sights	Standard Optics	—	—	—	—	—
Standard Stock	Standard Receiver	—	—	—	—	—
UDT Door Breacher Muzzle	Standard Muzzle	—	—	—	—	—
Lightweight Barrel + Contour Camera	Close-Quarters Barrel	−15%	—	+15%	—	—
Pink	Paint	—	—	—	—	—

STOCK WEAPON STATS

- EFFECTIVE RANGE
- MAGAZINE SIZE
- AGILITY
- MAGNIFICATION
- STEALTH

WEAPON ATTACHMENTS

ATTACHMENT	TYPE	ER	MS	A	M	S
Flash Hider	Standard Muzzle	—	—	—	—	—
SAS Standard Barrel	Close-Quarters Barrel	−15%	—	+15%	—	—
PDW Stock (Collapsed)	Close-Quarters Receiver	−10%	—	+20%	—	—
30-Round 5.56mm Magazine	Standard Magazine	—	—	—	—	—
Aimpoint Comp M4	Reflex Sight	—	—	−5%	—	—
Combat Beige	Paint	—	—	—	—	—

CANADIAN JTF-2 DEMOLITIONS

JTF-2 is an elite special operations force of the Canadian military specializing in counterterrorism. Although small in number, they make up for their size with relentless and aggressive suppressive firepower. These guys have your six.

GERMAN KSK DEMOLITIONS

This highly specialized, elite unit consists of the best of the best of Germany's special operations soldiers. Their small numbers are testament to a rigorous selection process. The KSK's five platoons can take the fight anywhere in the world—mountain to sea, pole to pole.

HECKLER & KOCH 416C JTF-2

STOCK WEAPON STATS

	0	1	2	3	4
EFFECTIVE RANGE (ER)					
MAGAZINE SIZE (MS)					
AGILITY (A)					
MAGNIFICATION (M)					
STEALTH (S)					

WEAPON ATTACHMENTS

ATTACHMENT	TYPE	ER	MS	A	M	S
Muzzle Brake	Standard Muzzle	—	—	—	—	—
Aimpoint Micro T-1	Reflex Sight	—	—	−5%	—	—
No Stock	Close-Quarters Receiver	−10%	—	+20%	—	—
Lightweight Barrel + LLM01 & PEQ-2	Close-Quarters Barrel	−15%	—	+15%	—	—
JTF-2 30-Round 5.56mm PMAG	Standard Magazine	—	—	—	—	—
Sand	Paint	—	—	—	—	—

HECKLER & KOCH 416C KSK

STOCK WEAPON STATS

	0	1	2	3	4
EFFECTIVE RANGE (ER)					
MAGAZINE SIZE (MS)					
AGILITY (A)					
MAGNIFICATION (M)					
STEALTH (S)					

WEAPON ATTACHMENTS

ATTACHMENT	TYPE	ER	MS	A	M	S
Muzzle Brake	Standard Muzzle	—	—	—	—	—
Standard Barrel + Contour Camera	Standard Barrel	—	—	—	—	—
PDW Stock (Partially Extended)	Standard Receiver	—	—	—	—	—
30-Round 5.56mm PMAG	Standard Magazine	—	—	—	—	—
Trijicon SRS02	Reflex Sight	—	—	−5%	—	—
Flat Brown	Paint	—	—	—	—	—

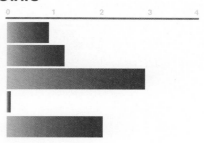

NORWAY FSK/HJK DEMOLITIONS

Although relatively new, these two units of Norway's Special Forces were born to counter terrorist threats to their nation. Since inception, they have been active in campaigns around the world, including Bosnia, Kosovo, and Afghanistan.

POLISH GROM DEMOLITIONS

GROM is Polish for "thunder." And that is what this SF unit brings to the table: they hit hard. Formed in 1990, they have earned the respect of every operator around the world for their tenacity.

MK16 PDW FSK/HJK

STOCK WEAPON STATS

	0 1 2 3 4
EFFECTIVE RANGE (ER)	
MAGAZINE SIZE (MS)	
AGILITY (A)	
MAGNIFICATION (M)	
STEALTH (S)	

WEAPON ATTACHMENTS

ATTACHMENT	TYPE	ER	MS	A	M	S
30-Round 5.56mm Magazine	Extended Magazine	−15%	+30%	—	—	—
Trijicon RMR	Reflex Sight	—	—	−5%	—	—
Standard Stock + 2-Tone Receiver	Standard Receiver	—	—	—	—	—
Muzzle Brake	Standard Muzzle	—	—	—	—	—
Lightweight Barrel	Close-Quarters Barrel	−15%	—	+15%	—	—
Flat White	Paint	—	—	—	—	—

HECKLER & KOCH 416C GROM

STOCK WEAPON STATS

	0 1 2 3 4
EFFECTIVE RANGE (ER)	
MAGAZINE SIZE (MS)	
AGILITY (A)	
MAGNIFICATION (M)	
STEALTH (S)	

WEAPON ATTACHMENTS

ATTACHMENT	TYPE	ER	MS	A	M	S
Muzzle Brake	Standard Muzzle	—	—	—	—	—
PDW Stock (Extended)	Standard Receiver	—	—	—	—	—
Lightweight Barrel + M720V Light	Close-Quarters Barrel	−15%	—	+15%	—	—
HK Diopter Iron Sights	Standard Optics	—	—	—	—	—
30-Round 5.56mm PMAG + Tab	Standard Magazine	—	—	—	—	—
OD	Paint	—	—	—	—	—

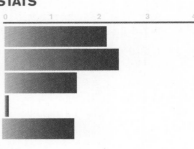

ROKN UDT/SEAL DEMOLITIONS

This Special Forces unit is part of the Republic of Korea Naval Special Warfare Flotilla. This unit is heavily modeled after the U.S. Navy's SEALs in training and tactics. They have already proved their skill in a number of successful maritime hostage rescues.

RU SPETSGRUPPA ALFA DEMOLITIONS

While there are many branches of the Russian Special Forces, the most famous is the Alpha Group. Specializing in counterterrorism, their training is some of the most rigorous in the military. Alphas are at home in a variety of environments and constantly conduct drills to hone their skills.

AA-12 ROKN

AKS-74U SUCHKA

STOCK WEAPON STATS

	0	1	2	3	4
EFFECTIVE RANGE (ER)					
MAGAZINE SIZE (MS)					
AGILITY (A)					
MAGNIFICATION (M)					
STEALTH (S)					

STOCK WEAPON STATS

	0	1	2	3	4
EFFECTIVE RANGE (ER)					
MAGAZINE SIZE (MS)					
AGILITY (A)					
MAGNIFICATION (M)					
STEALTH (S)					

WEAPON ATTACHMENTS

ATTACHMENT	TYPE	ER	MS	A	M	S
Standard Stock	Standard Receiver	—	—	—	—	—
8-Round 12 Ga. Box Magazine	Standard Magazine	—	—	—	—	—
UDT Door Breacher Muzzle	Standard Muzzle	—	—	—	—	—
Small Holographic	Reflex Sight	—	—	–5%	—	—
Lightweight Barrel + M952V Light & VFG	Close-Quarters Barrel	–15%	—	+15%	—	—
UDT Gray	Paint	—	—	—	—	—

WEAPON ATTACHMENTS

ATTACHMENT	TYPE	ER	MS	A	M	S
Kobra Red Dot	Reflex Sight	—	—	–5%	—	—
Krinkov Muzzle Brake	Standard Muzzle	—	—	—	—	—
30-Round 7.62mm Bakelite Magazine	Standard Magazine	—	—	—	—	—
SUCHKA Cord Wrapped Side Folding Stock	Close-Quarters Receiver	–10%	—	+20%	—	—
Lightweight Barrel	Close-Quarters Barrel	–15%	—	+15%	—	—
Light Gray	Paint	—	—	—	—	—

SWEDISH SOG DEMOLITIONS

Formed by the merging of the SSG (Special Protection Group) and SIG (Special Reconnaissance Group) in 2011 to provide a variety of strategic applications across many disciplines. In addition to conducting small-scale, low-profile ops, SOG operators can also be inserted as a component of large-scale conventional warfare operations.

U.S. ARMY SFOD-D DEMOLITIONS

SFOD-D is one of the United States' secretive Tier 1 counter-terrorism and Special Mission Units. Commonly known as The Unit, it was formed under the designation 1st SFOD-D, and has been involved in every U.S. ground operation since its inception.

AA-12 SOG

STOCK WEAPON STATS

	0	1	2	3	4
EFFECTIVE RANGE (ER)					
MAGAZINE SIZE (MS)					
AGILITY (A)					
MAGNIFICATION (M)					
STEALTH (S)					

WEAPON ATTACHMENTS

ATTACHMENT	TYPE	ER	MS	A	M	S
Door Breacher Muzzle	Standard Muzzle	—	—	—	—	—
Aimpoint CompCS	Reflex Sight	—	—	−5%	—	—
8-Round 12 Ga. Box Magazine	Standard Magazine	—	—	—	—	—
SOG Rear Shell Holder Stock	Standard Receiver	—	—	—	—	—
Standard Barrel + M952V Light	Standard Barrel	—	—	—	—	—
M90 Woodland	Paint	—	—	—	—	—

MK16 PDW SFOD-D

STOCK WEAPON STATS

	0	1	2	3	4
EFFECTIVE RANGE (ER)					
MAGAZINE SIZE (MS)					
AGILITY (A)					
MAGNIFICATION (M)					
STEALTH (S)					

WEAPON ATTACHMENTS

ATTACHMENT	TYPE	ER	MS	A	M	S
Lightweight Barrel + QD VFG	Close-Quarters Barrel	−15%	—	+15%	—	—
SFOD 30-Round 5.56mm Magazine	Extended Magazine	−15%	+30%	—	—	—
SCAR Iron Sights	Standard Optics	—	—	—	—	—
No Stock	Close-Quarters Receiver	−10%	—	+20%	—	—
Muzzle Brake	Standard Muzzle	—	—	—	—	—
Sky	Paint	—	—	—	—	—

U.S. NAVY SEAL DEMOLITIONS

Frogmen have the most grueling selection process in the military. Those who make it through become highly trained experts in assaults, hostage rescue, and counterterrorism. And expert snipers—just ask a pirate.

U.S. OGA DEMOLITIONS

Other Government Agency (OGA) Operators are recruited from the military's special operations community. They're nimble and use technology to their advantage in direct action and intelligence gathering.

AA-12 SEAL

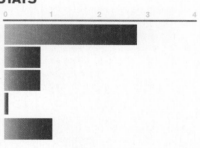

STOCK WEAPON STATS

MK16 PDW OGA

STOCK WEAPON STATS

WEAPON ATTACHMENTS

ATTACHMENT	TYPE	ER	MS	A	M	S
Standard Stock	Standard Receiver	—	—	—	—	—
8-Round 12 Ga. Box Magazine	Standard Magazine	—	—	—	—	—
SEAL Muzzle Brake	Standard Muzzle	—	—	—	—	—
Heavy Barrel	Precision Barrel	+20%	—	–10%	—	—
Trijicon 1x42	Reflex Sight	—	—	–5%	—	—
Chocolate Chip	Paint	—	—	—	—	—

WEAPON ATTACHMENTS

ATTACHMENT	TYPE	ER	MS	A	M	S
Lightweight Barrel + M720V	Close-Quarters Barrel	–15%	—	+15%	—	—
Aimpoint Micro T-1	Reflex Sight	—	—	–5%	—	—
20-Round 5.56mm Magazine	Standard Magazine	—	—	—	—	—
Surefire Suppressor	Silenced Muzzle	–15%	—	—	—	+60%
Standard Stock	Standard Receiver	—	—	—	—	—
Flat Gray	Paint	—	—	—	—	—

HEAVY GUNNER

A high rate of fire and large ammo supply make the Heavy Gunner a welcome addition to any Fireteam. The ability to deploy a bipod for supported shooting and increased accuracy only sweetens the deal.

Sidearm: Heckler & Koch 45CT

Grenade: Mini Frags

PERFORMANCE

	1	2	3	4	5
SPEED					
ARMOR					
FIREPOWER					

SUPPORT ACTIONS

Level	Points Req.	Offensive	Defensive
1	400	Blackhawk Transport	Smoke Screen
2	900	Mk19	Fireteam Replenish
3	1,500	MH-60L DAP Blackhawk	RQ-7 Shadow
4	2,300	Apache Pilot	Apache Pilot

The heavy gunner lugs around a massive light machine gun capable of sustained rapid fire, ideal for suppressing opponents or defending fixed positions. Due to the LMG's size, slow reload speed, and dreadful hip accuracy, the heavy gunner is a difficult class to play when your team is on the offensive. When possible, find a open sight line that allows you to cover your teammates from a distance. The heavy gunner is most effective in a defensive role, using their LMG's bipod to establish coverage of choke points and other narrow avenues of attack. When carrying the weapon, always take aim through the attached scope or iron sights to improve accuracy—you won't hit a thing firing from the hip. Sometimes it's better to equip your pistol when maneuvering in tight spaces. In addition to the light machine gun, the heavy gunner also carries a couple of Mini Frags. These unique fragmentation grenades are thrown in clusters of three, breaking apart and scattering before detonating in unison. This allows the grenades to cover a much wider area than a standard frag grenade. Although their individual blast radius is much smaller, their ability to saturate a wide area with shrapnel can be devastating to opposition Fireteams.

CLASS ABILITY: BIPOD SETUP

By deploying the bipod, the otherwise cumbersome and recoil-heavy light machine gun becomes noticeably stable and accurate, even when firing prolonged automatic bursts. This support stance ability also has another powerful benefit. While the bipod is deployed, the light machine gun has infinite ammo and does not need to be reloaded. While this may seem too good to be true, there are several major drawbacks to this ability. For one, the bipod locks you in a fixed position, either when prone or while crouched behind low cover. From this stationary position, you're vulnerable to flanking attacks, not to mention snipers. The bipod also locks the weapon down, only allowing it to rotate a few degrees, covering a rather narrow firing arc. As a result, only deploy when aiming down narrow sight lines and choke points. Once deployed, aim the weapon to the left and right to test the firing arc, ensuring you can cover all suitable angles. While reloading is unnecessary while the bipod is deployed, you do need to monitor your rate of fire to prevent the weapon's barrel from overheating. If the muzzle begins glowing red, ease off on the trigger until it cools down. You can prevent overheating by firing in short, controlled bursts.

UNIQUE SUPPORT ACTIONS

BLACKHAWK TRANSPORT

Support Action Points: 400

Calling in this support action summons the arrival of a Blackhawk helicopter at your position. Once the chopper arrives, you're immediately put behind the controls of its door-mounted minigun. The minigun has an incredible rate of fire, allowing you to mow down all opponents within view, racking up kill after kill. While in play, the Blackhawk also serves as a temporary spawn point for your teammates. When spawning on the Blackhawk, you enter the game on a fast rope line, sliding down to the battlefield. Since the Blackhawk hovers in one spot, it's a sitting duck for incoming fire, so if you're manning the minigun, don't expect to live very long. Enemy snipers and other opponents will most likely focus their fire on the gunner first before targeting the chopper itself. The chopper remains in play for approximately 60 seconds unless it sustains heavy damage, at which point it automatically retreats—it can't be destroyed outright. When calling in this support action, do so near your team's spawn point or along the perimeter of the map. This gives you the best view of the map from the gunner's position, allowing you to pick off targets at long range.

MK19

Support Action Points: 900

The Mk19 is an automatic 40mm grenade launcher that must be deployed from a stationary position. Before activating this support action, find a good defensible position where you're unlikely to be flanked. Consider backing up into a corner where you have a good view of an objective or another high-traffic area of the map. When activated, the Mk19 is automatically deployed on the ground, prompting your character to automatically sit down behind it. While behind the controls, you can pan and tilt the weapon to cover generous firing arc, but go easy on the trigger as this weapon fires explosives rounds at a rapid pace. Usually one grenade is more than enough to take out a single opponent. You can leave the weapon at any point and return to it later. If you suspect you're about to be flanked (or tomahawked from behind) don't get greedy. Leave the weapon behind and defend yourself. Or better yet, ask your Fireteam Buddy to watch your back while you're busy slinging an oppressive barrage of explosive rounds down range—it's the least they can do.

> **TIP**
> The heavy gunner can resupply all teammates with ammo, but they can only heal their Fireteam Buddy.

MH-60L DAP BLACKHAWK

Support Action Points: 1,500

Unlike the Blackhawk Transport, this support action is an air strike performed by a heavily armed Blackhawk variant equipped with high-explosive rockets and rapid-firing gun pods. This action is initiated much like a mortar strike through the use of a laser target designator. But instead of just pinpointing the target location, you must also designate the direction the Blackhawk should approach from as indicated by the green conical icon in the center of the sight. Setting the Blackhawk's approach vector can make a big difference in how the air strike plays out. For instance, if initiating a strike down a narrow street, it's best to have the Blackhawk fly over parallel with the street so it can focus its ordnance along a narrow corridor. Take a moment to determine the best angle of attack before designating the approach vector. Once the strike has begun, kick back and watch the fireworks. These Blackhawks may draw the fire of your opponents, but no amount of incoming fire will prevent the chopper from making its devastating strafing run.

UNIT PROFILES

AUSTRALIAN SAS-R HEAVY GUNNER

Quick and deadly, their motto is "Who Dares Wins." Formed in 1957 with just one company, and now boasting three Sabre Squadrons, OZ SAS-R are experts in reconnaissance missions, surveillance, and counterterrorism.

HECKLER & KOCH MG4 SAS-R

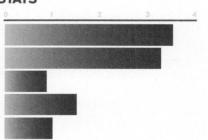

BRITISH SAS HEAVY GUNNER

"What color is the boathouse in Hereford?" These guys would know. Their tactics, training, and equipment have been the model for many other country's Special Forces including the U.S. Army's Delta Force. Their motto is "Who Dares Wins." These guys dare.

M240B

STOCK WEAPON STATS

EFFECTIVE RANGE (ER)	
MAGAZINE SIZE (MS)	
AGILITY (A)	
MAGNIFICATION (M)	
STEALTH (S)	

WEAPON ATTACHMENTS

ATTACHMENT	TYPE	ER	MS	A	M	S
Standard Stock	Standard Receiver	—	—	—	—	—
SAS-R Muzzle Brake	Standard Muzzle	—	—	—	—	—
Heavy Barrel +PEQ- 15	Precision Barrel	+20%	—	–10%	—	—
100-Round 5.56mm Magazine	Standard Magazine	—	—	—	—	—
M145	Low-Power Scope	—	—	–8%	+40%	—
Kangaroo	Paint	—	—	—	—	—

STOCK WEAPON STATS

EFFECTIVE RANGE	
MAGAZINE SIZE	
AGILITY	
MAGNIFICATION	
STEALTH	

WEAPON ATTACHMENTS

ATTACHMENT	TYPE	ER	MS	A	M	S
Flash Hider	Standard Muzzle	—	—	—	—	—
Lightweight Barrel	Close-Quarters Barrel	–15%	—	+15%	—	—
Lightweight Stock	Close-Quarters Receiver	–10%	—	+20%	—	—
SAS 100-Round 7.62mm Magazine	Standard Magazine	—	—	—	—	—
Trijicon SRS02	Reflex Sight	—	—	—	–5%	—
South African 2000	Paint	—	—	—	—	—

CANADIAN JTF-2 HEAVY GUNNER

JTF-2 is an elite special operations force of the Canadian military specializing in counterterrorism. Although small in number, they make up for their size with relentless and aggressive suppressive firepower. These guys have your six.

GERMAN KSK HEAVY GUNNER

This highly specialized, elite unit consists of the best of the best of Germany's special operations soldiers. Their small numbers are testament to a rigorous selection process. The KSK's five platoons can take the fight anywhere in the world—mountain to sea, pole to pole.

M249 JTF-2

HECKLER & KOCH MG4KE

STOCK WEAPON STATS

	0 1 2 3 4
EFFECTIVE RANGE (ER)	
MAGAZINE SIZE (MS)	
AGILITY (A)	
MAGNIFICATION (M)	
STEALTH (S)	

STOCK WEAPON STATS

	0 1 2 3 4
EFFECTIVE RANGE (ER)	
MAGAZINE SIZE (MS)	
AGILITY (A)	
MAGNIFICATION (M)	
STEALTH (S)	

WEAPON ATTACHMENTS

ATTACHMENT	TYPE	ER	MS	A	M	S
Lightweight Barrel +m700v	Close-Quarters Barrel	−15%	—	+15%	—	—
100-Round Ammo Bag	Standard Magazine	—	—	—	—	—
Muzzle Brake	Standard Muzzle	—	—	—	—	—
Trijicon TA11MGO-M249 + RMR	Low-Power Sight	—	—	−8%	+40%	—
JTF-2 Stock (Extended)	Precision Receiver	+15%	—	−15%	—	—
GROM Pixel	Paint	—	—	—	—	—

WEAPON ATTACHMENTS

ATTACHMENT	TYPE	ER	MS	A	M	S
KSK Muzzle Brake	Standard Muzzle	—	—	—	—	—
MG4 Scope	Low-Power Sight	—	—	−8%	+40%	—
150-Round 5.56mm Box Magazine	Extended Magazine	−15%	+30%	—	—	—
Standard Stock + Sling Strap	Standard Receiver	—	—	—	—	—
Lightweight Barrel + Handguard	Close-Quarters Barrel	−15%	—	+15%	—	—
Flecktarn	Paint	—	—	—	—	—

NORWAY FSK/HJK HEAVY GUNNER

Although relatively new, these two units of Norway's Special Forces were born to counter terrorist threats to their nation. Since inception, they have been active in campaigns around the world, including Bosnia, Kosovo, and Afghanistan.

POLISH GROM HEAVY GUNNER

GROM is Polish for "thunder." And that is what this SF unit brings to the table: they hit hard. Formed in 1990, they have earned the respect of every operator around the world for their tenacity.

M240 FSK/HJK

STOCK WEAPON STATS

	0 1 2 3 4
EFFECTIVE RANGE (ER)	
MAGAZINE SIZE (MS)	
AGILITY (A)	
MAGNIFICATION (M)	
STEALTH (S)	

WEAPON ATTACHMENTS

ATTACHMENT	TYPE	ER	MS	A	M	S
M240 Para Stock	Close-Quarters Receiver	–10%	—	+20%	—	—
Heavy Barrel w/Surefire M952V Light	Precision Barrel	+20%	—	–10%	—	—
Trijicon TA648MGO-M240 ACOG + RMR	Low-Power Sight	—	—	–12%	+50%	—
FSK/HJK 100-Round 7.62mm Magazine	Standard Magazine	—	—	—	—	—
Compensator	Standard Muzzle	—	—	—	—	—
Desert Spots	Paint	—	—	—	—	—

M249 GROM

STOCK WEAPON STATS

	0 1 2 3 4
EFFECTIVE RANGE (ER)	
MAGAZINE SIZE (MS)	
AGILITY (A)	
MAGNIFICATION (M)	
STEALTH (S)	

WEAPON ATTACHMENTS

ATTACHMENT	TYPE	ER	MS	A	M	S
Lightweight Barrel	Close-Quarters Barrel	–15%	—	+15%	—	—
Muzzle Brake	Standard Muzzle	—	—	—	—	—
Trijicon TA11MGO-M249 ACOG	Low-Power Sight	—	—	–8%	+40%	—
GROM Stock (Collapsed)	Standard Receiver	—	—	—	—	—
GROM 50-Round Ammo Box	Standard Magazine	—	—	—	—	—
Desert Spray	Paint	—	—	—	—	—

ROKN UDT/SEAL HEAVY GUNNER

This Special Forces unit is part of the Republic of Korea Naval Special Warfare Flotilla. This unit is heavily modeled after the U.S. Navy's SEALs in training and tactics. They have already proved their skill in a number of successful maritime hostage rescues.

RU SPETSGRUPPA ALFA HEAVY GUNNER

While there are many branches of the Russian Special Forces, the most famous is the Alpha Group. Specializing in counterterrorism, their training is some of the most rigorous in the military. Alphas are at home in a variety of environments and constantly conduct drills to hone their skills.

K3 SAW

PKP SPETSNAZ

STOCK WEAPON STATS

	0	1	2	3	4
EFFECTIVE RANGE (ER)					
MAGAZINE SIZE (MS)					
AGILITY (A)					
MAGNIFICATION (M)					
STEALTH (S)					

STOCK WEAPON STATS

	0	1	2	3	4
EFFECTIVE RANGE (ER)					
MAGAZINE SIZE (MS)					
AGILITY (A)					
MAGNIFICATION (M)					
STEALTH (S)					

WEAPON ATTACHMENTS

ATTACHMENT	TYPE	ER	MS	A	M	S
M249 Para Stock (Extended)	Precision Receiver	+15%	—	–15%	—	—
100-Round Ammo Pouch	Standard Magazine	—	—	—	—	—
Muzzle Brake	Standard Muzzle	—	—	—	—	—
Aimpoint CompM4	Reflex Sight	—	—	–5%	—	—
Heavy Barrel + Handguard	Precision Barrel	+20%	—	–10%	—	—
Jungle Path	Paint	—	—	—	—	—

WEAPON ATTACHMENTS

ATTACHMENT	TYPE	ER	MS	A	M	S
etsnaz Stock	Standard Receiver	—	—	—	—	—
Spetsnaz 100-Round 7.62mm Box Magazine	Standard Magazine	—	—	—	—	—
Lightweight Barrel + VFG & LLM01	Close-Quarters Barrel	–15%	—	+15%	—	—
SpecterDR	Low-Power Dual Sights	—	—	–12%	+50%	—
Muzzle Brake	Standard Muzzle	—	—	—	—	—
Snow Cell	Paint	—	—	—	—	—

SWEDISH SOG HEAVY GUNNER

Formed by the merging of the SSG (Special Protection Group) and SIG (Special Reconnaissance Group) in 2011 to provide a variety of strategic applications across many disciplines. In addition to conducting small-scale, low-profile ops, SOG operators can also be inserted as a component of large-scale conventional warfare operations.

U.S. ARMY SFOD-D HEAVY GUNNER

SFOD-D is one of the United States' secretive Tier 1 counter-terrorism and Special Mission Units. Commonly known as The Unit, it was formed under the designation 1st SFOD-D, and has been involved in every U.S. ground operation since its inception.

KSP 90

STOCK WEAPON STATS

	0 1 2 3 4
EFFECTIVE RANGE (ER)	
MAGAZINE SIZE (MS)	
AGILITY (A)	
MAGNIFICATION (M)	
STEALTH (S)	

WEAPON ATTACHMENTS

ATTACHMENT	TYPE	ER	MS	A	M	S
SOG Stock	Standard Receiver	—	—	—	—	—
Muzzle Brake	Standard Muzzle	—	—	—	—	—
SOG 50-Round Ammo Box	Standard Magazine	—	—	—	—	—
Aimpoint CompCS	Reflex Sight	—	—	–5%	—	—
Heavy Barrel	Precision Barrel	+20%	—	–10%	—	—
Black Spray	Paint	—	—	—	—	—

M240 MK243 MOD 1

STOCK WEAPON STATS

	0 1 2 3 4
EFFECTIVE RANGE (ER)	
MAGAZINE SIZE (MS)	
AGILITY (A)	
MAGNIFICATION (M)	
STEALTH (S)	

WEAPON ATTACHMENTS

ATTACHMENT	TYPE	ER	MS	A	M	S
Trijicon TA11H-308 + RMR	Low-Power Sight	—	—	–12%	+50%	—
SFOD 100-Round 7.62mm Magazine	Standard Magazine	—	—	—	—	—
Wooden Stock	Standard Receiver	—	—	—	—	—
Standard Barrel w/ PEQ-15	Standard Barrel	—	—	—	—	—
Compensator	Standard Muzzle	—	—	—	—	—
Finnish Snow	Paint	—	—	—	—	—

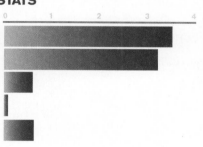

US NAVY SEAL HEAVY GUNNER

Frogmen have the most grueling selection process in the military. Those who make it through become highly trained experts in assaults, hostage rescue, and counterterrorism. And expert snipers—just ask a pirate.

U.S. OGA HEAVY GUNNER

Other Government Agency (OGA) Operators are recruited from the military's special operations community. They're nimble and use technology to their advantage in direct action and intelligence gathering.

M240L

STOCK WEAPON STATS

EFFECTIVE RANGE (ER)

MAGAZINE SIZE (MS)

AGILITY (A)

MAGNIFICATION (M)

STEALTH (S)

WEAPON ATTACHMENTS

ATTACHMENT	TYPE	ER	MS	A	M	S
Flash Hider	Standard Muzzle	—	—	—	—	—
SpecterDR	Low-Power Dual Sights	—	—	−12%	+50%	—
EAL 100-Round 7.62mm Magazine	Standard Magazine	—	—	—	—	—
Standard Stock	Standard Receiver	—	—	—	—	—
Standard Barrel w/ PEQ-2	Standard Barrel	—	—	—	—	—
AOR2	Paint	—	—	—	—	—

M249 MK46 MOD 1

STOCK WEAPON STATS

EFFECTIVE RANGE (ER)

MAGAZINE SIZE (MS)

AGILITY (A)

MAGNIFICATION (M)

STEALTH (S)

WEAPON ATTACHMENTS

ATTACHMENT	TYPE	ER	MS	A	M	S
M249 Para Stock (Collapsed)	Close-Quarters Receiver	−10%	—	+20%	—	—
100-Round Ammo Bag	Standard Magazine	—	—	—	—	—
Flash Hider	Standard Muzzle	—	—	—	—	—
SpecterDR	Low-Power Dual Sights	—	—	−12%	+50%	—
Lightweight Barrel + PEQ-15	Close-Quarters Barrel	−15%	—	+15%	—	—
Brazilian Lizard	Paint	—	—	—	—	—

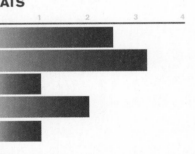

POINT MAN

Not only fleet on foot, the point man operator can unleash high power ammunition on the enemy. These rounds have more kick, inflict more damage, and can even drop the demolitions class while in their durable tank stance.

Sidearm: 870

Grenade: Flashbangs

PERFORMANCE

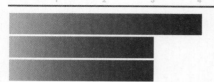

	1	2	3	4	5
SPEED					
ARMOR					
FIREPOWER					

SUPPORT ACTIONS

Level	Points Req.	Offensive	Defensive
1	400	RQ-11 Raven	Smoke Screen
2	900	Airburst Mortar	Fireteam Replenish
3	1,500	AH-6J Little Bird	RQ-7 Shadow
4	2,300	Apache Pilot	Apache Pilot

The point man class performs similarly to the assaulter, but is slightly more proficient in close-quarters combat thanks to their devastating 870 shotgun, which serves as their sidearm. At close range, the 870 is absolutely lethal, making it the perfect weapon for clearing buildings and other cramped spaces. All it takes is one hit from this bad boy to take down most opponents—it is less effective against the demolitions class, particularly when their ballistic armor is active. Fortunately, the point man's primary assault rifle provides another offensive option when range and penetration matter. All the available assault rifles in this class are deadly, precision instruments, perfect for engaging opponents at any range. Instead of carrying standard fragmentation grenades, the point man is equipped with flashbangs. As their name implies, these non-lethal diversionary devices emit a bright flash and loud bang, temporarily blinding and deafening all within their blast radius, including teammates. Be extremely careful when deploying these hand-tossed devices—blinding yourself, your Fireteam Buddy, or your teammates will not help your cause. For best results, toss flashbangs toward distant (or obscured) enemies prior to engaging them. When accurately deployed, a flashbang can blind an opponent (or anyone else) for as long as five seconds. Strike immediately after the flashbang detonates so you can mow down your blind opponents without facing much opposition.

> **TIP**
> If blinded by a flashbang, there's not much you can do to defend yourself, so immediately drop prone and remain motionless until you regain your sight. If you're lucky, your opponents may overlook your body or assume you're dead.

CLASS ABILITY: HIGH POWER AMMUNITION

The point man is equipped with one magazine of high power ammunition—high-damage output rounds capable of taking down even the most heavily armored opponents. While extra firepower is always welcome, prepare yourself for the harsh recoil exhibited by these rounds when fired through the point man's assault rifle. Muzzle climb is significant with each shot, making it difficult to accurately fire the weapon automatically. As a result, it's advised to switch your weapon to semi-automatic fire when high power ammunition is loaded, particularly when engaging opponents beyond ten meters. Firing one shot at a time makes it much easier to keep the weapon on target. High power ammunition is very effective against the demolitions class, even when their ballistic armor is active. Use the point man's speed to flank these slow-moving tanks while firing high power rounds into their helmet. Since you only have one magazine of heavy hitters at a time, resist the urge to reload after each kill. If you reload the high power ammunition magazine while it still holds ammo, your rifle will be loaded with a standard magazine.

UNIQUE SUPPORT ACTIONS

RQ-11 RAVEN

Support Action Points: 400

The RQ-11 is a small UAV capable of identifying hostile units in a limited radius. When the support action is activated, the RQ-11 temporarily replaces your selected weapon, prompting you to throw the UAV skyward. Before tossing the RQ-11, face the direction you want it to orbit. Unlike the RQ-7 Shadow, this UAV performs a tighter orbit over a relatively compact area. This makes it ideal for locating opponents near objectives or other high-traffic areas. This information is relayed to everyone on your team, allowing them to spot enemies on their minimap. When you throw the RQ-11, always aim up so the UAV can achieve its orbit without crashing into the side of a building or any other objects. If the UAV crashes, it's lost for good. Be careful where you aim that thing—it's possible to score a kill with the RQ-11 is you throw it directly at an enemy. The UAV remains airborne for approximately 60 seconds, giving you and your team a significant advantage when it comes to hunting down the opposing team.

AIRBURST MORTAR

Support Action Points: 900

This support action is deployed like all other mortar strikes. When activated, you must first designate the target area with a pair of binoculars—make sure your Fireteam Buddy watches your back while you call in the strike. As with most mortar strikes, try to target areas where you know enemies are present. Unlike traditional mortar rounds, which detonate upon impact with the ground, these mortar rounds explode a few meters above the ground, scattering shrapnel over a wide blast radius. This makes the support action extremely effective against opponents hiding behind walls and other solid forms of cover. Since the rounds explode above their heads, cover does very little to protect them unless they're within a building with a solid roof.

AH-6J LITTLE BIRD

Support Action Points: 1,500

The AH-6J Little Bird is similar to the heavy gunner's MH-60L DAP Blackhawk support action. Upon activating the support action, you're prompted to designate the target area using a laser target designator. Once the target area is selected, you're prompted to choose the Little Bird's approach vector as indicated by the green conical icon in the center of the designator's viewfinder. Soon after the target area is designated and the approach vector determined, the Little Bird appears in the distance and begins strafing the marked area with rapid-firing gunpods. Since the strafing run in linear, it's best to focus these strikes down narrow streets and alleys where opponents are clustered in large numbers. Properly aligning the chopper's approach vector is vital when focusing fire down narrow areas like this, so take your time calling in this strike to optimize its effectiveness.

UNIT PROFILES

AUSTRALIAN SAS-R POINT MAN

Quick and deadly, their motto is "Who Dares Wins." Formed in 1957 with just one company, and now boasting three Sabre Squadrons, OZ SAS-R are experts in reconnaissance missions, surveillance, and counterterrorism.

F88 AUSTEYR

BRITISH SAS POINT MAN

"What color is the boathouse in Hereford?" These guys would know. Their tactics, training, and equipment have been the model for many other country's Special Forces including the U.S. Army's Delta Force. Their motto is "Who Dares Wins." These guys dare.

F88 SAS

STOCK WEAPON STATS

	0	1	2	3	4
EFFECTIVE RANGE (ER)					
MAGAZINE SIZE (MS)					
AGILITY (A)					
MAGNIFICATION (M)					
STEALTH (S)					

STOCK WEAPON STATS

	0	1	2	3	4
EFFECTIVE RANGE (ER)					
MAGAZINE SIZE (MS)					
AGILITY (A)					
MAGNIFICATION (M)					
STEALTH (S)					

WEAPON ATTACHMENTS

ATTACHMENT	TYPE	ER	MS	A	M	S
SpecterDR	Low-Power Dual Sights	—	—	–12%	+50%	—
SAS-R Stock	Standard Receiver	—	—	—	—	—
Muzzle Brake	Standard Muzzle	—	—	—	—	—
42-Round 5.56mm Magazine	Extended Magazine	–15%	+30%	—	—	—
Heavy Barrel	Precision Barrel	+20%	—	–10%	—	—
Erbsent	Paint					

WEAPON ATTACHMENTS

ATTACHMENT	TYPE	ER	MS	A	M	S
30-Round 5.56mm Magazine	Standard Magazine	—	—	—	—	—
Muzzle Brake	Standard Muzzle	—	—	—	—	—
Trijicon TA31-Ch	Low-Power Sight	—	—	–8%	+40%	—
Lightweight Barrel + PEQ – 15	Close-Quarters Barrel	–15%	—	+15%	—	—
SAS Stock	Standard Receiver	—	—	—	—	—
Green Honeycomb	Paint					

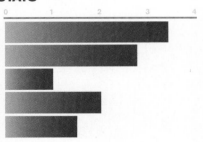
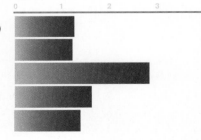

CANADIAN JTF-2 POINT MAN

JTF-2 is an elite special operations force of the Canadian military specializing in counterterrorism. Although small in number, they make up for their size with relentless and aggressive suppressive firepower. These guys have your six.

GERMAN KSK POINT MAN

This highly specialized, elite unit consists of the best of the best of Germany's special operations soldiers. Their small numbers are testament to a rigorous selection process. The KSK's five platoons can take the fight anywhere in the world—mountain to sea, pole to pole.

LARUE OBR 5.56 JTF-2

STOCK WEAPON STATS

	0	1	2	3	4
EFFECTIVE RANGE (ER)					
MAGAZINE SIZE (MS)					
AGILITY (A)					
MAGNIFICATION (M)					
STEALTH (S)					

WEAPON ATTACHMENTS

ATTACHMENT	TYPE	ER	MS	A	M	S
Flash Hider	Standard Muzzle	—	—	—	—	—
Trijicon TA31-Ch	Low-Power Sight	—	—	–8%	+40%	—
Standard Barrel +Contour	Standard Barrel	—	—	—	—	—
Magpul CTR Stock	Standard Receiver	—	—	—	—	—
30-Round 5.56mm Magazine	Standard Magazine	—	—	—	—	—
Gray Tiger	Paint	—	—	—	—	—

LARUE OBR 5.56 KSK

STOCK WEAPON STATS

	0	1	2	3	4
EFFECTIVE RANGE (ER)					
MAGAZINE SIZE (MS)					
AGILITY (A)					
MAGNIFICATION (M)					
STEALTH (S)					

WEAPON ATTACHMENTS

ATTACHMENT	TYPE	ER	MS	A	M	S
Flash Hider	Standard Muzzle	—	—	—	—	—
Magpul PRS Stock	Precision Receiver	+15%	—	–15%	—	—
Heavy Barrel	Precision Barrel	+20%	—	–10%	—	—
Aimpoint Micro T-1 + 3x Magnifier	Low-Power Sight	—	—	–8%	+40%	—
KSK 30-Round 5.56 PMAG	Standard Magazine	—	—	—	—	—
Flecktarn Urban	Paint	—	—	—	—	—

NORWAY FSK/HJK POINT MAN

Although relatively new, these two units of Norway's Special Forces were born to counter terrorist threats to their nation. Since inception, they have been active in campaigns around the world, including Bosnia, Kosovo, and Afghanistan.

POLISH GROM POINT MAN

GROM is Polish for "thunder." And that is what this SF unit brings to the table: they hit hard. Formed in 1990, they have earned the respect of every operator around the world for their tenacity.

F88 FSK/HJK

AK-103 GROM

STOCK WEAPON STATS

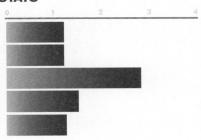

	0	1	2	3	4
EFFECTIVE RANGE (ER)					
MAGAZINE SIZE (MS)					
AGILITY (A)					
MAGNIFICATION (M)					
STEALTH (S)					

STOCK WEAPON STATS

	0	1	2	3	4
EFFECTIVE RANGE					
MAGAZINE SIZE					
AGILITY					
MAGNIFICATION					
STEALTH					

WEAPON ATTACHMENTS

ATTACHMENT	TYPE	ER	MS	A	M	S
30-Round 5.56mm Magazine	Standard Magazine	—	—	—	—	—
FSK/HJK Stock	Standard Receiver	—	—	—	—	—
Aimpoint CompM4 + 3x Magnifier	Low-Power Sight	—	—	–8%	+40%	—
Muzzle Brake	Standard Muzzle	—	—	—	—	—
Lightweight Barrel	Close-Quarters Barrel	–15%	—	+15%	—	—
Green Spots	Paint	—	—	—	—	—

WEAPON ATTACHMENTS

ATTACHMENT	TYPE	ER	MS	A	M	S
Heavy Barrel + Sure-fire M720v Light	Precision Barrel	+20%	—	–10%	—	—
30-Round 7.62mm Bakelite Magazine	Standard Magazine	—	—	—	—	—
AK Triangular Folding Stock	Close-Quarters Receiver	–10%	—	+20%	—	—
Compensator	Standard Muzzle	—	—	—	—	—
M145 (M4 Reticle)	Low-Power Sight	—	—	–8%	+40%	—
GROM Snow Puma	Paint	—	—	—	—	—

ROKN UDT/SEAL POINT MAN

This Special Forces unit is part of the Republic of Korea Naval Special Warfare Flotilla. This unit is heavily modeled after the U.S. Navy's SEALs in training and tactics. They have already proved their skill in a number of successful maritime hostage rescues.

RU SPETSGRUPPA ALFA POINT MAN

While there are many branches of the Russian Special Forces, the most famous is the Alpha Group. Specializing in counterterrorism, their training is some of the most rigorous in the military. Alphas are at home in a variety of environments and constantly conduct drills to hone their skills.

LARUE OBR 5.56 ROKN

AK-103 SPETSNAZ

STOCK WEAPON STATS

	0	1	2	3	4
EFFECTIVE RANGE (ER)					
MAGAZINE SIZE (MS)					
AGILITY (A)					
MAGNIFICATION (M)					
STEALTH (S)					

STOCK WEAPON STATS

	0	1	2	3	4
EFFECTIVE RANGE (ER)					
MAGAZINE SIZE (MS)					
AGILITY (A)					
MAGNIFICATION (M)					
STEALTH (S)					

WEAPON ATTACHMENTS

ATTACHMENT	TYPE	ER	MS	A	M	S
Flash Hider	Standard Muzzle	—	—	—	—	—
Trijicon SRS02	Reflex Sight	—	—	−5%	—	—
Magpul CTR Stock (Painted Receiver)	Standard Receiver	—	—	—	—	—
Lightweight Barrel + M952V Light	Close-Quarters Barrel	−15%	—	+15%	—	—
30-Round 5.56mm Magazine	Standard Magazine	—	—	—	—	—
Disruptive Brown	Paint	—	—	—	—	—

WEAPON ATTACHMENTS

ATTACHMENT	TYPE	ER	MS	A	M	S
AK-74 Muzzle Brake	Standard Muzzle	—	—	—	—	—
30-Round 7.62mm Magazine	Standard Magazine	—	—	—	—	—
Lightweight Barrel	Close-Quarters Barrel	−15%	—	+15%	—	—
Kobra Red Dot	Reflex Sight	—	—	−5%	—	—
Standard Stock + Sling Strap	Standard Receiver	—	—	—	—	—
Spetsnaz Jungle	Paint	—	—	—	—	—

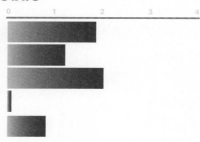

SWEDISH SOG POINT MAN

Formed by the merging of the SSG (Special Protection Group) and SIG (Special Reconnaissance Group) in 2011 to provide a variety of strategic applications across many disciplines. In addition to conducting small-scale, low-profile ops, SOG operators can also be inserted as a component of large-scale conventional warfare operations.

US ARMY SFOD-D POINT MAN

SFOD-D is one of the United States' secretive Tier 1 counter-terrorism and Special Mission Units. Commonly known as The Unit, it was formed under the designation 1st SFOD-D, and has been involved in every U.S. ground operation since its inception.

AK5C

LARUE OBR 5.56 SFOD-D

STOCK WEAPON STATS

	0	1	2	3	4
EFFECTIVE RANGE (ER)					
MAGAZINE SIZE (MS)					
AGILITY (A)					
MAGNIFICATION (M)					
STEALTH (S)					

WEAPON ATTACHMENTS

ATTACHMENT	TYPE	ER	MS	A	M	S
Lightweight Barrel	Close-Quarters Barrel	−15%	—	+15%	—	—
30-Round 5.56 Magazine	Standard Magazine	—	—	—	—	—
Muzzle Brake	Standard Muzzle	—	—	—	—	—
Aimpoint CompCS	Reflex Sight	—	—	−5%	—	—
Lightweight Stock	Close-Quarters Receiver	−10%	—	+20%	—	—
M90 Winter	Paint	—	—	—	—	—

STOCK WEAPON STATS

	0	1	2	3	4
EFFECTIVE RANGE					
MAGAZINE SIZE					
AGILITY					
MAGNIFICATION					
STEALTH					

WEAPON ATTACHMENTS

ATTACHMENT	TYPE	ER	MS	A	M	S
Trijicon 4x32ECOS + RMR	Low-Power Dual Sights	—	—	−12%	+50%	—
Flash Hider	Standard Muzzle	—	—	—	—	—
Maqpul CTR Stock	Standard Receiver	—	—	—	—	—
Heavy Barrel + M720V	Precision Barrel	+20%	—	−10%	—	—
SEAL 30-Round 5.56 PMAG	Standard Magazine	—	—	—	—	—
MOH Bowflage	Paint	—	—	—	—	—

U.S. NAVY SEAL POINT MAN

Frogmen have the most grueling selection process in the military. Those who make it through become highly trained experts in assaults, hostage rescue, and counterterrorism. And expert snipers—just ask a pirate.

U.S. OGA POINT MAN

Other Government Agency (OGA) Operators are recruited from the military's special operations community. They're nimble and use technology to their advantage in direct action and intelligence gathering.

LARUE OBR 5.56 SEAL

AK-103 OGA

STOCK WEAPON STATS

EFFECTIVE RANGE (ER)	
MAGAZINE SIZE (MS)	
AGILITY (A)	
MAGNIFICATION (M)	
STEALTH (S)	

STOCK WEAPON STATS

EFFECTIVE RANGE (ER)	
MAGAZINE SIZE (MS)	
AGILITY (A)	
MAGNIFICATION (M)	
STEALTH (S)	

WEAPON ATTACHMENTS

ATTACHMENT	TYPE	ER	MS	A	M	S
Trijicon 4x32ECOS + RMR	Low-Power Dual Sights	—	—	−8%	+40%	—
Flash Hider	Standard Muzzle	—	—	—	—	—
Maqpul CTR Stock	Standard Receiver	—	—	—	—	—
Lightweight Barrel	Close-Quarters Barrel	−15%	—	+15%	—	—
SEAL 30-Round 5.56mm PMAG	Standard Magazine	—	—	—	—	—
SEAL Brown	Paint	—	—	—	—	—

WEAPON ATTACHMENTS

ATTACHMENT	TYPE	ER	MS	A	M	S
AK-74 Muzzle Brake	Standard Muzzle	—	—	—	—	—
30-Round 7.62mm Magazine	Standard Magazine	—	—	—	—	—
Maqpul CTR Stock	Standard Receiver	—	—	—	—	—
Trijicon TA11J +RMR	Low-Power Sight	—	—	−8%	+40%	—
Heavy Barrel	Precision Barrel	+20%	—	−10%	—	—
Green Grunge	Paint	—	—	—	—	—

SNIPER

Long-range accuracy and a fully-automatic sidearm compliment the real threat posed by this operator. While in a supported stance, a long-range directional minimap leads the sniper to targets, with voice ISR correction and overhead icons.

Sidearm: G18

Grenade: Proximity Mines

PERFORMANCE

	1	2	3	4	5
SPEED					
ARMOR					
FIREPOWER					

SUPPORT ACTIONS

Level	Points Req.	Offensive	Defensive
1	400	Switchblade	Smoke Screen
2	900	81mm Mortar	Fireteam Replenish
3	1,500	Rocket Artillery	RQ-7 Shadow
4	2,300	Apache Pilot	Apache Pilot

Armed with a high-powered rifle, the sniper is the master of long-range combat. But this is a role that's difficult to fill, particularly given the compact size of the maps and lack of long sight lines. It's important to learn the maps and find those spots especially designed for this class—study the maps in the next section to find the key sight lines. Snipers must rely on their Fireteam buddies to provide rear security while lining up those perfect shots. When possible, always drop prone before taking a shot to improve your accuracy. Don't forget to hold your breath to stabilize the scope view before taking a shot—you can hold your breath by clicking down on the left control stick or by holding down the SHIFT key. Deploying the rifle's bipod is another way to stabilize the weapon, negating the need to hold your breath. Sniper rifles are long and cumbersome, making them practically worthless for close-quarters engagements. Fortunately the sniper is also equipped with a fully automatic G18 pistol. Always equip this pistol when moving around the map—it's a true beast in close-quarters firefights! Instead of standard grenades, the sniper is equipped with two proximity mines. Place these in narrow choke points or other high-traffic areas to score some sneaky kills. The proximity mines are also useful for covering your flanks when sniping. For example, when sniping from a second-story window, place a proximity mine on the staircase to cover your back.

CLASS ABILITY: REMOTE SPOTTER

Like the heavy gunner's LMGs, all sniper rifles are equipped with a bipod that can be deployed to stabilize the weapon. Bipods can be deployed while prone or when crouched behind low cover, but pick your position carefully before deploying the bipod and make sure your Fireteam Buddy stays nearby to guard you. You're extremely vulnerable while in the support stance, making it easy for opponents to take you out with their tomahawks. If you don't have a Fireteam Buddy, or if they're off doing their own thing, deploy a proximity mine behind you or on your flanks to ward off attackers. While the bipod is deployed, the sniper benefits from a special minimap. As the sniper sees opponents, these targets are called out and shown on the minimap as well as the minimaps of all teammates. In this sense, the sniper can serve as a spotter, directing teammates toward known enemy locations. When zooming in with the rifle's scope view, the weapon is completely stable, making it easy to line up lethal headshots without needing to hold your breath.

UNIQUE SUPPORT ACTIONS

SWITCHBLADE
Support Action Points: 400

The Switchblade performs like a miniature cruise missile, allowing the sniper to scan the map for potential targets before initiating a devastating dive-bomb attack. When equipped, the UAV-like device is prepped for launch. You must find a relatively open area to launch the Switchblade, with minimal overhead cover. A small rocket launches the Switchblade into the air, at which point your HUD is replaced with a camera view looking down at the map. The Switchblade travels in a straight line from the moment it's launched, so it's a good idea to deploy it from the perimeter of the map and aimed toward the general direction of enemy troops—when possible, launch it toward the opposing team's spawn point. The camera view allows you to see enemy troops scurrying about the map, indicated by red icons. Try to find a group of opponents before initiating the dive-bomb attack. At this point you have direct control of the Switchblade, much like the assaulter's Guided Missile. Guide the Switchblade into a large group of opponents to score multiple kills. If you don't initiate the dive-bomb sequence, the Switchblade will continue flying in a straight line, directly off the map.

81MM MORTAR
Support Action Points: 900

This support action functions identically to the 60mm Mortar offered by the assaulter class. Using a pair of binoculars you must designate the target area, after which mortar rounds begin falling. The 81mm rounds have a slightly larger blast radius than those of the 60mm rounds, spreading the shrapnel and destruction over a wider area. As usual, target areas where opponents have been located, such as objectives or narrow choke points. Avoid targeting areas close to buildings as many of the mortar rounds will strike rooftops, inflicting no damage on your intended targets. Also, be careful when peering through the binoculars, as your peripheral vision is significantly reduced. Ask your Fireteam Buddy to stand watch while you call in the strike—this is not a good time to get a tomahawk in the back.

ROCKET ARTILLERY
Support Action Points: 1,500

Rocket Artillery is yet another mortar-like offensive support action, but spread over a larger area. Like the other mortar strikes, this support action begins by designating a target area with a pair of binoculars. This particular strike is best directed at large open areas where the rockets are less likely to collide with overhead cover such as rooftops or trees. During Sector Control matches, consider launching a strike against flag locations when you suspect enemy troops are hiding nearby. Soon after the target is designated, rocket artillery begins slamming into the ground, killing any opponents unlucky enough to be caught in the wide blast radius.

UNIT PROFILES

AUSTRALIAN SAS-R SNIPER
Quick and deadly, their motto is "Who Dares Wins." Formed in 1957 with just one company, and now boasting three Sabre Squadrons, OZ SAS-R are experts in reconnaissance missions, surveillance, and counterterrorism.

LARUE OBR 7.62 SAS-R

BRITISH SAS SNIPER
"What color is the boathouse in Hereford?" These guys would know. Their tactics, training, and equipment have been the model for many other country's Special Forces including the U.S. Army's Delta Force. Their motto is "Who Dares Wins." These guys dare.

MCMILLAN CS5 SAS

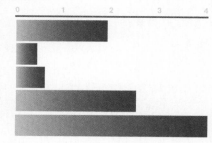

STOCK WEAPON STATS

EFFECTIVE RANGE (ER)	3
MAGAZINE SIZE (MS)	1
AGILITY (A)	1
MAGNIFICATION (M)	2.5
STEALTH (S)	4

WEAPON ATTACHMENTS

ATTACHMENT	TYPE	ER	MS	A	M	S
U.S. Optics ST-10 (MILDOT Reticle)	High-Power Dual Sights	—	—	−20%	+70%	—
Muzzle Brake	Standard Muzzle	—	—	—	—	—
Heavy Barrel	Precision Barrel	+20%	—	−10%	—	—
20-Round 7.62mm Magazine	Standard Magazine	—	—	—	—	—
Maqpul PRS Stock	Precision Receiver	+15%	—	−15%	—	—
DPM2	Paint	—	—	—	—	—

STOCK WEAPON STATS

EFFECTIVE RANGE	2
MAGAZINE SIZE	0.5
AGILITY	1
MAGNIFICATION	2
STEALTH	3.5

WEAPON ATTACHMENTS

ATTACHMENT	TYPE	ER	MS	A	M	S
Lightweight Barrel + Contor Camera	Close-Quarters Barrel	−15%	—	+15%	—	—
U.S. Optics ST-10 (JNG Reticle) + Camera	High-Power Dual Sights	—	—	−20%	+70%	—
Lightweight Stock (Collapsed)	Close-Quarters Receiver	−10%	—	+20%	—	—
5-Round .308Win Magazine	Standard Magazine	—	—	—	—	—
Compensator	Standard Muzzle	—	—	—	—	—
Tan HoneyComb	Paint	—	—	—	—	—

CANADIAN JTF-2 SNIPER

JTF-2 is an elite special operations force of the Canadian military specializing in counterterrorism. Although small in number, they make up for their size with relentless and aggressive suppressive firepower. These guys have your six.

GERMAN KSK SNIPER

This highly specialized, elite unit consists of the best of the best of Germany's special operations soldiers. Their small numbers are testament to a rigorous selection process. The KSK's five platoons can take the fight anywhere in the world—mountain to sea, pole to pole.

MCMILLAN TAC-50 WINTER

MCMILLAN TAC-50 KSK

STOCK WEAPON STATS

	0	1	2	3	4
EFFECTIVE RANGE (ER)					
MAGAZINE SIZE (MS)					
AGILITY (A)					
MAGNIFICATION (M)					
STEALTH (S)					

STOCK WEAPON STATS

	0	1	2	3	4
EFFECTIVE RANGE (ER)					
MAGAZINE SIZE (MS)					
AGILITY (A)					
MAGNIFICATION (M)					
STEALTH (S)					

WEAPON ATTACHMENTS

ATTACHMENT	TYPE	ER	MS	A	M	S
Stock Barrel	Standard Barrel	—	—	—	—	—
5-Round .50 Cal Magazine	Standard Magazine	—	—	—	—	—
Precision Stock (Collapsed)	Precision Receiver	+15%	—	−15%	—	—
U.S. Optics SN-8	High-Power Sight	—	—	−15%	+60%	—
Surefire Suppressor	Silenced Muzzle	−15%	—	—	—	+60%
Navy Tiger	Paint	—	—	—	—	—

WEAPON ATTACHMENTS

ATTACHMENT	TYPE	ER	MS	A	M	S
Heavy Barrel	Precision Barrel	+20%	—	−10%	—	—
U.S. Optics SN-3 5-25x T-PAL (MIL Scale Gap Reticle)	High-Power Dual Sights	—	—	−20%	+70%	—
Precision Stock (Position 3)	Precision Receiver	+15%	—	−15%	—	—
5-Round .50 Cal Magazine	Standard Magazine	—	—	—	—	—
Surefire Suppressor	Silenced Muzzle	−15%	—	—	—	+60%
Flecktarn Green	Paint	—	—	—	—	—

NORWAY FSK/HJK SNIPER

Although relatively new, these two units of Norway's Special Forces were born to counter terrorist threats to their nation. Since inception, they have been active in campaigns around the world, including Bosnia, Kosovo, and Afghanistan.

POLISH GROM SNIPER

GROM is Polish for "thunder." And that is what this SF unit brings to the table: they hit hard. Formed in 1990, they have earned the respect of every operator around the world for their tenacity.

MCMILLAN CS5 FSK/HJK

MCMILLAN TAC-50 GROM

STOCK WEAPON STATS

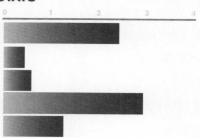

	0	1	2	3	4
EFFECTIVE RANGE (ER)					
MAGAZINE SIZE (MS)					
AGILITY (A)					
MAGNIFICATION (M)					
STEALTH (S)					

STOCK WEAPON STATS

	0	1	2	3	4
EFFECTIVE RANGE					
MAGAZINE SIZE					
AGILITY					
MAGNIFICATION					
STEALTH					

WEAPON ATTACHMENTS

ATTACHMENT	TYPE	ER	MS	A	M	S
Lightweight Barrel + LLM01	Close-Quarters Barrel	−15%	—	+15%	—	—
Lightweight Stock (Tan Receiver)	Close-Quarters Receiver	−10%	—	+20%	—	—
Muzzle Brake	Standard Muzzle	—	—	—	—	—
5-Round .308 Win Magazine + Tape	Standard Magazine	—	—	—	—	—
U.S. Optics SN-8	High-Power Dual Sights	—	—	−20%	+70%	—
Winter Night	Paint	—	—	—	—	—

WEAPON ATTACHMENTS

ATTACHMENT	TYPE	ER	MS	A	M	S
Precision Stock (Position 1)	Precision Receiver	+15%	—	−15%	—	—
Standard Barrel + Contour Camera	Standard Barrel	—	—	—	—	—
GROM Muzzle Brake	Standard Muzzle	—	—	—	—	—
5-Round .50 Cal Magazine	Standard Magazine	—	—	—	—	—
U.S. Optics ST-10 (MILDOT Reticle)	High-Power Dual Sights	—	—	−20%	+70%	—
GROM Puma	Paint	—	—	—	—	—

ROKN UDT/SEAL SNIPER

This Special Forces unit is part of the Republic of Korea Naval Special Warfare Flotilla. This unit is heavily modeled after the U.S. Navy's SEALs in training and tactics. They have already proved their skill in a number of successful maritime hostage rescues.

RU SPETSGRUPPA ALFA SNIPER

While there are many branches of the Russian Special Forces, the most famous is the Alpha Group. Specializing in counterterrorism, their training is some of the most rigorous in the military. Alphas are at home in a variety of environments and constantly conduct drills to hone their skills.

MCMILLAN TAC-300 ROKN

MCMILLAN TAC-300 SPETSNAZ

STOCK WEAPON STATS

	0	1	2	3	4
EFFECTIVE RANGE (ER)					
MAGAZINE SIZE (MS)					
AGILITY (A)					
MAGNIFICATION (M)					
STEALTH (S)					

WEAPON ATTACHMENTS

ATTACHMENT	TYPE	ER	MS	A	M	S
Heavy Barrel	Precision Barrel	+20%	—	−10%	—	—
Muzzle Brake	Standard Muzzle	—	—	—	—	—
U.S. Optics SN-3 5-25x T-PAL (MILDOT Reticle)	High-Power Dual Sights	—	—	−20%	+70%	—
Precision Stock	Precision Receiver	+15%	—	−15%	—	—
5-Round .300 WM Magazine	Standard Magazine	—	—	—	—	—
Tiger Call Winter	Paint	—	—	—	—	—

STOCK WEAPON STATS

	0	1	2	3	4
EFFECTIVE RANGE					
MAGAZINE SIZE					
AGILITY					
MAGNIFICATION					
STEALTH					

WEAPON ATTACHMENTS

ATTACHMENT	TYPE	ER	MS	A	M	S
Muzzle Brake	Standard Muzzle	—	—	—	—	—
Heavy Barrel	Precision Barrel	+20%	—	−10%	—	—
U.S. Optics ST-10 (MILDOT Reticle) + BUIS	High-Power Sight	—	—	−15%	+60%	—
Precision Stock	Precision Receiver	+15%	—	−15%	—	—
5-Round .300 WM Magazine	Standard Magazine	—	—	—	—	—
Spetsanz Red	Paint	—	—	—	—	—

SWEDISH SOG SNIPER

Formed by the merging of the SSG (Special Protection Group) and SIG (Special Reconnaissance Group) in 2011 to provide a variety of strategic applications across many disciplines. In addition to conducting small-scale, low-profile ops, SOG operators can also be inserted as a component of large-scale conventional warfare operations.

U.S. SFOD-D SNIPER

SFOD-D is one of the United States' secretive Tier 1 counter-terrorism and Special Mission Units. Commonly known as The Unit, it was formed under the designation 1st SFOD-D, and has been involved in every U.S. ground operation since its inception.

MCMILLAN TAC-300 SOG

LARUE OBR 7.62 SFOD-D

STOCK WEAPON STATS

EFFECTIVE RANGE (ER)	
MAGAZINE SIZE (MS)	
AGILITY (A)	
MAGNIFICATION (M)	
STEALTH (S)	

STOCK WEAPON STATS

EFFECTIVE RANGE	
MAGAZINE SIZE	
AGILITY	
MAGNIFICATION	
STEALTH	

WEAPON ATTACHMENTS

ATTACHMENT	TYPE	ER	MS	A	M	S
Heavy Barrel	Precision Barrel	+20%	—	−10%	—	—
U.S. Optics ST-10 (MOA Scale Reticle)	High-Power Dual Sights	—	—	−20%	+70%	—
Muzzle Brake	Standard Muzzle	—	—	—	—	—
5-Round .308 WM Magazine + Tape	Standard Magazine	—	—	—	—	—
Standard Stock	Standard Receiver	—	—	—	—	—
Safari	Paint	—	—	—	—	—

WEAPON ATTACHMENTS

ATTACHMENT	TYPE	ER	MS	A	M	S
Maqpul CTR Stock +RISR	Standard Receiver	—	—	—	—	—
Lightweight Barrel	Close-Quarters Barrel	−15%	—	+15%	—	—
Trijicon TA648-308 + RMR	Low-Power Dual Sights	—	—	−12%	+50%	—
20-Round 7.62mm Magazine	Standard Magazine	—	—	—	—	—
Surefire Suppressor	Silenced Muzzle	−15%	—	—	—	+60%
Grass	Paint	—	—	—	—	—

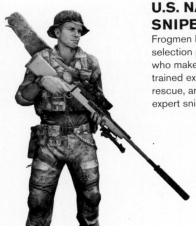

U.S. NAVY SEAL SNIPER

Frogmen have the most grueling selection process in the military. Those who make it through become highly trained experts in assaults, hostage rescue, and counterterrorism. And expert snipers—just ask a pirate.

U.S. OGA SNIPER

Other Government Agency (OGA) Operators are recruited from the military's special operations community. They're nimble and use technology to their advantage in direct action and intelligence gathering.

MCMILLAN TAC-300 SEAL

MCMILLAN CS5 OGA

STOCK WEAPON STATS

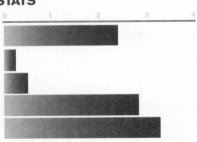

EFFECTIVE RANGE (ER)
MAGAZINE SIZE (MS)
AGILITY (A)
MAGNIFICATION (M)
STEALTH (S)

STOCK WEAPON STATS

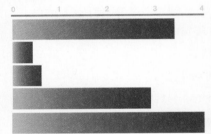

EFFECTIVE RANGE
MAGAZINE SIZE
AGILITY
MAGNIFICATION
STEALTH

WEAPON ATTACHMENTS

ATTACHMENT	TYPE	ER	MS	A	M	S
Standard Barrel + ConTour Camera	Standard Barrel	—	—	—	—	—
U.S. Optics SN-8	High-Power Dual Sights	—	—	–20%	+70%	—
Surefire Suppressor	Silenced Muzzle	–15%	—	—	—	+60%
Standard Stock	Standard Stock	—	—	—	—	—
5-Round .300 WM Magazine	Standard Magazine	—	—	—	—	—
Black and Tan	Paint	—	—	—	—	—

WEAPON ATTACHMENTS

ATTACHMENT	TYPE	ER	MS	A	M	S
U.S. Optics SN-3 5-25x T-PAL (MILDOT Reticle)	High-Power Dual Sights	—	—	–20%	+70%	—
Lightweight Stock (Extended)	Precision Receiver	+15%	—	–15%	—	—
5-Round .308Win Magazine	Standard Magazine	—	—	—	—	—
Compensator	Standard Muzzle	—	—	—	—	—
Lightweight Barrel + M952V Light	Standard Barrel	—	—	—	—	—
Dark Grunge	Paint	—	—	—	—	—

SPEC OPS

Swift operator that makes up for lack of weapon punch with a compliment of tools, like thermal ISR (Intelligence, Reconnaissance, and Surveillance) vision, which can detect targets through obstacles.

Sidearm: G23

Grenade: M67 Frag

PERFORMANCE

	1	2	3	4	5
SPEED					
ARMOR					
FIREPOWER					

SUPPORT ACTIONS

Level	Points Req.	Offensive	Defensive
1	400	Radar Jammer	Smoke Screen
2	900	120mm Dragon Fire	Fireteam Replenish
3	1,500	A-10 Warthog	RQ-7 Shadow
4	2,300	Apache Pilot	Apache Pilot

The spec ops class is fast and nimble, perfect for staging raids on enemy held-positions, using their signal scan ability to gain the upper hand. The submachine guns (SMGs) offered by this class have amazingly high rates of fire, but lack accuracy and stopping power at ranges beyond 20 meters. As a result, spec ops soldiers are at a serious disadvantage when engaging opponents at intermediate to long ranges. For this reason, always avoid areas with long sight lines, such as streets or long alleyways—you won't win a duel against a sniper or assaulter soldier in these wide-open spaces. Instead, move through buildings and other tight spaces where the SMG can chew up targets at close range. Like the assaulter, the spec ops class is equipped with two M67 fragmentation grenades. These grenades are perfectly suited for the close-quarters engagements the spec ops soldier is designed for. While moving through structures, use the signal scan ability to locate enemies and then deploy grenades by banking them off walls or through doorways. This allows you to engage enemies without exposing yourself to incoming fire. For best results, cook the grenades to give your opponents little time to run away.

CLASS ABILITY: SIGNAL SCAN

Of all the class abilities, signal scan is the most unique, giving the spec ops soldier a brief glimpse of nearby enemies. This ability detects the heat signatures of nearby enemy troops, briefly appearing as red silhouettes on the HUD. While the ability is only active for a couple of seconds, it's more than enough time to spot enemies hiding behind walls and other pieces of cover. Once you've identified enemy positions, it's much easier to plan your attack or call in an offensive support action. Signal scan has a rather limited range, allowing you to only detect enemy heat signatures within approximately a 50-meter radius. But since the spec ops soldier usually operates in tight, confined spaces, signal scan's range is usually more than sufficient for dealing with immediate threats. Upon spawning into a match, signal scan isn't available—it must charge for a few seconds before it can be activated. Likewise, after each use, signal scan requires a recharging period before it can be used again. The high-pitched tone emitted by this ability can be heard by teammates and opponents alike. If you hear this sound, it's a good indication that an enemy spec ops soldier is nearby and that your location has been compromised—be ready to move out!

UNIQUE SUPPORT ACTIONS

RADAR JAMMER

Support Action Points: 400

This sneaky device emits an electromagnetic pulse that scrambles the minimap display of all nearby opponents. This is a great way to counter UAVs deployed by the opposing team, allowing your teammates to remain undetected as long as they stay within the jammer's range. Jammers can also detonate nearby enemy explosives, potentially killing opponents who deploy them. When defending during Combat Mission or Hotspot, consider deploying these devices near the objective in an effort to remain concealed. Once activated, it takes a few seconds to deploy this device on the ground, so make sure your Fireteam Buddy or a teammate is nearby to provide cover. Jammers deployed by the opposing team can be destroyed—just shoot them.

120MM DRAGON FIRE

Support Action Points: 900

Of all the artillery-based offensive support actions, this one is the most impressive, raining down massive mortar rounds on the designated target area. When activated, the strike is initiated by designating the target area through a pair of binoculars. As usual, don't attempt to initiate a strike until you're certain your flanks are clear of opponents—have a buddy stand guard to watch your back while you designate the target. Like the sniper's Rocket Artillery, use this support action in wide-open areas where the incoming rounds have plenty of overhead clearance. Mortar rounds that explode on rooftops or trees do no damage to opponents on the ground.

A-10 WARTHOG

Support Action Points: 1,500

Watching an A-10 conduct a low-altitude strafing run never gets old, especially when you're the one scoring all the points for the kills. Initiating close air support from the A-10 is just like calling in a strike for the point man's AH-6J Little Bird. Using a laser target designator, you must first select a target area. Once the target area is chosen, you're prompted to select the A-10's approach vector—this determines at what angle the aircraft begins its strafing run. Soon after air strike has been initiated, an A-10 appears in the distance and begins a strafing run along the approach vector you designated. You can make the most of these strafing runs by lining them up along streets or other narrow, high-traffic areas.

UNIT PROFILES

AUSTRALIAN SAS-R SPEC OPS

Quick and deadly, their motto is "Who Dares Wins." Formed in 1957 with just one company, and now boasting three Sabre Squadrons, OZ SAS-R are experts in reconnaissance missions, surveillance, and counterterrorism.

BRITISH SAS SPEC OPS

"What color is the boathouse in Hereford?" These guys would know. Their tactics, training, and equipment have been the model for many other country's Special Forces including the U.S. Army's Delta Force. Their motto is "Who Dares Wins." These guys dare..

HECKLER & KOCH G36 SAS-R

DANIEL DEFENSE MK18 SAS

STOCK WEAPON STATS

	0	1	2	3	4
EFFECTIVE RANGE (ER)					
MAGAZINE SIZE (MS)					
AGILITY (A)					
MAGNIFICATION (M)					
STEALTH (S)					

STOCK WEAPON STATS

	0	1	2	3	4
EFFECTIVE RANGE					
MAGAZINE SIZE					
AGILITY					
MAGNIFICATION					
STEALTH					

WEAPON ATTACHMENTS

ATTACHMENT	TYPE	ER	MS	A	M	S
Trijicon RMR	Reflex Sight	—	—	-5%	—	—
Muzzle Brake	Standard Muzzle	—	—	—	—	—
30-Round 5.56mm Magazine	Standard Magazine	—	—	—	—	—
No Stock	Close-Quarters Receiver	–10%	—	+20%	—	—
G36 Barrel	Standard Barrel	—	—	—	—	—
SAS-R	Desert Sand	—	—	—	—	—

WEAPON ATTACHMENTS

ATTACHMENT	TYPE	ER	MS	A	M	S
Maqpul UBR	Stock Standard Receiver	—	—	—	—	—
Aimpoint CompM4	Reflex Sight	—	—	-5%	—	—
Muzzle Brake	Standard Muzzle	—	—	—	—	—
Lightweight Barrel + QD VFG	Close Quarters Barrel	-15%	—	+15%	—	—
30-Round 5.56mm Magazine	Standard Magazine	—	—	—	—	—
SAS Green	Paint	—	—	—	—	—

CANADIAN JTF-2 SPEC OPS

JTF-2 is an elite special operations force of the Canadian military specializing in counterterrorism. Although small in number, they make up for their size with relentless and aggressive suppressive firepower. These guys have your six.

GERMAN KSK SPEC OPS

This highly specialized, elite unit consists of the best of the best of Germany's special operations soldiers. Their small numbers are testament to a rigorous selection process. The KSK's five platoons can take the fight anywhere in the world—mountain to sea, pole to pole.

DANIEL DEFENSE MK18 JTF-2

HECKLER & KOCH G36 KSK

STOCK WEAPON STATS

EFFECTIVE RANGE (ER)

MAGAZINE SIZE (MS)

AGILITY (A)

MAGNIFICATION (M)

STEALTH (S)

STOCK WEAPON STATS

EFFECTIVE RANGE

MAGAZINE SIZE

AGILITY

MAGNIFICATION

STEALTH

WEAPON ATTACHMENTS

ATTACHMENT	TYPE	ER	MS	A	M	S
Magpul MOE Stock	Close-Quarters Receiver	−10%	—	+20%	—	—
Iron Sights	Standard Optics	—	—	—	—	—
Flash Hider	Standard Muzzle	—	—	—	—	—
30-Round 5.56mm PMAG	Standard Magazine	—	—	—	—	—
Lightweight Barrel +VFG	Close-Quarters Barrel	−15%	—	+15%	—	—
Tan Tiger	Paint	—	—	—	—	—

WEAPON ATTACHMENTS

ATTACHMENT	TYPE	ER	MS	A	M	S
KSK Lightweight Barrel	Close-Quarters Barrel	−15%	—	+15%	—	—
Muzzle Brake	Standard Muzzle	—	—	—	—	—
30-Round 5.56mm Magazine	Standard Magazine	—	—	—	—	—
Standard Stock	Standard Receiver	—	—	—	—	—
Small Holographic	Reflex Sight	—	—	−5%	—	—
Grass Dunes	Paint	—	—	—	—	—

NORWAY FSK/HJK SPEC OPS

Although relatively new, these two units of Norway's Special Forces were born to counter terrorist threats to their nation. Since inception, they have been active in campaigns around the world, including Bosnia, Kosovo, and Afghanistan.

POLISH GROM SPEC OPS

GROM is Polish for "thunder." And that is what this SF unit brings to the table: they hit hard. Formed in 1990, they have earned the respect of every operator around the world for their tenacity.

HECKLER & KOCH G36 FSK/HJK

STOCK WEAPON STATS

	0	1	2	3	4
EFFECTIVE RANGE (ER)					
MAGAZINE SIZE (MS)					
AGILITY (A)					
MAGNIFICATION (M)					
STEALTH (S)					

WEAPON ATTACHMENTS

ATTACHMENT	TYPE	ER	MS	A	M	S
FSK/HJK Lightweight Barrel	Close-Quarters Barrel	–15%	—	+15%	—	—
30-Round 5.56mm Magazine + Tape	Standard Magazine	—	—	—	—	—
Muzzle Brake	Standard Muzzle	—	—	—	—	—
FSK/HJK Stock	Standard Receiver	—	—	—	—	—
Trijicon 1x42	Reflex Sight	—	—	–5%	—	—
Finnish Snow Night	Paint	—	—	—	—	—

AK-103 BULLPUP GROM

STOCK WEAPON STATS

	0	1	2	3	4
EFFECTIVE RANGE					
MAGAZINE SIZE					
AGILITY					
MAGNIFICATION					
STEALTH					

WEAPON ATTACHMENTS

ATTACHMENT	TYPE	ER	MS	A	M	S
Standard Barrel + VFG & M952V Light	Close-Quarters Barrel	–15%	—	+15%	—	—
Trijicon 1x42	Reflex Sight	—	—	–5%	—	—
30-round 7.62mm Bakelite Magazine	Standard Magazine	—	—	—	—	—
Bullpup Stock + Sling Strap	Standard Receiver	—	—	—	—	—
AK-74 Muzzle Brake	Standard Muzzle	—	—	—	—	—
Green	Mesh Paint	—	—	—	—	—

ROKN UDT/SEAL SPEC OPS

This Special Forces unit is part of the Republic of Korea Naval Special Warfare Flotilla. This unit is heavily modeled after the U.S. Navy's SEALs in training and tactics. They have already proved their skill in a number of successful maritime hostage rescues.

RU SPETSGRUPPA ALFA SPEC OPS

While there are many branches of the Russian Special Forces, the most famous is the Alpha Group. Specializing in counterterrorism, their training is some of the most rigorous in the military. Alphas are at home in a variety of environments and constantly conduct drills to hone their skills..

HECKLER & KOCH MP7 ROKN

STOCK WEAPON STATS

EFFECTIVE RANGE (ER)	
MAGAZINE SIZE (MS)	
AGILITY (A)	
MAGNIFICATION (M)	
STEALTH (S)	

WEAPON ATTACHMENTS

ATTACHMENT	TYPE	ER	MS	A	M	S
40-Round 4.6mm Magazine	Standard Magazine	—	—	—	—	—
MP7 Stock (Collapsed)	Close-Quarters Receiver	–10%	—	+20%	—	—
Flash Hider	Standard Muzzle	—	—	—	—	—
Trijicon RMR	Reflex Sight	—	—	–5%	—	—
Lightweight Barrel + PEQ-15	Close-Quarters Barrel	–15%	—	+15%	—	—
Digital Forest Tiger	Paint	—	—	—	—	—

AK-103 BULLPUP SPETSNAZ

STOCK WEAPON STATS

EFFECTIVE RANGE	
MAGAZINE SIZE	
AGILITY	
MAGNIFICATION	
STEALTH	

WEAPON ATTACHMENTS

ATTACHMENT	TYPE	ER	MS	A	M	S
Compensator	Standard Muzzle	—	—	—	—	—
Lightweight Barrel +VFG & PEQ-15	Close-Quarters Barrel	–15%	—	+15%	—	—
Kobra Red Dot	Reflex Sight	—	—	–5%	—	—
30-Round 7.62mm Magazine	Standard Magazine	—	—	—	—	—
Bullpup Stock	Standard Receiver	—	—	—	—	—
Spetsnaz Urban	Paint	—	—	—	—	—

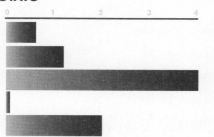

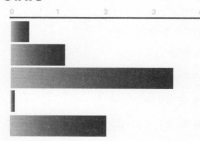

SWEDISH SOG SPEC OPS

Formed by the merging of the SSG (Special Protection Group) and SIG (Special Reconnaissance Group) in 2011 to provide a variety of strategic applications across many disciplines. In addition to conducting small-scale, low-profile ops, SOG operators can also be inserted as a component of large-scale conventional warfare operations..

.

U.S. ARMY SFOD-D SPEC OPS

SFOD-D is one of the United States' secretive Tier 1 counter-terrorism and Special Mission Units. Commonly known as The Unit, it was formed under the designation 1st SFOD-D, and has been involved in every U.S. ground operation since its inception.

C8

DANIEL DEFENSE MK18 SFOD-D

STOCK WEAPON STATS

	0 1 2 3 4
EFFECTIVE RANGE (ER)	
MAGAZINE SIZE (MS)	
AGILITY (A)	
MAGNIFICATION (M)	
STEALTH (S)	

STOCK WEAPON STATS

	0 1 2 3 4
EFFECTIVE RANGE	
MAGAZINE SIZE	
AGILITY	
MAGNIFICATION	
STEALTH	

WEAPON ATTACHMENTS

ATTACHMENT	TYPE	ER	MS	A	M	S
Maqpul CTR Stock	Standard Receiver	—	—	—	—	—
Flash Hider	Standard Muzzle	—	—	—	—	—
30-Round 5.56mm PMAG	Standard Magazine	—	—	—	—	—
Lightweight Barrel + VFG	Close-Quarters Barrel	–15%	—	+15%	—	—
Small Holographic	Reflex Sight	—	—	–5%	—	—
M90 Night	Paint	—	—	—	—	—

WEAPON ATTACHMENTS

ATTACHMENT	TYPE	ER	MS	A	M	S
Lightweight Barrel + M952V Light	Close-Quarters Barrel	–15%	—	+15%	—	—
Aimpoint Micro T-1	Reflex Sight	—	—	–5%	—	—
30-Round 5.56mm PMAG	Standard Magazine	—	—	—	—	—
Buffer Tube Cover	Close-Quarters	–10%	—	+20%	—	—
Surefire Suppressor	Silenced Muzzle	–15%	—	—	—	+60%
Disruptive Gray	Paint	—	—	—	—	—

US NAVY SEAL SPEC OPS

Frogmen have the most grueling selection process in the military. Those who make it through become highly trained experts in assaults, hostage rescue, and counterterrorism. And expert snipers—just ask a pirate.

U.S. OGA SPEC OPS

Other Government Agency (OGA) Operators are recruited from the military's special operations community. They're nimble and use technology to their advantage in direct action and intelligence gathering.

HECKLER & KOCH MP7 SEAL

HECKLER & KOCH MP7 OGA

STOCK WEAPON STATS

	0	1	2	3	4
EFFECTIVE RANGE (ER)					
MAGAZINE SIZE (MS)					
AGILITY (A)					
MAGNIFICATION (M)					
STEALTH (S)					

STOCK WEAPON STATS

	0	1	2	3	4
EFFECTIVE RANGE					
MAGAZINE SIZE					
AGILITY					
MAGNIFICATION					
STEALTH					

WEAPON ATTACHMENTS

ATTACHMENT	TYPE	ER	MS	A	M	S
40-Round 4.6mm Magazine	Standard Magazine	—	—	—	—	—
Small Holographic	Reflex Sight	—	—	−5%	—	—
Standard Barrel + LLM01	Standard Barrel	—	—	—	—	—
Surefire Suppressor	Silenced Muzzle	−15%	—	—	—	+60%
MP7 Stock (Extended)	Standard Receiver	—	—	—	—	—
Zen Garden	Paint	—	—	—	—	—

WEAPON ATTACHMENTS

ATTACHMENT	TYPE	ER	MS	A	M	S
40-Round 4.6mm Magazine + Tape	Standard Magazine	—	—	—	—	—
MP7 Stock (Collapsed)	Close-Quarters Receiver	−10%	—	+20%	—	—
Surefire Suppressor	Silenced Muzzle	−15%	—	—	—	+60%
Lightweight Barrel + M952V Light	Close-Quarters Barrel	−15%	—	+15%	—	—
Aimpoint Micro T-1	Reflex Sight	—	—	−5%	—	—
Winter Grunge	Paint	—	—	—	—	—

[NO...]
F

[SWEDISH]
SOC...

[CANADIAN]
JTF-2

[BRITISH]
SAS

[US]
SEAL

[US]
OGA

[US]
SFOD-D

"AL FARA CLIFFSIDE" 208

"BASILAN AFTERMATH" 220

"HARA DUNES" 232

"NOVI GRAD WARZONE" 244

MULTIPLAYER
MAPS

/HJK

SK

[POLISH]
GROM

[RUSSIAN]
SPETSNAZ
ALFA GROUP

[SOUTH KOREAN]
UDT/SE

"SARAJEVO STADIUM" 254

"SHOGORE VALLEY" 266

"SOMALIA STRONGHOLD" 278

"TUNGAWAN JUNGLE" 290

R

AL FARA CLIFFSIDE

Located in the perilous mountains of northern Yemen, this cliffside village is known as Al Fara. Many conquerors have come and gone in its long history, but the village remains where is has been perched for centuries. Rumors state that every army that passed through its valley never suffered a defeat if their cause was honorable and just.

AL FARA CLIFFSIDE TACTICAL

Choke Point
1

Overwatch Position
1

Sightline
1

TACTICAL OVERVIEW

This ancient village is dominated by a massive cistern near the middle of the map, offering plenty of subterranean pathways ideal for flanking opponents or simply avoiding conflict on the upper level. The cistern has a large opening near the center of the village, allowing players to drop down to the lower level—but expect to take fall damage. This skylight-like feature is also a good way for players to monitor movement on the map's lower level, particularly during Hotspot and Combat Mission matches. The paths and alleys flanking the cistern are quite cramped, leading to intense point-blank firefights—choose your class and weapons accordingly.

CHOKE POINTS

RECOMMENDED WEAPONS
Proximity Mines, Shotgun, SMG, LMG

Only during Combat Mission is this choke point viable. Its tight space and darkness are ideal for a proximity mine. Attackers rushing bomb site A via the southern flank might be too hasty to notice any mines. Defenders will be more occupied with a full-frontal assault, so having this path flanked is a good idea. The hallway also makes for some close-quarters combat with only corners to hide behind for cover. However, if you are at the right position, you can stand farther back to put some suppressive fire down the hall. But there are also quite a few long sight lines here that snipers and heavy gunners can utilize to lock down key areas of the map.

RECOMMENDED WEAPONS
Explosives, Assault Rifle, LMG, Sniper Rifle

This choke point, available in all modes, overlooks an objective area/ high-traffic path. This becomes a choke point due to the cover the wall provides from incoming enemy fire. It's also a tight space, so any cooked grenades that land at the top of the stairs will most definitely kill you. The top of the staircase is also a three-way intersection, with one path having a long line of sight, causing the position to receive a good deal of crossfire from behind and below. Use mid- to long-range weapons to fire up into or down from this position. The best method of getting below would be to use an alternate path.

RECOMMENDED WEAPONS
Explosives, Assault Rifle, Shotgun, SMG, LMG

While defending the objective in Combat Mission, Sector Control, Hotspot, or perhaps at some point in Team Deathmatch, enemies are going to come from the bridge and use this alley to flank would-be defenders of the North Base area. Put some proximity mines along that alley, find some cover, and get ready. Once enemies have made it to this alley they'll move in quickly if defenders aren't paying attention. Defending here can also be dangerous if flanked from the rear. Throw in grenades, and push enemies back with short- to mid-range weapons.

RECOMMENDED WEAPONS
Explosives, Assault Rifle, LMG, SMG, Sniper Rifle

This pathway is the lower path headed toward bomb site B in Combat Mission. Snipers will likely fire into combat as others push toward the point to arm the charge. Defensive snipers should plant proximity mines in as many of these lower paths as possible or directly on the objective. Mines will likely go unnoticed given the urgency required just to get to the objective. Lean from the side of walls or use wooden crates for cover. While defending this point, be aware of the firefight on the upper level, because you may be flanked from above if enemies jump down. Attackers will also flank from the tunnel to the right.

RECOMMENDED WEAPONS
Explosives, SMG, Shotgun, Assault Rifle, LMG

During Team Deathmatch, Hotspot, and Home Run, this alley is often a high-traffic path between objectives where you'll likely meet enemies, so use short- to mid-range weapons coming through here. This path mainly becomes a choke point during Sector Control when enemies come from South Base upstairs, or south spawn to capture Center Base. Center Base defenders are often too preoccupied with people on the upper stairway choke point to notice anyone coming through the alleys. As defenders at Center Base, throw cooked grenades into this lower alley to keep people off of Center Base coming from this direction.

RECOMMENDED WEAPONS
Explosives, LMG, Assault Rifle

At bomb site B in Combat Mission, enemies will come along this path to flank the objective from the alleyway or by way of the upper area. Taking up a more forward position as a defender here will choke attackers off from those two paths. This position is fairly close to the enemy spawn point, so know when to fall back to the bomb site. During Hotspot, this position is near a bomb site so the paths around this cliffside will become congested quickly. Use mid- to long-range weapons in the area.

RECOMMENDED WEAPONS
7
Explosives, Assault Rifle, Shotgun, SMG, LMG

During Combat Mission and Hotspot, these passages may see heavy traffic due to the nearby objectives. Litter these pathways with proximity mines or other explosives.

Lean around corners during engagements and use short- to mid-range weapons while snipers should hang back to take pot shots down the passages.

RECOMMENDED WEAPONS
8
Explosives, Assault Rifle, LMG, Sniper Rifle (supported)

This lesser-travelled choke point, or flanking path, is found in all modes. The northern end of the path has a great second-story window for any sniper or deployed LMG to fire from. The southern end of the path meets with the upper level staircase choke point thereby creating a good deal of enemy movement. This pathway offers little in the way of cover, so make sure your gun is fully loaded before making use of it.

OVERWATCH POSITIONS

RECOMMENDED WEAPONS
9
Explosives, Smoke Screen, Assault Rifle, LMG, SMG, Sniper Rifle

At bomb site A during Combat Mission, the attacking team face an uphill battle to secure a foothold here, only to face a volley of grenades and bullets as they attempt to arm the first charge. Have a sniper post up on this building, going prone, while a Fireteam Buddy protects the sniper from anyone flanking on the right. Drop smoke and lay down cover fire to arm the point. Spare no grenade, even if you don't see anyone, because there's probably someone behind every wall.

RECOMMENDED WEAPONS
11
Grenades, Assault Rifle, LMG, SMG

In every mode besides Combat Mission, this area becomes hotly contested while defending an objective or simply passing through. These ruins are your best bit of cover. Use cooked grenades and mid- to long-range weapons to take care of anyone on the upper staircase and anyone in the lower passages. You're likely to receive a fair amount of damage, so resupply your buddy often.

RECOMMENDED WEAPONS
10
Explosives, Assault Rifle, SMG, LMG

During Combat Mission, whichever team has secured the upper area overlooking bomb site B will be able to take out anyone attempting to arm the point very quickly. Throw down grenades and shoot the proverbial fish in a barrel. It is essential for attackers to occupy the upper area if they are to have any hope of arming the bomb. The major down side of shooting over this ledge would be that you've now left yourself entirely open to any enemies in the above area.

RECOMMENDED WEAPONS
12
Grenades, LMG, Sniper Rifle (supported)

During all game modes besides Home Run, this point offers a good elevated viewpoint looking directly over the appropriate objective. It also benefits from the advantage, or disadvantage, of being directly across from another window in the alley, thereby creating excellent friendly crossfire (or possible enemy fire). This window is great for mounting the LMG or for posting snipers, but be sure to take care of any enemies coming up the staircase from behind.

RECOMMENDED WEAPONS

Assault Rifle, LMG, Sniper Rifle (supported)

13

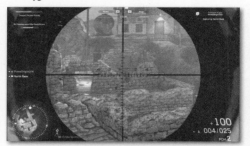

This second-story window is available in all modes besides Home Run. This window looks out over the bridge leading toward the ruins of Sector Control's Center Base area. Anyone using these ruins for cover or hoping to cross the bridge will be sorely disappointed. Put the hurt down with a mounted LMG or sniper rifle. When crossing the bridge, be sure no one is posted up in the building's window.

RECOMMENDED WEAPONS
14
Explosives, Assault Rifle, LMG, Sniper Rifle (supported)

While playing any game mode besides Home Run, a wise flanker or defender would post up in this window for taking out enemies near the objective or passing through the alley. If a teammate takes position in the window across the way from the objective, then a good crossfire can be achieved. Cover is fairly slim and the window is rather open, so be careful about staying in one spot. Shut

RECOMMENDED WEAPONS

Explosives, LMG, Sniper Rifle (supported)

15

Combat Mission's bomb site A is a very exposed approach for attackers. Do your best to cover teammates as they assault the objective. If the broken building to the right is crawling with enemies, this position should be good enough to post up on to lay down some suppressive fire. Move up more toward the objective once it's clear enough.

SIGHT LINES

RECOMMENDED WEAPONS
16
Sniper Rifle

During Combat Mission, Team Deathmatch, and Sector Control, this sight line, within a ruined structure on the upper level, offers a sweeping view across the entire area. During Combat Mission, while defending the path looking toward the attacker's spawn point, enemies may also come from the flank across the terrace. Fall back into the ruins to look through the rubble to view any attacker attempting to flank. During Sector Control, this position will look directly at South Base.

RECOMMENDED WEAPONS

Sniper Rifle

17

This line of sight is available in all game modes and should be used when your position goes unnoticed. There is a nook on the terrace large enough to hide in. Pull out a sniper rifle and aim all the way down the passage toward the stairway choke point. It may be an easy kill or two, but once you're noticed, move on.

SIGHT LINES

RECOMMENDED WEAPONS
Sniper Rifle

18

This sight line is available for all modes except Home Run. While aiming past the courtyard of what would be the North Base, potential target, or bomb site C, a sniper will have a clear path of enemies funneling through a choke point. While teammates handle them at closer range, take your time and pick them off.

RECOMMENDED WEAPONS
Sniper Rifle, LMG (supported)

20

During all game modes besides Home Run, if you're along the middle of the bridge or along the alley parallel to the bridge, you'll be given a clear view of either position. While running through these areas, take a moment to look across the divide. If an enemy is in view, set up shop and let him know you're open for business.

RECOMMENDED WEAPONS
Sniper Rifle

19

During the first phase of Combat Mission, this sight line, from the defenders' point of view, looks down the upper-level alley directly toward the truck at bomb site B. Enemies arming the truck with a charge will post up within the area in an effort to secure the bomb site. From this point a sniper is given free rein to take out anyone extending too far forward from the truck.

RECOMMENDED WEAPONS
Assault Rifle, LMG, Sniper Rifle

21

During all game modes besides Home Run, there is a bit of rock to peer over within the ruins between Sector Control's Center Base and the bridge. This sight line, with plenty of cover, is hardly noticeable while firing on anyone at the top of the stairway choke point.

COMBAT MISSION

C

B

A

Attacker Spawn

Defender Spawn

Bomb Site

At the start of this battle, the attackers are at a distinct disadvantage as they attempt to gain entry into the village. The first bomb site (A) is located at the main gate. Instead of staging a frontal assault, the attackers should attempt to flank from the west and sneak up on the defenders from behind. The second bomb site (B) is positioned at the bottom of the cistern in the center of the map. Both teams should attempt to control the underground tunnels as well as the large skylight-like opening above the bomb site. With so many possible paths and approaches, this can be a tough bomb site for the defenders to lock down. They'll have a much better time guarding the third and final bomb site (C) by taking up positions in the surrounding buildings. As a result, the attackers need to approach this area cautiously. If the area can't be secured, always utilize a Smoke Screen support action before attempting to plant a charge.

HOTSPOT

Attacker Spawn

Defender Spawn

Potential Target

In Hotspot, the attackers start to the south and the defenders spawn on the north side, with the five potential targets spread out across the center of the map. As in all Hotspot matches, the defenders know ahead of time which potential target will be chosen. This gives them the chance to establish a perimeter around each target and dig in before the attackers even know where to go. However, the attackers have plenty of paths available to choose from when it comes to approaching each target. Instead of locking down each target area, the defenders should consider defending the nearby choke points. Cramped paths and blind corners offer great opportunities for staging ambushes or setting booby traps, like proximity mines. As a result, the attackers must move in cautiously. In most cases, the most direct path to a target is not the safest. So take your time inching in toward the target until your team can safely plant a charge and prevent it from being disarmed.

SECTOR CONTROL

Legend:
- ◯ Spawn Point
- ◈ N North Base
- ◈ C Center Base
- ◈ S South Base

Regardless of which side of the map you find yourself on during Sector Control, make an effort to capture and control a minimum of two bases. As usual the Center Base is the most hotly contested area of the map. This is located in a cramped courtyard in the center. At the start of the match, most of your team should rush for the Center Base and try to capture it before the opposing team can—a single Fireteam will have no problem capturing the base closest to your team's starting spawn point, so don't waste too many resources on this location. But don't get greedy. If your team establishes a perimeter around the Center Base, it's possible to cut off all traffic in this area, preventing the opposing team from reaching the base closest to your starting spawn point. Instead of trying to capture and defend all bases, settle on holding the Center Base and the one closest to your team's starting position. Hunker down at these two bases until you have a significant score advantage. Then (and only then) make a move for the third base.

HOME RUN

Attacker Spawn

Defender Spawn

Flag

Much of the fighting in Home Run is centered around the large cistern in the center of the map. While neither flag is present in this subterranean passage, it's a popular path for the attacking team whether heading for Flag A or Flag B. As a result, the defending team should consider deploying some forward skirmishers to deal with the attackers in these tunnels—SMGs and proximity mines are very effective down here. But it's equally important for the defenders to stay posted near the two flags, as it's impossible to tell which one the attackers will go after. If the attackers manage to capture one of the flags, they usually race through the underground cistern passage as it's the most direct route to their home base. Defenders should prepare for this possibility, keeping troops posted in this oft-traveled passage. But if you're carrying the flag and most of your team is dead, take your time getting back to your base. Consider taking the high ground, moving across the upper level instead of running the risk of getting ambushed in the dark tunnels below.

TEAM DEATHMATCH

○ Spawn Point

If you like gritty, urban combat, this map is tough to beat when it comes to Team Deathmatch. Naturally, much of the combat gravitates around the cistern on the south side of the map. The tunnels down here are death traps favoring those with quick reflexes and close-quarters weapons (like SMGs) with high rates of fire. If you choose to fight down here, avoid the central area where opponents can fire down at you through the large, circular opening in the ceiling. If you prefer more house-to-house style fighting, stick to the north side of the map. Here you can find several accessible buildings, including some with second floors. As a result, many of these second floors are occupied by snipers, so be mindful of areas with long sight lines. If you're the one doing the sniping, make sure your Fireteam Buddy watches your back while you peer out windows. At the very least deploy a proximity mine on the staircase to deter any would-be attackers eager to sink their tomahawk into the back of your head.

BASILAN AFTERMATH

Basilan is the largest southern island of the Philippines. Having been a magnet for tourists, this idyllic location was recently devastated by a tsunami. Its once pristine beaches are covered in debris and its world-famous hotels cater to nothing but rats. Peace and beauty may yet return to this region, but only if victory can.

BASILAN AFTERMATH TACTICAL

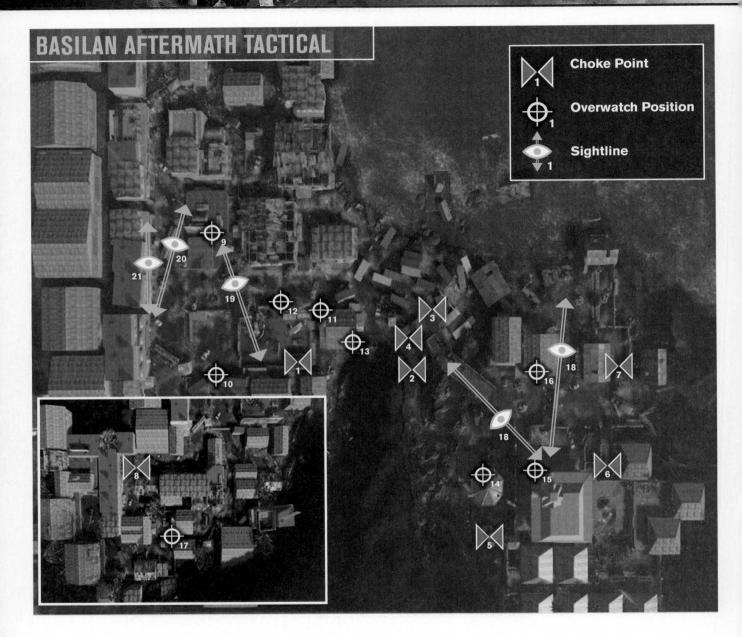

⋈ 1	**Choke Point**
⊕ 1	**Overwatch Position**
◈ 1	**Sightline**

TACTICAL OVERVIEW

It'll be a while before any tourists send home a postcard from this once popular resort destination. The powerful tsunami has transformed this once bustling section of the city into a debris-filled ghost town. Abandoned cars and buses fill the streets near the western gas station, offering decent cover while limiting sight lines. At the center of the map are a jumble of shipping containers, tossed into precarious piles by the now receded waters, forming a tight maze of debris where deadly close-quarters engagements are common. The hotel and gazebo on the east side of the map are two of the few structures that escaped with minimal damage. The upper floors of these structures are popular sniper perches, so be careful when moving about this part of town. Expect heavy fighting here during Sector Control and the last phase of Combat Mission matches.

CHOKE POINTS

RECOMMENDED WEAPONS
Assault Rifle, LMG, Proximity Mines

In Combat Mission, this stairway is an excellent flank for attackers leading upstairs toward the helicopter at bomb site A. Attackers will often catch defenders off guard if they approach from these stairs, so as a defender it's important to have the stairs covered as much as possible. Use close-quarters firearms or proximity mines to handle any attackers approaching from this staircase.

RECOMMENDED WEAPONS
LMG, Assault Rifle, SMG

During Combat Mission, this choke point looking toward the approaching attackers is perfect for catching a lot of people within the blast radius of explosive weapons like grenades, proximity mines, and offensive support actions. Do not stay within the field of view of the attacker's overwatch position. While covering this route, use LMGs and assault rifles to push up through the path. Do not stay within this path for any longer than necessary as it's a complete meat grinder.

RECOMMENDED WEAPONS
Grenades, Proximity Mines, Shotgun, SMG, LMG

As a defender and attacker during Combat Mission, cover as many of these choke points in between the shipping crates as much as possible with proximity mines, grenades, offensive support actions, and cover fire. Be prepared for close-quarters encounters when moving in between the crates. Moving through the crates is a dangerous but necessary proposition to reach the objective or to simply defend it.

RECOMMENDED WEAPONS
Proximity Mines, Grenades, Assault Rifle, LMG, Sniper Rifle

In Combat Mission matches, this intersection is high traffic and high maintenance. As a defender, ensure this flank is being covered, perhaps from the sandbags or farther back along the bridge out of view from the attackers' window perch overlooking this path. Attackers won't have enough time to notice any proximity mines placed along the path entering into the truck site as they'll be too busy handling incoming fire.

RECOMMENDED WEAPONS
Explosives, SMG, LMG, Assault Rifle, Shotgun

During Combat Mission and Sector Control, the stairway from the gazebo leading up toward the hotel will often be a choke point with a moderate amount of traffic, since it's the only way from that direction leading up to the South Base or bomb site C. During Sector Control, if the northern team possess the Center Base, then this staircase will be hotly contested. Close-quarters to mid-range classes are advised to take point upon passing through the staircase.

RECOMMENDED WEAPONS
Explosives, SMG, LMG, Assault Rifle, Shotgun

During Combat Mission and Sector Control, defenders will have to watch this point well, as enemies will start to pile through to get to the final objective or South Base. North Base attackers will find stiff resistance as defenders in the hotel will be often be firing upon this location from above. Defenders should keep pressure on this point with plenty of proximity mines and other explosives. Toss a remote charge over the wall in either direction for what is often an easy kill.

RECOMMENDED WEAPONS

Assault Rifle, LMG, SMG, Sniper Rifle

During Sector Control, enemies will often rush this choke point near the North Base. Throw down explosives if you can while attacking or defending in this area. The southern team should move in with assault rifles or LMGs, providing cover fire for close-range classes to move in. Defenders of North Base have fair warning of anyone approaching, so any long-range classes should have a good chance to wound or kill anyone advancing from the south, using sheds for cover. Also watch the northeast entrance for anyone trying to flank.

RECOMMENDED WEAPONS

Assault Rifle, LMG, SMG, Semi-Auto Sniper Rifle

During Home Run, this choke point provides adequate cover among the rubble. Use short- to mid-range weaponry to push through. Flag defenders will have a bit of elevated advantage. Attackers can counter this with the use of explosives.

OVERWATCH POSITIONS

RECOMMENDED WEAPONS

LMG (SUPPORTED)

This position on top of the gas station provides excellent field of fire overlooking a high-traffic area. In Combat Mission, it also provides overwatch of the bomb site for the attackers. Hold here to prevent any defenders from disarming the bomb. Set up your LMG with your bipod to provide covering fire for your team. There's only one way up on your six, so be aware of any advancing footsteps.

RECOMMENDED WEAPONS
LMG, Assault Rifle

This overwatch position covers most of the approaching area leading up to the bomb site A during Combat Mission matches. This position is best for unsupported LMGs and assault rifles for mid-range engagements. Since enemies often approach your six using the stairs behind you, use of proximity mines or grenades to cover the stairway is also recommended.

RECOMMENDED WEAPONS
LMG (SUPPORTED)

In Combat Mission, this position is found close to the defenders' spawn point. Set up the LMG's bipod on the wall for greater control to take out advancing enemies heading to bomb site A. Be aware of enemy snipers positioned on the gas station's rooftop across the street, and use this position to countersnipe them, along with any other snipers you find.

RECOMMENDED WEAPONS
Shotgun, SMG, LMG, Assault Rifle

Lean out from beneath the fallen billboard for a good view of the street. There's a good amount of cover and you're largely cloaked in darkness until you fire on your target. Drop prone to maintain less visibility, but be wary of the warehouse flanking your right as enemies will push that flank aggressively as well. In Combat Mission, use close- to mid-range weapons when covering this first floor below bomb site A as enemies will be running through here often.

RECOMMENDED WEAPONS
13 *LMG (supported), Sniper Rifle (supported)*

Once bomb site A blows up in Combat Mission and the attackers are advancing, this position inside the building overlooking bomb site B becomes an excellent spot to deploy the LMG or sniper rifle to provide covering fire. Defenders are sure to use this path in an attempt to defend, but your cover fire will make them think twice. You might have a relatively far back position, but if your teammates aren't filling up that choke point, you will be drawing attention to yourself.

RECOMMENDED WEAPONS
14 *LMG, Sniper Rifle (supported)*

In Combat Mission, set up shop using the bipod of the LMG or sniper rifle on the second level of the gazebo to fire on anyone attempting to plant the charge on the truck at bomb site B. The gazebo is made of wood and painted white so you're fairly open, but you may be far back enough from bomb site B to take out anyone trying to venture near your position through the path on left, the bridge, the water beneath the bridge, or the far right flanking path. In Sector Control, this position overlooks the Center Base and the approach from the North Base. Cover the water under the bridge and the far right path from the bridge.

RECOMMENDED WEAPONS
15 *LMG, Assault Rifle, Sniper Rifle*

During Combat Mission and Sector Control, the hotel balcony is a good overwatch position for LMGs, assault rifles, and sniper rifles. However, enemies will be expecting you to be there, so keep your Fireteam Buddy close for support. If things get dicey, run inside for cover and resupply. Enemies will be constantly funneling in through the hotel, so keep on the move to check your flanks, and place proximity mines if you're a sniper.

RECOMMENDED WEAPONS
16 *LMG, Sniper Rifle (supported)*

During Combat Mission and Sector Control, this position is a great overwatch spot to counter anyone taking up position on the hotel's balcony or to simply cover any teammates planting the final charge during Combat Mission. If you have the opportunity, deploy your bipod while prone to take full advantage of the provided cover. During Sector Control, peek over the wall, mount your rifle, and use it to fire on anyone at the Center Base.

RECOMMENDED WEAPONS
17 *LMG, Sniper Rifle, Assault Rifle, Proximity Mines*

During Home Run, this fantastic overwatch position can be used to either attack or defend Flag A. Easily take out enemies from this perch. Do not lock yourself down with a bipod as anyone seeking to flank you will approach your rear quickly. Booby trap possible approaches with proximity mines or monitor footsteps and your minimap carefully for anyone approaching.

SIGHT LINES

RECOMMENDED WEAPONS
18   *Sniper Rifle (supported)*

During Sector Control, this sniper position from the balcony of the large white hotel is a great line of sight directly toward the attackers' spawn point near the North Base. Defensively, this position leaves you fairly exposed. Have a squad mate nearby providing support. During Combat Mission, a clear view of attackers can be had covering the truck bomb site (B). At this distance the bipod is recommended for better accuracy.

RECOMMENDED WEAPONS
20   *Sniper Rifle, Assault Rifle, LMG*

This sight line provides an elevated sniping advantage over anyone attempting to take cover behind cars or pillars, however it does leave you exposed. Plant proximity mines on the scaffolding leading up to the gas station to thwart any would-be assailants. When using this position, ensure your Fireteam Buddy is laying down covering fire so you aren't completely open. Use the billboard as well for additional cover.

RECOMMENDED WEAPONS
19   *LMG, Assault Rifle, SMG*

This defensive position is primarily for keeping enemy snipers off the gas station and covering the left of bomb site A during Combat Mission. Always be on the move and aware of your right flank where enemies will approach from the downed billboard. Use this position sparingly as it will often get you pinned between two flanks.

RECOMMENDED WEAPONS
21   *LMG, Sniper Rifle, Assault Rifle, Grenades*

Use this position to take out any defenders hoping to surprise attackers with sniper fire along the sidewalk. This sight line also provides exceptional crossfire to take out any defenders attempting to take cover behind cars and pillars during Combat Mission matches. If you have teammates covering the nearby sight lines, the enemy is not going to last long. This position is better for clearing out defenders and moving on than setting up shop. Use your leaning keys to stay behind cover as much as possible as you're highly visible.

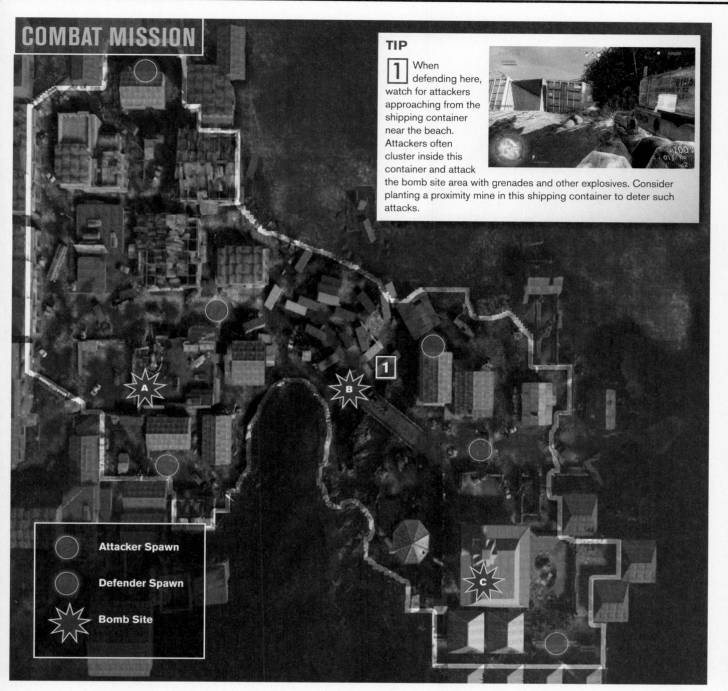

COMBAT MISSION

TIP

1 When defending here, watch for attackers approaching from the shipping container near the beach. Attackers often cluster inside this container and attack the bomb site area with grenades and other explosives. Consider planting a proximity mine in this shipping container to deter such attacks.

Legend:

- ● Attacker Spawn
- ● Defender Spawn
- ✦ Bomb Site

During the first phase of Combat Mission, the action centers around the helicopter crash site near the gas station on the west side of the map. Since bomb site A is located on a rooftop, the defending team should cover all access points to the roof in an effort to prevent the attackers from setting a charge. Expect rooftop-to-rooftop fighting between the gas station and bomb site, but don't let these duels make you lose sight of the objective. In the second phase of the battle, the bomb site (B) is located on a truck near the center of the map. The fighting here often takes place at point-blank range as attackers funnel in among the maze of shipping containers—choose your weapons accordingly. The final bomb site (C) is located within the hotel on the east side of the map. The defenders have the upper hand here since all they have to do is control entry into the hotel. As a result, the attackers should be prepared to bring in heavy firepower to help push the defenders away from their strong defensive positions near the hotel's courtyard and nearby gazebo.

SECTOR CONTROL

Spawn Point

N North Base

C Center Base

S South Base

For a Sector Control map, the boundaries here are very tight, with fighting mostly centered around the hotel and gazebo on the east side. The team spawning near the South Base has a slight advantage as they can cut through the nearby hotel to reach the gazebo, not far from the Center Base flag. The narrow stairway between the hotel and gazebo is an absolute meat grinder during this game mode as it's the quickest path between the South Base and Center Base. It's much safer to find another path. The South Base flag is positioned in a courtyard outside the hotel. There is very little cover near the flag and it can easily be defended from the hotel balcony. So when attacking here, make an effort to clear the second floor of the hotel before approaching the flag. The North Base is relatively isolated and usually controlled by the team attacking from the north side. Still, any team that holds the North Base should make an effort to defend it, otherwise it's an easy capture for the opposing team as the majority of the fighting rages to the south.

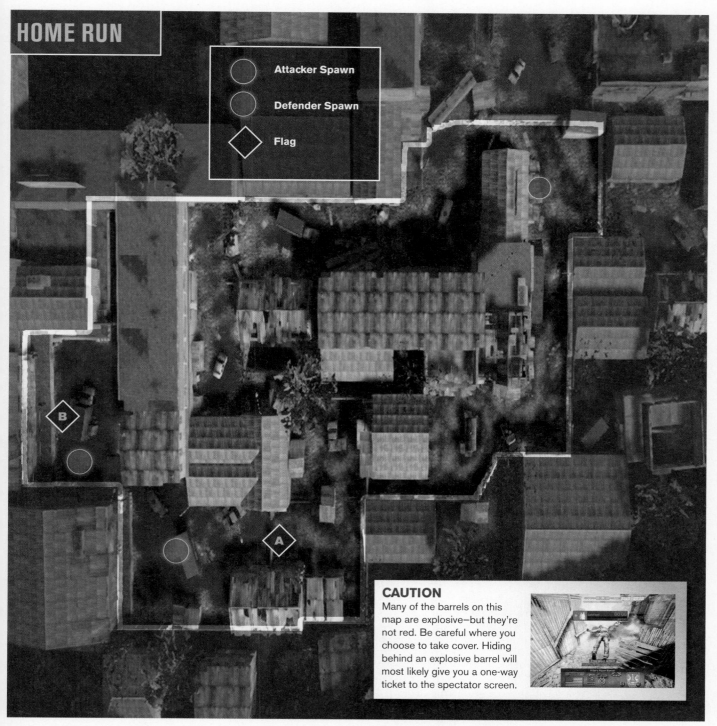

HOME RUN

Attacker Spawn

Defender Spawn

Flag

B

A

CAUTION

Many of the barrels on this map are explosive—but they're not red. Be careful where you choose to take cover. Hiding behind an explosive barrel will most likely give you a one-way ticket to the spectator screen.

The map area in Home Run is entirely unique to this game mode, giving players the chance to explore an industrial area of the island which is off-limits in all other modes. But the environment still feels like Basilan Aftermath, complete with debris-filled streets and other tsunami-related damage. The attacking team deploys from the east, moving toward the flags on the west. The long street leading to Flag B is often the site of some long-range engagements—bring along an assault or sniper rifle to deal with threats here. The direct path leading to Flag B is more broken up, with blind corners as well as a two-story building that can be used as an overwatch position by either team when securing the area around the flag. Choose your class and weapons carefully based on which flag you're planning to attack or defend. Given the long sight lines afforded here, you can never go wrong with the always versatile assaulter class. Still, the signal scan of the spec ops class can make a huge difference here whether attacking or defending.

TEAM DEATHMATCH

○ **Spawn Point**

Team Deathmatch is centered around the gas station and surrounding structures on the north side of the map. Across the street from the gas station is the large building with the crashed helicopter on its rooftop. These two structures are usually the focal point of the action in this game mode, with snipers posted on both rooftops taking shots at each other. So if you're wandering about the streets and alleys, avoid walking between these two key structures. Likewise, steer clear of the street on the west side of the map. The long sight lines afforded by this street make it another popular kill zone for snipers and other sharpshooters posted to the north or south. To avoid sniper fire, stick to the alleys and building interiors, such as the warehouse on the gas station's eastern flank. This large structure can actually serve as a decent "Alamo" if you have the assistance of other Fireteams to lock down the building's entry points. The adjacent alleys can also serve as deadly choke points, so be ready for close quarter engagements when operating in this cramped area.

HARA DUNES

For centuries the cistern in Hara was a place of relief for pilgrims traveling across the scorching desert. But history and tradition has been lost to time as the waters ran dry and the desert reclaimed its prize. This cistern now offers little more than shelter, meaning only one side will drink from the chalice of victory.

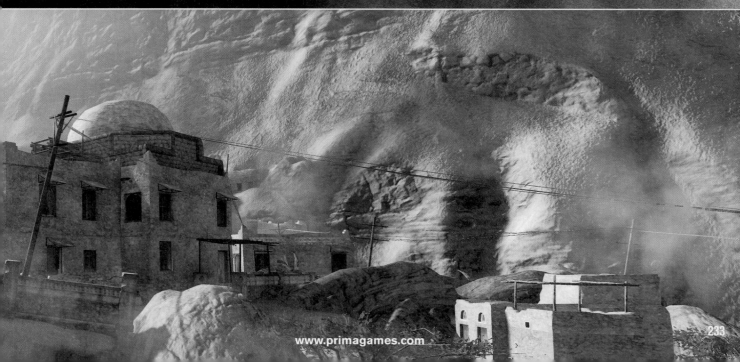

HARA DUNES TACTICAL

⋈ 1	Choke Point
⊕ 1	Overwatch Position
👁 1	Sightline

TACTICAL OVERVIEW

The sand from the nearby dunes isn't the only thing that has invaded this ancient village. Establishing control on this map means securing cramped buildings and narrow alleyways. The terrain on the south and west sides of the map is fairly flat, offering relatively long sight lines down the various streets and alleys. House-to-house fighting is common here, so choose your class and weapons accordingly for better performance among the blind corners and narrow doorways—the spec ops class performs very well in this environment. The terrain on the northern and eastern sides of the map is much rockier and uneven as

the structures adhere to the rise in elevation. While there's fewer structures in this area, there are just as many choke points given the numerous paths cutting through the rocky terrain. During Hotspot, Sector Control, and Combat Mission, the fighting is often intense around the large supply cache on the north side of the map.

CHOKE POINTS

RECOMMENDED WEAPONS
Explosives, Shotgun, SMG

During Combat Mission and Team Deathmatch, this hallway becomes a great high-traffic close-quarters thoroughfare. Sufficient cover is provided while pushing through, but be careful of proximity mines as they may be hard to detect in such a confined space while in a firefight. Use of plenty of explosives is advised to take out any mines and enemies within this hall.

RECOMMENDED WEAPONS
Explosives, LMG (supported), Assault Rifle, SMG

During Combat Mission and Team Deathmatch, this stairway and the other one just like it provide a good place to lay down some heat on any unsuspecting enemies as they move through this contested street and head for the nearby bomb site. The element of surprise will quickly dissipate, and once your position is known it's likely to receive one or two grenades. With this position's usefulness spent, vacate the area ASAP, and find another point of ambush. Using either of these stairways can result in being flanked from the other.

RECOMMENDED WEAPONS
Explosives, LMG (supported), Assault Rifle, Sniper Rifle

During Combat Mission and Team Deathmatch, the team spawning from the east will use the southern flank to get into the house overlooking the street, so covering the halls leading to it is a necessity. If the enemy gets a foothold on the overwatch then it may be tough to take back. Defending the hall from anyone attempting to move through here is crucial, and shouldn't take more than a couple people with the use of sufficient LMG suppressive fire and plenty of explosives. Use lean to engage from the doorway. Staying here can result in being flanked from the rear, so having someone cover your six is very important.

RECOMMENDED WEAPONS
Explosives, LMG (supported), Assault Rifle, SMG, Shotgun

During Combat Mission's second phase, this path sees plenty of movement. Use the provided cover and elevated advantage to hold attackers at bay. Use of supported LMGs is possible, but it would be best to remain mobile. Hold it down with a Fireteam Buddy if you hope to keep the position. Place a proximity mine right next to the doorway. It's important to cover this less likely flank if only for its proximity to the objective.

RECOMMENDED WEAPONS
Proximity Mines, Shotgun, LMG, SMG, Assault Rifle

During the Combat Mission (bomb site B) and Sector Control, this house becomes a great alternate path from the southern main street used in order to reach the South Base or bomb site B. This is ideal as a quick path if the building is secured by friendlies, but could prove difficult to pass through if proximity mines are located within. The team defending the objective should fire down from atop the staircase using the windowsill for cover. If attackers make it up this staircase, they can make this their stronghold and use it to lay down cover fire for their teammates planting on the point.

RECOMMENDED WEAPONS
Explosives, LMG, Assault Rifle, Sniper Rifle

During Combat Mission and Sector Control, this path might have light foot traffic, but teams will be vying for the overwatch building. During Combat Mission, this path should be used to flank bomb site B. The path is tight with plenty of cover, so lean around those corners. Throw grenades liberally along with heavy mid- to long-range weapon fire.

MEDAL OF HONOR WARFIGHTER

RECOMMENDED WEAPONS
7 *Explosives, Shotgun, SMG, LMG, Assault Rifle*

During Sector Control and Hotspot, this door will become congested with plenty of bodies. Bust through here, moving between objectives, using short- to mid-range weapons. This point is made for proximity mines to catch those foolish enough to move through this doorway quickly. Doors like this are grenade magnets, so do not attempt to use it if an enemy is aware of your intent to move through. Rather than fall prey, use this door to lie in wait for anyone blitzing through.

RECOMMENDED WEAPONS
9 *Explosives, Shotgun, SMG, LMG, Assault Rifle*

This area covers the other side of the hotly contestable Center Base during Sector Control, or a potential target during Hotspot. Use the ruins for cover to fire on anyone in the open as they offer very little cover comparatively. Stay mobile as enemies can flank the left, right, or rear approaching from South Base. Stay mobile and maintain a line of sight with your Fireteam Buddy for resupply. Also watch out for incoming grenades. With its low walls and tight spaces, grenade usage is very common here.

OVERWATCH POSITIONS

RECOMMENDED WEAPONS
10 *Explosives, Assault Rifle, LMG, Shotgun, Sniper Rifle, SMG*

In Combat Mission, this position is found close to the defenders' spawn point. Set up the LMG's bipod on the wall for greater control to take out advancing enemies heading to bomb site A. Be aware of enemy snipers positioned on the gas station's rooftop across the street, and use this position to countersnipe them, along with any other snipers you find.

RECOMMENDED WEAPONS
8 *Explosives, Assault Rifle, LMG, SMG, Sniper Rifle*

During Sector Control and Hotspot, this is a high-traffic area as players transition between bases and potential targets. Enemies will come around the corner of the building coming from the large door. This spot also doubles as a decent overwatch position too, with clear views of the Center Base and the nearby potential target. The window is also ideal for a deployed LMG to lay waste to any enemies too preoccupied with engagements on the lower level. After taking down a couple tangos from this elevated perch it's time to beware of revengers attempting to flank your six.

RECOMMENDED WEAPONS
11 *Explosives, Assault Rifle, LMG, SMG, Sniper Rifle*

During Combat Mission and Team Deathmatch, this overwatch is just as viable as the last. This is another window that attackers will use to cover anyone arming the first charge during Combat Mission. Drop that bipod and fire on anyone in the courtyard, ruins, or the other building's windows. Enemies will have a clear view of you sitting in this window from a long distance, so try to remain clandestine prior to engaging the enemy. This position can be flanked from the rear, so consider this while your mind goes into adrenaline-induced slow motion.

RECOMMENDED WEAPONS
12 *LMG, Sniper Rifle (supported)*

During Combat Mission, this road will see heavy traffic coming from the attackers' spawn point. Take position behind the sandbags for some cover. Mounting the LMG is possible, but stay mobile. Once attackers see that the road is being covered they will try to flank from the house to the left and you will want to cover that building with plenty of grenades. Enemies can also flank from the building to the left, so watch that doorway.

RECOMMENDED WEAPONS

LMG, Assault Rifle, Sniper Rifle

During Combat Mission, Hotspot, and Sector Control, this overwatch covers bomb site B, a potential target, or South Base. Defenders might be spread thin during Combat Mission covering most of the other choke points, so it's advantageous for attackers to get a sniper or LMG into the building to provide covering fire for anyone planting a charge on bomb site B. During Sector Control and Hotspot, this window has a clear view of the path between two key locations. This position is easily flanked from the staircase behind, so listen carefully.

RECOMMENDED WEAPONS

Assault Rifle, LMG (supported), Sniper Rifle

During Combat Mission, this is a good post for the high-traffic road approaching bomb site B. Defenders are flanked from the staircase pathway, while attackers can use it for suppressive fire. Keep a Fireteam Buddy close by for support. While playing Sector Control, this position overlooks South Base. While playing Hotspot, it overlooks a potential target. This is ideal for the southern team to defend South Base, but watch out for snipers in the buildings or approaching paths from Center Base.

RECOMMENDED WEAPONS

Explosives, Assault Rifle, LMG, Sniper Rifle, SMG

During Combat Mission, this doorway overlooks a high-traffic path. Move back inside the building and through the other door to cover the other path. It's important to cover these flanks fluidly as enemies are likely to move into this building to take hold of the upstairs overwatch. Using the doorway, or the more forward position near the truck, defend this pathway, but also pay attention to the window in the adjacent building. If attackers are coordinated enough to push at the same time into the house, this position could be flanked from both sides. Booby trap the doorways when possible.

RECOMMENDED WEAPONS

Grenades, Assault Rifle, LMG (supported), Sniper Rifle

Consider this point predominately useful for those spawning at the northern spawn point. During Combat Mission, this position looks directly over bomb site C while also providing exceptional cover and superior elevation. Enemies will have trouble detecting your presence until they're in the killbox at bomb site C, but a sniper in the building with the dome roof will have no trouble finding anyone camping here. During Sector Control, this point covers a high-traffic path between North Base and Center Base. An enemy would have to go out of the way to flank from the rear. During Hotspot, this point is located at a potential target, so use this overwatch loosely while defending other paths leading into the site.

RECOMMENDED WEAPONS

Grenades, Assault Rifle, Sniper Rifle, LMG (supported)

This point will undoubtedly be used to assault bomb site C during Combat Mission, and perhaps even to get a couple kills while people use the area as a path between points in Sector Control or Hotspot. Snipe defenders without worries by dropping a proximity mine, since it's a tight space dark enough to go unnoticed in a rush.

RECOMMENDED WEAPONS

Explosives, Assault Rifle, Sniper Rifle, LMG (supported)

During the assault on bomb site C in Combat Mission, this point should be used in tandem with the overwatch in the building to the immediate right. Defenders will be attempting to take out your teammate in the other building while this position will provide enough crossfire to push them back. These two overwatches should be enough to cover anyone planting a charge. This position can be flanked from the rear via a small path.

SIGHT LINES

RECOMMENDED WEAPONS
Grenades, Assault Rifle, LMG, Sniper Rifle

During Combat Mission and Team Deathmatch, take cover behind the cab of the half-buried truck in order to gain adequate cover with a good perspective of the entire road. This position has a open view of bomb site A during Combat Mission, but should be considered tentative as it leaves you exposed to the various windows and alleys from all sides. The road is a high-traffic area good for a few kills, but bug out quickly to avoid a bullet to the head from the window on the left. Do not tie yourself down by using a bipod.

RECOMMENDED WEAPONS
Sniper Rifle (supported)

While playing Combat Mission, Hotspot, and Sector Control, this sight line looks directly into the respective objective points. Snipers are given a wide field of view of the area, covering plenty of points of interest. To further drive the point home, it's nearly impossible to get flanked during Combat Mission. During Hotspot, this position is very near a potential target and overlooking another, so it would be good to use against any enemies out of range of the position.

RECOMMENDED WEAPONS
Assault Rifle, Sniper Rifle

Considerably a great point for anyone protecting an objective in Combat Mission, Sector Control, and Hotspot. There's some room for ground movement to get a clear shot of enemies in the area while maintaining a good deal of cover. Use of sniper rifles and assault rifles would be advised. However, it can be flanked from an elevated position on the right from a path leading to a ruined house. Enemy snipers will be searching this area as well, so be aware of enemy sight lines.

RECOMMENDED WEAPONS
Grenades, Sniper Rifle

During Combat Mission, this far back sight line can be used to cover bomb site B or to fire down while falling back to bomb site C. During Hotspot and Sector Control, a sniper can peer directly into a potential target or into South Base. While the position provides a good long-range advantage, it can be flanked easily by enemies on foot or by countersnipers.

RECOMMENDED WEAPONS
Sniper Rifle

During Combat Mission, Sector Control, or Hotspot, this window provides a clear sight line of anyone taking the path on the right while also covering the ruined house enemies will attempt to fire from. During Hotspot and Sector Control, this path will have a good deal more foot traffic than in Combat Mission. The roof in this building has zero ceiling, so don't think you're protected from mortars, because you're not.

RECOMMENDED WEAPONS
Assault Rifle, LMG (supported), Sniper Rifle

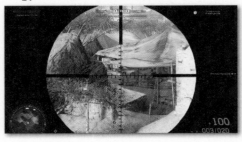

These second-story windows cover a good view of Combat Mission's bomb site C, Sector Control's North Base, and a potential target in Hotspot. When firing down from these sight lines it's good to consider the sight lines other snipers might have, specifically the ruined house and the domed building. As soon as an enemy sniper makes an appearance, the sniper should take priority over other targets in the field.

COMBAT MISSION

- ● Attacker Spawn
- ● Defender Spawn
- ✦ Bomb Site

In Combat Mission, the battle starts out on the west side of the map as both teams struggle for control of bomb site A. When attacking here, always look for flanking paths to avoid getting killed in the narrow choke points between your team's spawn point and the first bomb site. The defending team should prepare for such flanking attacks by moving some of their troops to monitor the street and buildings to the north. Securing the approaches is equally important when the battle moves on to bomb site B, near the center of the map. In addition to choke points, there are several useful overwatch positions both teams should attempt to leverage whether attempting to arm or disarm a charge. The final bomb site (C), is among the large ammo cache on the north side of the map. An array of suspended tarps shade this area, limiting sight lines—but you can still shoot through these overhead awnings. This often leads to intense firefights among the crates as both teams fight for control of this final bomb site.

HOTSPOT

During Hotspot, the western side of the map is cordoned off, focusing the action on the eastern and northern areas of the village. The five potential targets are scattered across this rocky and uneven portion of the map, allowing the defenders to leverage the challenging terrain, choke points, and plentiful cover to their advantage. As usual, both teams should move toward the center of the map early during the round in an effort to establish a foothold near the potential targets. This is particularly important for the attackers. If the attackers loiter near their spawn point until the first target is revealed, the defending team will have an easy time locking down the target. It's best to challenge the defenders early and often in the center of the map so they can't establish a solid foothold near any of the targets. This is also the best way to prevent the defenders from laying siege to the attackers' spawn area on the south side of the map. So spread out and take the fight to the enemy, even when there is no target declared.

SECTOR CONTROL

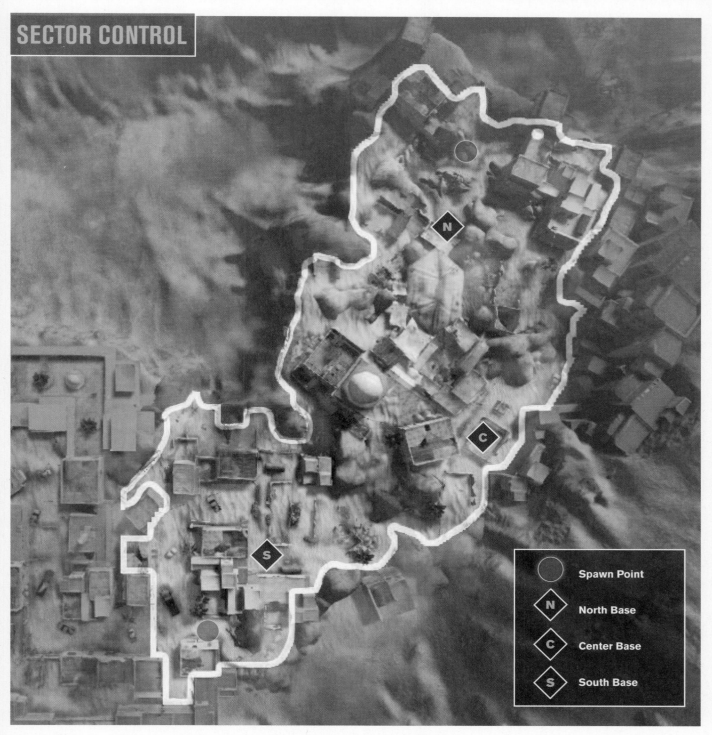

Spawn Point

N North Base

C Center Base

S South Base

As in Hotspot, the action in Sector Control is restricted to the east side of the map. But this time the objective areas are far more focused. In most matches, the North and South Bases are controlled by the teams who spawn nearby. That leaves the contentious Center Base up for grabs. The flag for the Center Base is situated within the ruins of a small structure along the eastern edge. To capture the Center Base you must enter through one of four narrow doorways and hold near the flag pole. Converting this flag is one of the most nerve-racking experiences during this game mode as you can't spot nearby enemies until they come barging through one of the doors. As a result, consider using proximity mines or remote charges to help defend this location against attack. While most fighting occurs near the Center Base, there's plenty of space to slip past this area and capture the North or South Bases. These bases are rarely defended, making them easy to capture—just be ready for the inevitable counterattack approaching from the opposing team's nearby spawn point.

TEAM DEATHMATCH

Spawn Point

Team Deathmatch takes place on the west side of the map, among the cramped buildings, dusty streets, and narrow alleyways. If playing on a full server with 20 players, this map feels very, very small. Upon spawning into the match, you're likely to come face-to-face with your first opponent in a few seconds. While close-quarters weapons like SMGs and shotguns work well for these point-blank encounters, you'll want something more versatile when it comes to engaging opponents in the streets. The assault rifles provided by the assaulter or point man classes are good choices for a variety of tactical situations. However, think twice before choosing the sniper class unless you plan on using the G18 automatic pistol and proximity mines for the duration of the match. The map is too small and the pace is way too fast to set up an effective sniping position. In fact, there aren't too many safe locations to hold out at. Instead, stay close to your Fireteam Buddy and keep moving, sticking to the buildings and alleyways to boost your team's score.

NOVI GRAD WARZONE

Sarajevo paid dearly during the war that ravaged the populace and surrounding region. Blatant disregard for collateral damage spared no district or neighborhood from the systematic destruction applied through the civil war. Recently, fires continue to destroy what little is left of its structures and history.

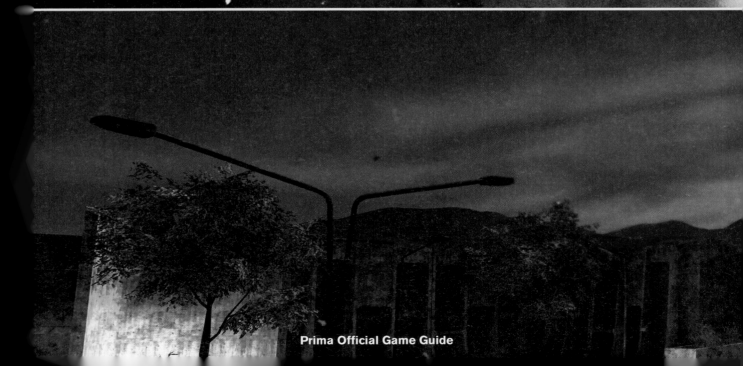

NOVI GRAD WARZONE TACTICAL

Choke Point

Overwatch Position

Sightline

TACTICAL OVERVIEW

Smoldering fires and a smoke-filled sky cast an eerie red glow across this war-torn part of the city, giving it the feel of a nightmarish underworld. The fighting here takes place at night, further reducing visibility as both teams attempt to exert control over this urban wasteland. What is not apparently clear by looking at the map is the shift in elevation between the three distinct areas. To the east is a warehouse complex situated around a large, outdoor loading dock filled with numerous crates. This is the lowest spot on the map—everything to the west is uphill, giving teams that spawn on the west side of the map a significant advantage. At the center of the map is a small, damaged restroom, once part of the surrounding park. This structure sits

atop the hill and is often the site of some intense close-quarters battles, particularly during Combat Mission and Hotspot. To the west is a large office park dominated by a skyscraper engulfed in flames. The fire is contained to the upper floors, leaving the bottom two floors accessible during Combat Mission and Team Deathmatch.

CHOKE POINTS

RECOMMENDED WEAPONS
Remote Charges, Proximity Mines, SMG, Sniper Rifle

During Combat Mission, Sector Control, and Hotspot, there is little cover along the small trails. Throw down proximity mines in the darker choke points. Sections of these dark paths funnel together, making unnoticed proximity mines unavoidable. If you backed up a bit to monitor the proximity mine, take out any stragglers that survive the explosion. Alternatively, the demolition class's remote charge also works well.

RECOMMENDED WEAPONS
Remote Charges, Proximity Mines, Assault Rifle, SMG, Sniper Rifle

This often trekked path is useful in Combat Mission, Sector Control, and Hotspot. Booby trap the path choke points between two bases, potential targets, or paths used to flank bomb site C. Your Fireteam Buddy and you should distract enemies enough as they advance for them to not notice any proximity mines or charges. Pick off survivors of the explosive blast.

RECOMMENDED WEAPONS
Explosives, Assault Rifle, LMG, SMG, Sniper Rifle

Much like the last point, this choke point in Combat Mission, Sector Control, and Hotspot is a great place to throw down a proximity mine. This specific point bears a mention as it's a high-traffic, three-way intersection while teams are defending Combat Mission's bomb site B and a potential target during Hotspot. A mine placed directly in front of this spot will go completely unnoticed as enemies come around the sandbags. While moving through these trails, use mid- to long-range weapons as enemies can be far off behind cover.

RECOMMENDED WEAPONS
Explosives, SMG, LMG, Sniper Rifle

While playing Combat Mission, Sector Control, or Hotspot, this little path is a particularly nasty proximity mine spot. Throw proximity mines under the fallen tree and they're practically invisible. Enemies within the open area are exposed while you may have better cover. While crouched, lean and peek around the rock for cover or wait for enemies to come through for an ambush. Be careful of enemies flanking your six.

RECOMMENDED WEAPONS
Explosives, Shotgun, SMG, LMG

While defending Combat Mission's bomb site C, hold the hallway by laying prone with a supported LMG in the dark for enemies flanking the defending team's left side. Fire at will as enemies charge in. Have your Fireteam Buddy cover your exposed rear with perhaps an SMG or assault rifle. Once you've fired, enemies will know your position and likely throw grenades from around the corner.

RECOMMENDED WEAPONS
Explosives, LMG, Assault Rifle, Sniper Rifle

During Combat Mission's bomb site C or in Team Deathmatch, this ramp will be a constant source of enemies, so bomb site defenders will have to cover this heavily. Its openness is great for throwing grenades up to and down from. Anyone caught on the ramp won't have any cover, so be reasonably sure enemies aren't within the area before climbing up or down. Alternate paths may be more efficient when assaulting bomb site C.

RECOMMENDED WEAPONS
Explosives, LMG, Assault Rifle, Sniper Rifle

During Combat Mission, this staircase will be essential for defenders to hold. Attackers assaulting this position will have poor cover, while defenders will have a good overwatch of incoming enemies. Attackers will want to use this staircase due to the proximity of the bomb site directly at the top. Attackers can roll grenades down the stairs while defenders may be able to flank opponents with grenades. Defenders should use medium- to long-range weapons to defend against enemies coming from a distance, while attackers that have made it this far will likely want to use short-range weapons for pushing up the staircase.

OVERWATCH POSITIONS

RECOMMENDED WEAPONS

Grenades, Sniper Rifle, LMG (supported)

This overwatch is useful during Combat Mission, Sector Control, and Hotspot. During Combat Mission and Sector Control, a supported sniper rifle or LMG has a clear view of the entire area. Post up here for a superb view of bomb site A during Combat Mission or to defend South Base during Sector Control. The window provides good cover as enemies become easy to pick off if they are too engaged with your teammates. Use grenades to flank anyone in this position. During Hotspot, it can look over two potential target areas.

RECOMMENDED WEAPONS

9 *Sniper Rifle, LMG (supported)*

While within the restroom during Combat Mission, Sector Control, or Hotspot, climb on the TV below this window to get a clear view of anyone running up or across this center path. Enemies will have some cover using this uphill climb, but from this position any supported sniper rifle or LMG will have enough time to take them out. This position can be flanked from the left or right alternate paths into the building, so plant proximity mines.

RECOMMENDED WEAPONS

10 *Explosives, LMG, Sniper Rifle (supported)*

This window overwatch near the loading dock is a viable option for defending or attacking two of Hotspot's potential targets. During Combat Mission and Sector Control, it can be useful while attacking bomb site A or the South Base. Deploy a sniper rifle or LMG bipod for optimal results. Anyone using this window can be flanked from the stairs behind or simply shot from the first floor of the building. Place proximity mines to protect your flanks.

RECOMMENDED WEAPONS

11 *Explosives, Assault Rifle, LMG, Sniper Rifle (supported)*

While defending bomb site B in Combat Mission or the North Base in Sector Control, take up a position on the sandbags looking down this path to keep an eye on this intersection. The cover is good and provides a supported fire position, and the uphill advantage should be enough to defend the point. Enemies can flank on the left. Use mid- to long-range weapons if your teammate is deployed at this position.

RECOMMENDED WEAPONS

12 *Explosives, Assault Rifle, LMG, Sniper Rifle (supported)*

During Combat Mission, Sector Control, and Hotspot, defend bomb site B, the North Base, or a potential target in Hotspot using this sandbag. Enemies on the path below can be seen from a good distance, so deploy a bipod for either a sniper rifle or LMG. The sandbags should provide enough cover from enemies attempting to run the gauntlet up the hill.

RECOMMENDED WEAPONS

13 *All Weapons*

During Combat Mission, Sector Control, and Hotspot, defend bomb site B, the North Base, or a potential target in Hotspot using this sandbag. Enemies on the path below can be seen from a good distance, so deploy a bipod for either a sniper rifle or LMG. The sandbags should provide enough cover from enemies attempting to run the gauntlet up the hill.

RECOMMENDED WEAPONS
Assault Rifle, LMG (supported)

During Combat Mission or Team Deathmatch, there is a small break in the wall good for defending bomb site C or to take out anyone in the area. A bipod is a viable option for longer-range shots or LMG suppressive fire. Enemies will come from the left and behind. During Combat Mission, watch out for enemy snipers in the building across the way.

RECOMMENDED WEAPONS
LMG, Sniper Rifle (supported)

During Combat Mission and Team Deathmatch, deploy a bipod-supported sniper rifle or LMG on the staircase opposite of bomb site C. It's a clear view of the parking lot for the LMG to handle, while a sniper rifle can pick off enemies beyond the parking lot. Move on quickly as it's easily flanked from the left and right. Countersnipers will be aware of your position once you've taken a few shots, so move out quickly. Have a Fireteam Buddy nearby for support.

SIGHT LINES

RECOMMENDED WEAPONS
LMG, Sniper Rifle (supported)

During Combat Mission, Sector Control, or Hotspot, hop up this truck's bumper and climb up to the roof. Lay prone with a bipod on top of the truck for a good sight looking toward the path coming from Combat Mission's bomb site A, a potential target in Hotspot, or Sector Control's South Base. The distance is such that any enemies coming from the paths beyond the buildings won't even see anyone on the truck. The down side is that once enemies see you, you'll be flanked by enemy fire from everywhere.

RECOMMENDED WEAPONS
Sniper Rifle

During Combat Mission, Sector Control, or Hotspot, while in the middle path, there's a clear sight line looking far down the middle path and little to the right. While looking down the center path toward the South Base, climb up onto the centered sandbags to the left. You're given a little cover, but not much. The elevated position is great for taking out enemies moving on a potential target or while defending bomb site B from enemies just leaving their spawn point. Don't stay exposed for long, as you'll likely be flanked from the left and right paths.

COMBAT MISSION

Attacker Spawn

Defender Spawn

Bomb Site

This battle starts out on the east side of the map, with bomb site A located on the large loading dock area. The maze of crates surrounding the bomb site often leads to point-blank engagements. If they fail to rush the site early on, the attackers must conduct a coordinated attack in an effort to overwhelm the defenders here before they can plant a charge. Deploying a Smoke Screen and/or UAV can definitely aid both teams in their effort to secure the loading dock. In the second phase of the battle, bomb site B is located within the restroom at the center of the map. Here the defenders have the upper hand, holding the high ground as the attackers charge up the crooked hillside paths. These narrow paths serve as excellent choke points for the defenders, ideal for stopping the attackers once and for all. Instead of charging up the center path, the attackers should look for flanking paths along the north or south sides. If the attackers manage to detonate bomb site B, the final fight takes place at the skyscraper to the west. Bomb site C is located on the second floor of this building, prompting heated firefights along the stairways and ramps leading up to this floor. While long-range engagements are frequent outside the building, the fighting that takes place indoors is point-blank, often benefiting from the close-quarters weapons of the point man or spec ops class.

HOTSPOT

Attacker Spawn

Defender Spawn

Potential Target

In Hotspot, the office park to the west is off-limits, with the bulk of the fighting occurring between the hilltop restroom and the warehouse complex's loading dock to the east. Given their nearby spawn point, the attackers have a good chance of securing the two potential targets near the loading dock. But the attackers can't assume either of these nearby targets will be randomly chosen, particularly at the beginning of the match. As a result, they should try to break out of the loading dock and establish a presence near the potential targets on the hillside and restroom. If the defending team manages to lock down the hill, reaching these three potential targets can be extremely difficult. Early on the defenders should work on securing the hillside while establishing a perimeter around the first potential target. If the first target is located near the loading dock, it will be difficult to get in position as the attackers stream from their spawn point toward the hill. Consider holding back on the hillside and let the attackers take out the first target if it's near their team's spawn point. Controlling the hill (and its three potential targets) is more important than defending the two targets near the loading dock.

SECTOR CONTROL

Spawn Point

N North Base

C Center Base

S South Base

Sector Control takes place within the same boundary as Hotspot, with the majority of the fighting taking place on the hillside between the restroom and the loading dock. The North Base is located only a few meters from the restroom, giving the team who spawns nearby a good chance of controlling this base throughout the match. The South Base is located at the loading dock, well within striking distance of the other team's spawn point. That leaves the Center Base on the hillside in the middle of the map as the most contentious spot during this battle. The team that spawns near the restroom has the best chance of controlling the Center Base, since they attack downhill. For those spawning near the loading dock, capturing the Center Base is literally an uphill battle. Instead of trying to charge up the hill toward this base, consider flanking along the path to the south. If you want to avoid the constant grind at the Center Base, consider moving along the south side of the hill in an attempt to move between the North Base and South Base. There is far less traffic along this side of the hill, making it easy to sneak in and capture the base closest to the opposing team's spawn point.

TEAM DEATHMATCH

Spawn Point

In Team Deathmatch, the battle is contained within the office park on the west side of the map. The obvious focal point on this map is the skyscraper, with both teams attempting to take control of this landmark. Holding out at the skyscraper isn't a bad strategy, especially if your team can lock down the second floor. This means defending the various staircases and ramps leading upstairs—these spots are deadly choke points ideal for scoring large numbers of kills. But maintaining control of the second floor for any significant duration is extremely difficult unless the entire team is on the same page. If this is your team's strategy, consider opening VOIP to the whole team so you can stay in constant contact with your teammates. While most of the fighting takes place in and around the skyscraper, the open areas to the east and west lend themselves to long-range combat, where assault and sniper rifles are very effective. Consider holding near your team's spawn point and engage the chaotic traffic raging around the skyscraper. You can also look for spots to engage cross-traffic as opponents rush from their team's spawn point toward the skyscraper.

SARAJEVO STADIUM

Once a great monument to the spirit of competition, now the stadium stands as a testament to the horrors of the 1990s civil war that ravaged the country that was once Yugoslavia. Ethnic cleansing and fighting has reduced this arena of sport to nothing more than a tattered mess of concrete and steel. Competition still rages here, but of a different kind.

255

SARAJEVO STADIUM TACTICAL

▷◁ 1	**Choke Point**
⊕ 1	**Overwatch Position**
◉ 1	**Sightline**

TACTICAL OVERVIEW

Like Novi Grad Warzone, this is another map set in the war-torn city of Sarajevo. While there's no fires or smoke, the action does take place at night, making visibility a challenge. The fighting is centered around an old sports complex featuring a stadium and heavily damaged bobsled track. The stadium occupies much of the map's south side, giving fights here an arena-like feel during Team Deathmatch and Combat Mission. At the center of the map is a small building topped with an old scoreboard. As a central location, the scoreboard structure sees plenty of action during Combat Mission, Hotspot, and Sector Control—use the less-traveled east and west flanking paths when moving to or past this contentious location. A damaged tower dominates the debris-filled landscape on the north side of the map—unfortunately, you cannot climb the tower for a better view of the map. One of the most unique features on this map is the bobsled track, which twists and turns from the stadium on the south side all the way to the tower to the north. This damaged concrete track often serves as highway, funneling traffic from one end to the other. Cracks and holes in the track also provide some wonderful overwatch positions and sight lines. But avoid loitering in the track too long as it's a high-traffic thoroughfare.

CHOKE POINTS

RECOMMENDED WEAPONS

Explosives, Assault Rifle, Grenade Launcher, SMG, LMG

During Combat Mission, looking toward bomb site A from the shipping container, there's a narrow path created by rubble within the stadium. From here you'll have a good view of the bomb site, but no cover while within the path. It's a high-traffic area, so proximity mines and grenade launchers are very effective. Mow down enemies caught in the path using an LMG, but be careful as you could be flanked from the rear. It's not the range of the gun here that really matters, but how you use it. This spot is also effective during Team Deathmatch, but don't loiter here very long.

RECOMMENDED WEAPONS

Explosives, Shotgun, SMG, LMG

During Combat Mission and Team Deathmatch, this small opening, offering little in the way of cover, is useful for keeping attackers from using the path as a flank. Stay here long and you'll be flanked from the rear and from the left. Use an LMG, or another short- to mid-range weapon, to dispatch would-be flankers. Have your Fireteam Buddy close for support.

RECOMMENDED WEAPONS

Explosives, Assault Rifle, SMG, LMG

During Combat Mission and Hotspot, be careful passing under here. The ditch is a great dark place to hide a proximity mine or remote charge, or to wait for someone to walk in as you'll see them before they see you. If you intend on ambushing someone from here, then be aware of your flanks. There's also a hole in the cement that an enemy can fire on from. Use short- to mid-range weapons when engaging.

RECOMMENDED WEAPONS

Explosives, Explosives, Assault Rifle, SMG

During Combat Mission, Hotspot, and Sector Control, this break in the wall makes an excellent, well-covered ambush point to take out enemies as they come up the adjacent high-traffic path. Even though you'll be directly in front of an enemy, they likely won't see you aiming through this hole in the bobsled track. Put a proximity mine or remote charge at the opening. SMGs and short, controlled rifle bursts will work well to finish enemies off. Watch your left and right flanks along the track.

RECOMMENDED WEAPONS

Explosives, Assault Rifle, LMG (supported)

During Combat Mission, Sector Control, and Hotspot, this path under the broken bobsled track will become highly trafficked in an effort to reach objectives— toss a proximity mine under the track. There's plenty of cover among the broken-down trucks. Enemies may engage from the track, firing between the cracks, so take on enemies from cover. Use the truck to mount an LMG for a wide field of fire to take out advancing enemies. Keep watch of the flank on your right while here.

RECOMMENDED WEAPONS

Explosives, Assault Rifle, SMG, LMG, Sniper Rifle

This choke point within Combat Mission, Sector Control, and Hotspot is a constant nuisance, with opponents coming through fairly quickly, so pay attention to the minimap and sounds of footsteps to avoid getting flanked. Attacking demolitions soldiers on the track area should throw remote charges over the wall to take out enemies waiting in ambush on the other side. Cover the broken track as much as possible, without exposing your flank to it, if you're distracted by an enemy coming from another direction. Cover the area with medium- to long-range weapons.

RECOMMENDED WEAPONS

Explosives, Shotgun, SMG

While playing Home Run and Team Deathmatch move through the destroyed bathroom area carefully. Check your corners and lay plenty of remote charges or proximity mines.

Use short-range weapons within these close quarters. Be careful of enemies flanking by way of the inner area that circles around.

RECOMMENDED WEAPONS

Explosives, Assault Rifle, Shotgun, SMG

During Home Run, while moving through the southern broken building check your corners, throw plenty of grenades, and watch your six as enemies can easily escape your vision. Through here spec ops are key to knowing where the enemy may be and taking them out before they can ambush. Use short-range weapons moving through the walls. Approach Flag B ready for more short- to long-range engagements.

RECOMMENDED WEAPONS

Explosives, LMG, Sniper Rifle (supported)

In Combat Mission, Sector Control, and Hotspot, have your Fireteam Buddy set up with an LMG on the nearby truck while you drop prone on this small hill for a little more concealment. From here a sniper can fire a few rounds before the enemy is too close to notice. You'll also have a clear view of the hole in the track wall enemies may use to fire from. Be careful not to be flanked from the left, from the truck, or from behind.

OVERWATCH POSITIONS

RECOMMENDED WEAPONS

Explosives, LMG, Sniper Rifle (supported)

During Combat Mission, this stadium overwatch spot is well suited for taking out opponents in the adjacent overwatch window and for dropping enemies near bomb site A. From here, it's best to use long-range weaponry to engage distant targets. Enemies can flank this position from the right and throw grenades up through the window. Jump off this ledge to land on the scaffolding if you need to get closer to bomb site A while maintaining an elevated position. Enemies probably won't notice your transition if you stay low. This spot is also accessible during Team Deathmatch, but don't hold here long—take a few shots at opponents on the stadium floor and then move on before they can return fire.

RECOMMENDED WEAPONS

Explosives, LMG, Sniper Rifle (supported)

During Combat Mission, this overwatch position has about the same vantage point over bomb site A as the previous window overwatch, only from the opposite angle. Monitor the other window, and take out any enemies that show up in its frame. Take out any enemies that are planting or disarming a charge from here. This overwatch perch is also available in Team Deathmatch, serving as an ideal spot for monitoring enemy movement along the stadium floor.

RECOMMENDED WEAPONS

12 *Grenades, Assault Rifle, LMG, Sniper Rifle (supported)*

During Combat Mission, Sector Control, and Hotspot, this spot mainly defends a high-traffic area mostly near the stadium. It's also a decent spot for snipers when covering a Hotspot potential target or Combat Mission's bomb site B. It's hard to be flanked from here, but there's a wall behind this spot that acts like a backboard for grenades. Try not to linger long and be ready to scoot if you take incoming sniper fire.

RECOMMENDED WEAPONS

13 *Explosives, Assault Rifle, LMG (supported)*

During Combat Mission, get up to this elevated position within the scoreboard structure to look down on this high-traffic area. You'll have good enough cover to surprise enemies as they walk toward bomb site B via the eastern flank, but don't hang out for long because enemies will likely flank the door right behind you. This is a prime position to fire your rifle or grenade launcher from.

RECOMMENDED WEAPONS

14 *Explosives, Assault Rifle, SMG*

While playing any game mode besides Home Run, a wise flanker or defender would post up in this window for taking out enemies near the objective or passing through the alley. If a teammate takes position in the window across the way from the objective, then a good crossfire can be achieved. Cover is fairly slim and the window is rather open, so be careful about staying in one spot. Shut enemies down using mid- to long-range weapons.

RECOMMENDED WEAPONS

15 *Explosives, Assault Rifle, Grenade Launcher, LMG, Sniper Rifle*

This major path sees heavy traffic during Combat Mission, Team Deathmatch, and Hotspot due to its direct passage among the various objectives. This is a long walk for anyone passing through without a Fireteam Buddy. The path is fairly open with narrower side branches opponents are likely to attack from. There's plenty of opportunities to flank and be flanked by snipers, LMGs, and grenade launchers while walking through here. Check holes in the bobsled track and walls for enemies, observe proximity mines in the tight spots, and maintain a line of sight with your Fireteam.

RECOMMENDED WEAPONS

16 *Explosives, Assault Rifle, LMG, Sniper Rifle (supported)*

This position is a little bit of everything in Combat Mission, Sector Control, and Hotspot. Near the bomb site C area in Combat Mission, lay down here for cover and deploy the bipod for long-distance shots. The path has a long sight line and covers an often-used approach. Use mid- to long-range weapons to cover the path, but be careful here because enemies can flank your rear from the left and right paths behind this position.

RECOMMENDED WEAPONS

17 *Assault Rifle, Sniper Rifle*

While in Combat Mission, Hotspot, or Sector Control, if any enemies are on the eastern path, defending an objective or passing through, sneak up to this hole in the track's wall and go for some headshots. The hole provides exceptional cover, but you can be flanked easily from the left and right sides if enemies are on the track with you. It's best to use rifles here for cleaner kills.

RECOMMENDED WEAPONS
Assault Rifle, Sniper Rifle

During Home Run, as an attacker, if your teammates have taken Flag A and they're on the final stretch, try to crouch in this corner behind some bushes and rubble. From here you should be substantially camouflaged while given a clear view of the entrance enemies might pursue your teammates from as well as a clear line of sight of the finish line. There's little cover here, so make your shot count with long-range weapons.

RECOMMENDED WEAPONS
Explosives, Shotgun, SMG

During Home Run, as a defender, hide to the left of the wall and crouch behind a bush for a good hidden point to ambush attackers from. This position should also provide a good view of the halls and the stairs to the north east. Use close-range weapons to handle anyone coming through, and watch the stairs in case enemies have pushed through. Throw down grenades and remote charges to take out enemies coming through the halls.

RECOMMENDED WEAPONS
Explosives, Shotgun, SMG

During Home Run, guard the flag from a distance by hiding in the camouflage of bushes. From here you'll have a clear view of Flag A and the lower open area. Watch the door and wait until enemies come out in the open for a clear shot. It is advisable to go prone with long-range supported weapons, but it's also wise to remain unsupported just in case you need to move out quickly. Watch your right as enemies might come from the stairs if they've cleared out your teammates.

SIGHT LINES

RECOMMENDED WEAPONS
Explosives, Assault Rifle, SMG, LMG, Sniper Rifle

During Combat Mission, quickly hide in the rubble for a direct line of sight on bomb site A to flank anyone arming or disarming the charge. Movement is minimum here, and you can be flanked easily, but you're pretty concealed. Get in and get out once you've made your kill. At this close range, any weapon should be acceptable to take out opponents at the bomb site.

RECOMMENDED WEAPONS
Proximity Mines, Assault Rifle, LMG, Sniper Rifle

Exclusive to Home Run, this sight line provides an excellent defensive position looking through the northern door in the wall. From here, you're fairly concealed in darkness and have some cover behind the counter. Pick off attackers as they walk through the door or attempt to take the flag back to their base. You can be flanked from behind if you aren't paying attention. Place proximity mines along the blind corners leading up to the flag to cover your back and score some sneaky kills.

COMBAT MISSION

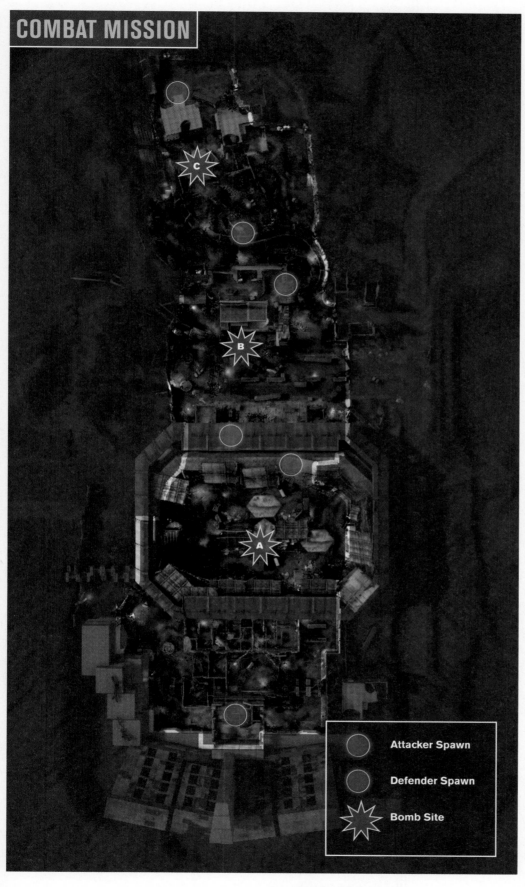

Attacker Spawn

Defender Spawn

Bomb Site

The first bomb site (A) is located in the center of the stadium, making it a tough spot to reach for the attackers. Here the defenders can lock down the stadium by covering all the southern entry points—don't forget to cover that sneaky flanking path on the west side too. An early push by the attackers allows them to infiltrate the stadium before the defenders can dig in. If an early attack isn't successful, the attackers should attempt to flank from the west instead of grinding against the stadium's southern entrances. In the second phase of the battle, bomb site B is located within the building beneath the scoreboard. With numerous approaches available, the attackers have an easier time of reaching this bomb site—flank from the east or west when possible to catch the defenders off-guard. If possible, the defenders should try to ambush the attackers when they exit the stadium. This is much easier than defending the numerous paths leading to bomb site B. The final bomb site (C) is located beneath the tower on the north side of the map. Once again, the attackers should utilize the east and west flanking paths when approaching this location. The majority of the defending team should stay near the tower and babysit the bomb site while a couple of Fireteams secure the flanking paths.

HOTSPOT

- ⬤ Attacker Spawn
- ⬤ Defender Spawn
- ✴ Potential Target

In Hotspot, the stadium is cordoned off, limiting the action to the areas around the scoreboard and tower. As in all Hotspot matches, the defenders should make a beeline toward the first target and secure it before the attackers arrive. The attackers shouldn't waste much time either. They should make an effort to establish a presence near the map's center. The centrally located scoreboard structure makes a perfect base of operations given its close proximity to all five potential targets. This structure can also serve as a good cut-off point for either side when attempting to contain the opposing team to its starting side of the map. This tactic can serve the attackers well, especially if either of the two potential targets near the stadium are randomly chosen—the same can be said for the defenders if the two targets near the tower become active. Whichever targets are chosen, utilize the map's various paths as well as the bobsled track to approach each target from unique angles. This is particularly important for the attackers, since the defending team is likely prepared for any direct assaults.

SECTOR CONTROL

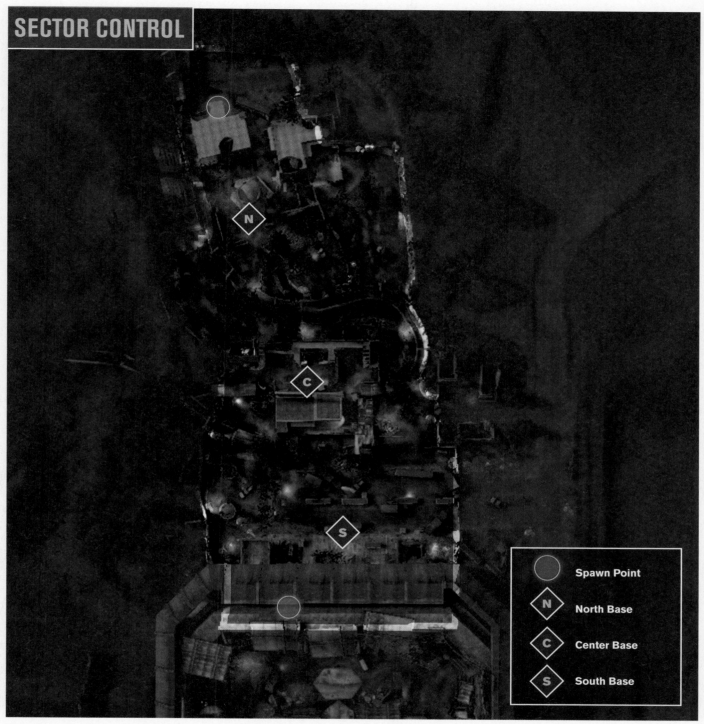

⬤	**Spawn Point**
◇ N	**North Base**
◇ C	**Center Base**
◇ S	**South Base**

The Sector Control map is approximately the same size as the Hotspot variant, with bases located at the stadium's entrance, the scoreboard structure, and the tower. The North Base at the tower and the South Base at the stadium's entrance are only a few meters away from each team's respective spawn point. As a result, these two bases probably won't change hands much during the course of the battle. The real fight occurs at the Center Base as both teams jockey for control of the scoreboard. The team approaching from the north has a good chance of rushing this base first. However, those approaching from the south have a better chance of occupying the scoreboard structure, giving them a distinct advantage when it comes to converting the flag. Since the North and South Bases are rarely defended, look for opportunities to slip past the fighting at the scoreboard and make a move for one of these oft-neglected flags. But don't expect to hold the flag closest to the opposing team's spawn point unless you have some serious backup. Two Fireteams working together can usually lock down the North or South Base, effectively trapping the opposing team at its spawn point.

HOME RUN

●	**Attacker Spawn**
●	**Defender Spawn**
◆	**Flag**

Home Run features a unique area of the map located on the south side of the stadium. The attacking team spawns on the west side of the map, while the defenders and flags are located to the east. Flag A is located on the north side, not far from the stadium. Players here should prepare for close-quarters engagements as there's plenty of debris and blind corners, giving the defending team many opportunities to ambush. The area around Flag B is a bit more open, offering some good sight lines. Given the numerous hiding spots around each flag, neither one is particularly easy to capture. Instead of rushing toward any specific flag, attackers should attempt to draw out the defenders by rushing down the center of the map. This is the best way to whittle away the defenders, leaving at least one of the flags open to capture. When rushing the flag back to your team's base, always use the paths on the north or south sides of the map, as they offer the most cover, especially if defenders are chasing you. However, defenders can prevent a capture by camping the southwest corner of the map, gunning down the flag carrier and any escorts just before they can reach safety.

TEAM DEATHMATCH

Spawn Point

Team Deathmatch takes place entirely within the stadium, making for a truly chaotic gameplay experience when playing on a full server with 20 players. There really are no safe spots to hold out on this map, so staying alive often comes down to staying mobile and having quick reflexes. While the stadium floor may look open, it's actually filled with all sorts of cover, offering decent protection while limiting sight lines. Fighting on the cluttered stadium floor often occurs at short to medium range, so consider bringing along an assault rifle or SMG. The corridors on the north and south sides of the stadium are also accessible. Instead of trying to dominate the stadium floor, try to control the stadium entrances adjacent to the opposing team's spawn point. The entry points into the stadium are deadly choke points, and if properly covered, your team can score multiple kills at each spot—grenades, proximity mines, and remote charges are all effective in these narrow doorways. Locking down these choke points is far more preferable than running around the map looking for random targets.

SHOGORE VALLEY

Eclipsed between the towering mountain ranges of the Chitral region is a deserted hillside village. Perched on a steep hill covered in thick woods with a river at its base, the ruins have a commanding view of the valley. A new outpost is being erected over the old town in an attempt to monitor the area and provide security for this isolated region.

SHOGORE VALLEY TACTICAL

Choke Point 1

Overwatch Position 1

Sightline 1

TACTICAL OVERVIEW

The stone structures of this hillside village offer a commanding view of the surrounding mountains. The map is divided into three distinct areas, some of which are only accessible in specific game modes. For instance, the rocky hillside in the southeast corner serves as the attacking team's spawn point in both Combat Mission and Hotspot. Climbing this rocky incline puts soldiers spawning here at a significant disadvantage, especially when taking fire from the high ground to the west. At the center of the map is a more modern area of the village, as evident by cars and trucks parked along the central dirt road. The village's ancient ruins are located on the north side of the map. Most of the buildings here have crumbled over time, leaving a maze of stone walls as well as the remains of an old cistern. An ancient domed temple overlooks this side of the map, carved out of the nearby mountain. This impressive structure cannot be accessed, so don't waste your time trying to climb the out-of-reach staircase on the map's northern edge.

CHOKE POINTS

RECOMMENDED WEAPONS
Explosives, Assault Rifle, Shotgun, SMG, LMG

The rock-covered hillside during Combat Mission easily becomes a cover-filled choke point. Defenders of bomb site A will have the elevated advantage while the attackers will need to push with plenty of grenades. This path can be used to hold cut off attackers from the bomb site, however if attackers have made it up the left path, then this defensive position can be flanked from the rear. Use short- to mid-range weapons to take care of enemies as engagements within the rocks can be up close and personal.

RECOMMENDED WEAPONS
Assault Rifle, SMG, Shotgun, LMG (supported)

During Sector Control and Combat Mission, attackers will use this path to flank the Center Base or bomb site B from higher ground. While defending from attackers or enemies coming from the South Base, push forward up to this truck and mount an LMG with a bipod on the barrels. Wait in ambush as enemies come around the wall. Have your Fireteam Buddy cover you with short- to mid-range weapons. It's possible to be flanked from the rear during Sector Control, but it's not as likely during Combat Mission.

RECOMMENDED WEAPONS
Explosives, SMG, Shotgun, LMG

While playing Combat Mission, Sector Control, and Hotspot, this building becomes a major path between objectives or leading to bomb sites/bases. Someone will always be in here, so throw down proximity mines. The mines will be more of a warning as flankers try to pass through. The windows can be used to flank enemies from or to flank enemies passing through the building. Try to keep a low profile while in here. Use short-range weapons while engaging within.

RECOMMENDED WEAPONS
Explosives, Shotgun, SMG, LMG

During Sector Control and Combat Mission, enemies will be trapped within the ruins if they meet any opposition directly outside. Check your corners while moving through. Have a teammate draw enemies in with fire to give away his position, stay low, and ambush the enemies from behind as they pass by. Don't get caught in the ruins, as enemies will throw grenades over the low walls and will often ambush you while exiting them. If you can, do your best to go around this area, unless it's unguarded. .

RECOMMENDED WEAPONS
Explosives, Assault Rifle, SMG, Shotgun

During Combat Mission, Home Run, and Team Deathmatch, the tighter paths to the east will see plenty of movement. As a defender, it's good to cover this entrance and the western open area. While operating in this area, keep moving to avoid being flanked. If an enemy knows you're within this area, watch out for grenades coming over the low walls. Use close-quarters weapons while covering these tight paths, and assault rifles while covering the more open western area near bomb site C.

RECOMMENDED WEAPONS
Explosives, Assault Rifle, Shotgun, SMG, LMG

Bomb site C in Combat Mission is going to be rough. Attackers will have to jump down into the cistern where defenders will be able to ambush them with short- to mid-range weapons. Anyone in the pit-like cistern is going to receive a heavy amount of grenades. The upper area must be secure to either plant or disarm the charge. Make sure your Fireteam Buddy is with you for cover fire as you move down here.

RECOMMENDED WEAPONS
Explosives, SMG, Pistol

During Combat Mission, this alley of debris is often used to flank bomb site C. This spot can also be used to flank enemies posted up within the scaffolding that overlooks the attackers' approach and bomb site. Enemies are likely to come from the stairs leading down from the scaffolding, from the doorway leading to bomb site C, or over the planks from their spawn point. Move through here quickly with your Fireteam using SMGs or side arms. Heavy gunners can toss their mini frags to carpet the enemy if they are numerous.

RECOMMENDED WEAPONS

Explosives, Assault Rifle, SMG, LMG

This area may become a choke point as enemies funnel over the planks. Once an enemy is out in the open area, there's little cover for them. Hang back behind rocks for some cover or use an assault rifle to take them out from a distance.

During Combat Mission, bomb site C attackers won't likely come this way, but they may attempt to snipe defenders out of their spawn point. While defending, if you see opponents in that area, throw a few grenades just over the scaffolding.

RECOMMENDED WEAPONS

Explosives, Assault Rifle, LMG

At Combat Mission's bomb site A and Sector Control's South Base, hide behind the wood debris to fire down toward the objective as teammates plant a charge or defend the flag. Lay down suppressive fire with an LMG or assault rifle. Monitor the path across the way for enemies rushing in.

OVERWATCH POSITIONS

RECOMMENDED WEAPONS

Assault Rifle, LMG, Sniper Rifle

During Combat Mission or Sector Control, hop onto the fallen tree and move all the way out to the branches. As long as you've gone unnoticed while climbing out to the branches, you'll be able to surprise one or two enemies from this perch. But be quick, because you won't have much time to do this. Don't take a shot unless you know you'll make a clean kill. The major down side to this location is its little to no cover.

RECOMMENDED WEAPONS

LMG, Sniper Rifle (supported)

At bomb site A during Combat Mission, drop prone with a sniper rifle or LMG next to the stone building. Considering the window's position, it would be best to remain prone to avoid being seen. Deploy here to either take out planting attackers or surprise a few defenders. Once you've given away your position, you'll need to leave quickly because there's no cover.

RECOMMENDED WEAPONS

Assault Rifle, LMG, Sniper Rifle

While defending bomb site A in Combat Mission, you'll approach a tight path with a good view of the objective. There should be adequate cover here, but there may be grenades thrown in this tight spot, so be careful.

Firing from this position is a good option for an LMG or sniper rifle to cover teammates defending the bomb site. Attackers have a good overwatch directly across from this position, so be sure to take anyone out who is about to use that cover. During Sector Control, use this spot while pushing the South Base team back to their spawn point, but be careful of the flank on the right.

RECOMMENDED WEAPONS

Assault Rifle, LMG, Sniper Rifle (supported)

During Combat Mission bomb site B, Sector Control, or Hotspot, deploy your bipod in the second-story window to cover the east side of the village. The elevation and cover will be good for supported sniping against incoming attackers. Slow down enemy movement using an LMG to give your teammates enough time to flank enemy positions. The windows are easy to throw grenades through and stairs are easily flanked by enemies, so pay close attention.

RECOMMENDED WEAPONS

Assault Rifle, LMG, Sniper Rifle

This spot is useful in Combat Mission, Sector Control, or Hotspot. While attacking bomb site B in Combat Mission, attackers can take the second-story building for their own in order to hold down the area as teammates move in to arm a charge. It's best to pop smoke in the area to give teammates further cover against defenders. Any sniper up here would also be good for taking out any enemy planting or disarming the bomb. During Sector Control, use this window to fire on enemies coming from the North Base. During Hotspot, use the window to cover potential targets in the area. Be careful of enemy snipers on the roof or in the windows of the building across the way.

RECOMMENDED WEAPONS

15 *Explosives, Assault Rifle, LMG, Sniper Rifle (supported)*

While playing Combat Mission, Sector Control, or Hotspot, use the sandbags on the building's roof for cover. Deploy a bipod with an LMG while defending bomb site B, the Center Base in front, the North Base behind, or while assaulting or defending Hotspot targets. Snipers can run up here quickly enough to take out enemies in the building across the way. Enemies can flank from behind or throw grenades on the position easily.

RECOMMENDED WEAPONS

16 *Assault Rifle, Sniper Rifle*

During Combat Mission, Sector Control, and Hotspot, jump on this fallen tree. Climb out to the end of the tree to hide among the branches. You'll be able to climb out far enough to shoot down at enemies unaware of your position, but make it count, because there's no cover up here. The position provides a good sight line of nearly the entire village. Use it to quickly flank an enemy from above or for a single sniper rifle round.

RECOMMENDED WEAPONS
17 Explosives, Sniper Rifle, LMG, Mk19

 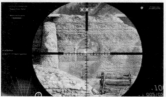

At Combat Mission's bomb site C, post up in the scaffolding within the ruins for an overwatch of the area. Move between the eastern overwatch and the southern overwatch covering the flanking approach. Go prone and deploy the bipod with a sniper rifle or LMG to cover the southern approach with deadly accuracy. During Team Deathmatch, the overwatches provide good positions to maintain map superiority. Have your Fireteam Buddy close by to cover the ramp behind you. Use the perch during Home Run to cover teammates bringing the flag back.

RECOMMENDED WEAPONS

18 *Explosives, Assault Rifle, Sniper Rifle*

While playing Combat Mission, Team Deathmatch, or Hotspot, use this point to cover the contestable area and to snipe enemies that take the scaffolding overwatches. While covering bomb site C in Combat Mission, use the top of these stairs to quickly move into the bomb site in case anyone is arming or disarming the charge. Remain mobile, stay behind cover, and watch the left and right flanking paths. Use the grenade launcher for crowd control or the sniper rifle for taking out enemies at the bomb site.

RECOMMENDED WEAPONS

19 *Explosives, Assault Rifle, LMG, Sniper Rifle*

During all modes except Hotspot, access this slightly elevated point simply for pot shots. Hop into the crumbling building covered in scaffolding near the maze-like walls and climb along the wall. You can get a small elevated advantage to take out opponents engaging your teammates. However, you are fully exposed on all sides, so get down quickly. These ruins are also great for ambushing people coming out of the nearby maze-like alley.

RECOMMENDED WEAPONS
20 *Explosives, Assault Rifle, LMG, Sniper Rifle*

While attacking in Combat Mission at bomb site C, set up on these sandbags to spot enemies and cover teammates as they approach the bomb site. Keep enemies from moving past the walls with grenades and suppressive fire. Snipers can easily pick off opponents coming out of their spawn point. Firing from here will leave you exposed, and snipers will take you out. Use mid-range weapons to take out enemies behind the walls, and long-range weapons for enemies near bomb site C.

SIGHT LINES

RECOMMENDED WEAPONS

21

Sniper Rifle, LMG (supported)

During Combat Mission, attackers will likely push toward this building in order to flank bomb site A. Defenders should take up a supported stance with a sniper rifle or LMG to keep enemies at bay. This high-traffic tight trail lines up enemies easily, making it a walk in the park for LMGs.

RECOMMENDED WEAPONS

22

LMG, Sniper Rifle

The rock-covered mountainside is treacherous for attackers approaching bomb site A in Combat Mission. Make things easier for teammates by providing sniper fire as they attempt to storm the house at the top of the hill. LMGs might work, but won't be as effective as sniping enemies out of windows.

RECOMMENDED WEAPONS

23

LMG, Sniper Rifle (supported)

This sight line, along the western wall, is useful in Combat Mission (bomb site C) and Team Deathmatch, where enemies are visible enough for long-distance engagements. Attacking enemies may often try to approach the scaffolding via this clearing by moving cover to cover. Go prone with a supported LMG or sniper rifle to take care of anyone moving within this sight line.

RECOMMENDED WEAPONS

24

Assault Rifle, LMG, Sniper Rifle

At bomb site C during Combat Mission, this eastern flank is a popular approach for the attackers. The space is fairly open with mostly low walls and short buildings for cover. This sight line looks toward the defenders' spawn point, so pick off opponents from this position while your teammates flank from the south. As you fire on enemies, have your Fireteam Buddy lob grenades and flank enemies from the other side of the buildings.

COMBAT MISSION

⬤	Attacker Spawn
⬤	Defender Spawn
✦	Bomb Site

At the start of Combat Mission, the attacking team is tasked with charging up the rocky hillside in an effort to reach bomb site A. The climb alone is challenging enough, but the difficulty only intensifies once the defenders take up positions at the top of the hill. As a result, the attackers should rush bomb site A as soon as the match begins in an effort to gain a foothold on top of the hill before the defending team can get situated. Defenders, on the other hand, should do their best to keep the attackers pinned at the bottom of the hill. If the attackers succeed in detonating bomb site A, the action shifts to the nearby village where bomb site B is located. This is a more even fight, featuring plenty of house-to-house engagements as both teams attempt to secure the bomb site. The long sight lines offered by the dirt road often push most movement to the periphery, with attackers flanking from the north or south. In the final phase of the battle, the action shifts to the ancient ruins, where bomb site C is located within the central cistern. This compact hole in the ground is an absolute deathtrap, likely booby trapped by the defenders. Attackers must approach cautiously and secure the cistern's perimeter before dropping down in the hole to arm a charge.

HOTSPOT

○	Attacker Spawn
●	Defender Spawn
✷	Potential Target

The action in Hotspot is restricted to the modern section of the village, with the five potential targets scattered about the various structures. The attackers approach from the east side and must work quickly to establish a presence within the village. Consider taking up positions within the buildings on the east side of the map while waiting for the first target to be declared—by watching the defenders' movements its possible to predict what the first target will be. Both teams should avoid the dirt road running through the center of the village. Despite the long sight lines and numerous overwatch positions covering this road, it remains a dangerous high-traffic area and the site of many deaths. It's much safer to travel along the northern and southern flanking paths. Of the two, the northern path, set along the hillside, offers the most cover in the form of large boulders. The southern path running parallel to the river is a bit more dangerous given the long sight lines—expect plenty of sniper duels here. Overall, the plentiful cover and accessible buildings give both teams a fair chance of securing a win on this map.

SECTOR CONTROL

Legend:
- Spawn Point
- **N** North Base
- **C** Center Base
- **S** South Base

Similar to Hotspot, Sector Control is focused mostly within the modern part of the village. The North Base is located on the southern edge of the ancient ruins—the surrounding walls and narrow choke points make this a relatively easy base to defend, assuming anyone bothers. The South Base is located on the east edge of the village, not far from the rocky hillside. This base can be watched from several angles, including from within the nearby buildings. Given their close proximity to the team spawn points, the North Base and South Base usually don't change hands very often, especially if they're defended. Like most Sector Control matches, the bulk of the fighting occurs around the Center Base. The flag here is positioned next to the two-story house on the south side of the road. The eastern and western avenues of attack are the most common here, as both teams rush in a straight line from their team's spawn point toward the Center Base. As a result, traffic along the northern and southern flanking paths is sparse, making them ideal for bypassing the fight in the center of the map and making a move for the North or South Base. These flanking paths can also be utilized to defend or reinforce the Center Base. In particular, the hillside positions to the north have a good view of the Center Base.

HOME RUN

Attacker Spawn

Defender Spawn

Flag

A

B

Home Run takes place entirely within the confines of the ancient ruins, requiring both teams to become familiar with the maze-like layout of this archeological site. The attacking team starts out on the west side, with Flag A and Flag B both located along the hillside to the east. Regardless of which flag they go for, the attackers should always hook around the northern and southern sides of the map. It's important to avoid the low ground around the cistern at all costs. The attackers can also make use of the structure near their spawn point to gain overwatch. Get at least one soldier on the rooftop of this building to provide covering fire while the rest of the team advances on the flags. The defending team should never wander far from the flags, as it's difficult to predict which direction the attackers will approach from—unless using the spec ops signal scan ability. When the two teams eventually encounter each other, fighting usually occurs at close range, so choose your class and weapon accordingly.

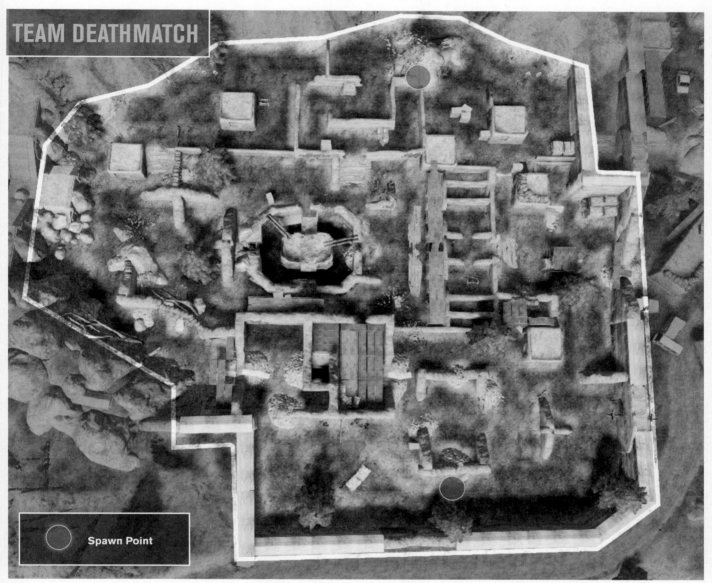

TEAM DEATHMATCH

Spawn Point

Like Home Run, Team Deathmatch also takes place among the ancient ruins. This is a very small area when playing on a full server with 20 players. Expect movement to gravitate toward the west side of the map as both teams fight for control of the rooftop position. While this rooftop offers an excellent view of the map, it is not a very good defensive position. The lack of overhead cover makes players posted here vulnerable to incoming grenades as well as offensive support actions. Instead of camping any one position on the map, it's best to stay on the move. Traffic usually flows in both directions along the perimeter of the map. Always stay within close range of your Fireteam Buddy so you can support, resupply, and heal each other. In many instances you'll round a corner and come face-to-face with an opponent. In these common situations, it's best to have a buddy to help you eliminate the threat and assist in your recovery immediately following the engagement. Stick to the perimeter of the map, avoiding the center (and cistern) at all costs.

SOMALIA STRONGHOLD

The seas surrounding Somalia have long been the feeding grounds of local pirates. Using inland strongholds and hideouts they have been able to run unchallenged, until now. Task Force Atlas has been dispatched to address this international problem. Their orders are clear; penetrate as far inland as necessary and destroy any and all threats, assets, and personnel associated to this band of criminals.

SOMALIA STRONGHOLD TACTICAL

Legend:
- ⋈ Choke Point 1
- ⊕ Overwatch Position 1
- 👁 Sightline 1

TACTICAL OVERVIEW

This crumbling town is dominated by a massive lighthouse situated on the southern coast. But modern sailors should steer clear, as they won't find safe harbor in this pirate haven. There are three core areas of this map: the lighthouse to the south, the supply truck to the west, and the antenna to the north. Given the long sight lines and elevated windows, sniper duels are common around the lighthouse—the small windows on the lighthouse's second floor are almost always occupied as are those of the nearby burning building. The courtyard where the supply truck is located is another high-traffic area likely to see plenty of action across most game modes. This area is dominated by tight choke points, making it a popular ambush spot. The antenna site to the north is another area to familiarize yourself with

if you're looking for more choke points as well as some significant sight lines and overwatch positions. Overall, the combat on this map is varied, with engagements occurring at various ranges. If you don't have an assault or sniper rifle, stay away from the wide open spaces, particularly around the lighthouse.

CHOKE POINTS

RECOMMENDED WEAPONS
Remote Charge, Proximity Mines, Assault Rifle, LMG

While playing Combat Mission, defenders should cover this path to prevent the attackers from flanking bomb site A. Firing from the broken wall provides considerable cover while crouching or leaning, but loitering can result in being flanked quickly from behind. Use assault rifles and LMGs for optimal results. If you're demolitions or sniper class, lay a charge or proximity mine at the edge of the corner, get back to the hole, and detonate when someone rounds the corner.

RECOMMENDED WEAPONS
Explosives, Assault Rifle, Shotgun, SMG

During Combat Mission, there is a small staircase with a wall to hide behind for exceptional cover as your team pushes back enemies that overextend on this path. Use short- to mid-range weapons to help support your team while taking this path. As an attacker, you won't be flanked from this position, but bear in mind attackers can still receive grenades and mortar fire.

RECOMMENDED WEAPONS
Explosives, Assault Rifle, LMG, SMG

During all game modes aside from Home Run, use these walls as temporary cover to flank enemies running through the path, but don't leave your body completely exposed. Lean out from the sides of the walls before engaging the enemy. Firing from this position will leave the left and right flanks completely exposed to the enemy. Enemies using the open road are easy pickings, so lay down as much fire and grenades as possible.

RECOMMENDED WEAPONS
Explosives, Assault Rifle, LMG, SMG

Within this path or around the open area, this path covers every game mode except Home Run. With a Fireteam Buddy, this position should be good for catching enemy teams passing through the open area unaware. Firing from this position provides moderate corner cover. Coordinate with another Fireteam located in another position to get a good crossfire going. Lingering too long may result in being flanked from the right.

RECOMMENDED WEAPONS
Grenades, Assault Rifle, LMG

The lighthouse will be a hotly contested area, and vied for as a firing position in Team Deathmatch, Sector Control, Combat Mission, and Hotspot. Enemies defending the lighthouse will have a clear overwatch to take out advancing enemies. Grenades and support actions will dominate the area, so when pushing in move in as a team. One to three defenders can hold the position well, so lob grenades through the doors before entering to plant a charge. Use of LMG and rifles will work very well within this area. While attacking this point, enemies may flank from the left side.

RECOMMENDED WEAPONS
Grenades, Assault Rifle, Shotgun, SMG, LMG

During Combat Mission, Team Deathmatch, Sector Control, and Hotspot, this tight path, providing plenty of cover using the corners, debris, and a burned-out truck, will be a good pathway to lay in ambush for approaching enemies. Lob grenades over short walls toward the enemy. An LMG can hold this path well enough, but enemies can counter with grenades easily, so keep that in mind.

RECOMMENDED WEAPONS
Explosives, Assault Rifles, LMG, Sniper Rifle

During all game modes, this becomes a tight passage where proximity mines can easily be undetected in a rush. Ambush passing enemies from the windows. Lean around the corners if enemies are approaching. By engaging the enemy from this firing position, you can be flanked on the right side. Enemies at the other end of the passage can be flanked from either the left or right. Let your buddy engage as you resupply him from behind. When he needs to reload, switch places.

OVERWATCH POSITIONS

RECOMMENDED WEAPONS
Proximity Mines, Assault Rifles

During all game modes besides Team Deathmatch, this overwatch is likely to receive enemies passing through the village courtyard often. It's a major thoroughfare between objectives and to be considered a valuable position with adequate cover. Combat Mission, in particular, overlooks the first bomb plant site. Watch for enemies flanking fairly quickly from the western side of the building or through the southern door of the building. Patrol often to ensure this position is a fairly clear place to engage the enemy. Use the LMG or assault rifle to cover the courtyard or possibly a sniper rifle to cover the roads and nearer choke points.

RECOMMENDED WEAPONS
Explosives, Assault Rifle, LMG, SMG

This position will likely be most useful during Combat Mission, looking over bomb site A. Use the window for cover by crouching or leaning. This position is ideal for attackers to provide elevated cover fire while assaulting bomb site A. Defenders can use this position to wipe out attackers. While in the window, be mindful of incoming grenades. Use rapid-fire assault rifles or LMGs.

RECOMMENDED WEAPONS
Grenades, Assault Rifle, LMG (supported)

This window within the burning building overlooks Combat Mission's bomb site A. Crouch behind the hole in the wall for some cover, then mount an LMG or simply use an assault or sniper rifle to take out enemies extending too far from the bomb site or while enemies attack bomb site B. Attackers can use this position as well to clean shop on any defenders on bomb site A. Keep in mind that anyone can flank from behind.

RECOMMENDED WEAPONS
LMG, Sniper Rifle (supported)

During Combat Mission, deploy a bipod with your LMG or sniper rifle on this wall for suppressive fire for teammates to move up onto the point. Continue suppressive fire until the bomb detonates. Keep in mind that snipers can pick you off from a good distance. Enemies can come flanking from the right, but it's unlikely if teammates are keeping up pressure.

RECOMMENDED WEAPONS
Assault Rifle, Sniper Rifle

During Combat Mission, drop prone and deploy your sniper rifle's bipod behind the wall surrounding the lighthouse to score some kills at bomb site A. Enemies are hard pressed to see you at such a distance all the while dealing with the more forward defenders. You might also use an assault rifle to provide some fire for more medium-range targets.

RECOMMENDED WEAPONS
Explosives, Assault Rifle, SMG, Shotgun, LMG

While defending bomb site A in Combat Mission, hop over the rubble and onto the side of the building to look over the wall to lay down some suppressive fire to keep attackers from rushing the bomb site. Crouch behind the wall for cover. Do not stay long as you can be flanked from the rear or become an easy target for sniper fire. Use short- or mid-range weaponry to fire down from the wall.

RECOMMENDED WEAPONS
Proximity Mines, LMG (supported)

During all game modes, access this house, break the window open, deploy the LMG's bipod, and use it for a second-story ambush on anyone passing through this high-traffic area. They might have some walls for cover, but it'll be too late unless they already know you're there. Proximity mine the staircase or throw down grenades on enemies flanking from the stairs.

RECOMMENDED WEAPONS
Explosives, Assault Rifle, LMG, Sniper Rifle (supported)

15

During all modes but Home Run, this torn-down wall will provide an excellent elevated position to take out anyone near the antenna. Go prone as a sniper with a bipod for headshots on anyone planting or defusing the bomb. Set up proximity mines at the stairs as enemies might flank them. Enemies can shoot you out of the hole in the wall if you've leaned too far out over it. Have your Fireteam Buddy cover the ground level on the left to avoid unwanted company.

RECOMMENDED WEAPONS
Explosives, Assault Rifle, SMG, LMG, Sniper Rifle (supported)

16

During all modes, this window covers a well-tread path that also leads toward another second-story overwatch. Deploy the LMG's bipod and fire at unsuspecting enemies below. Keep proximity mines or your buddy at the top of the stairs and be aware of your six while up here. Be advised, the bar in front of your view is not destructible, so it may stop bullets from reaching your target.

RECOMMENDED WEAPONS
Explosives, Assault Rifle, LMG, Sniper Rifle

17

During Sector Control and Hotspot, this second-story overwatch covers Center Base and a supply truck potential target. The window provides exceptional cover while firing on anyone moving within the area. Tangos can be brought down with mid- to long-range weapons fire. During Combat Mission, use this as a fallback position after attackers have taken out bomb site B. Enemies will be passing through to reach bomb site C, and using this window will catch a few enemies off guard.

RECOMMENDED WEAPONS
Grenades, Assault Rifle, LMG (supported), SMG

18

This position is available in all modes except Home Run. This upstairs window overlooks a path that is often used to pass from one objective to the next. During Combat Mission, use this as a defensive position to take out enemies coming from bomb site B to bomb site C. Supported LMGs are ideal for this situation. Enemies will flank from the staircase to the right.

SIGHT LINES

RECOMMENDED WEAPONS
Sniper Rifle, LMG (supported)

19

During Sector Control and Hotspot, this point covers the South Base or two potential targets. The window provides great advantage in height while maintaining a good deal of cover. Snipers will find this site ideal for taking out other snipers in the burning building across the way, while LMGs will be able to lay down suppressing fire. Enemies have two ways to flank, so use proximity mines as a warning.

RECOMMENDED WEAPONS
Sniper Rifle, Assault Rifle

20

During all game modes but Home Run, the burning building and the lighthouse have a clear view of one another. Both landmarks provide excellent sniping positions for either attacking or defending an objective or while enemies move between points. The first priority is to take out other enemy snipers in the windows. The second priority is to take out enemies on the ground. A sniper rifle is recommended for the long-range shots, but a good marksman can also use a single-shot assault rifle to take down enemies.

RECOMMENDED WEAPONS
Sniper Rifle, LMG (supported)

21

During all modes except Home Run, a prone supported sniper rifle is given a clear view of objectives located at the antenna site while hiding within a house. From this point, the sight line extends to the eastern path, so any enemy attempting to flank along this path, provided they've made it without dying, can be put down quickly. Move out from the house a little more to have a wider field of view to cover the rest of the area. Alternatively, lie down with an LMG to provide suppressive fire to defend the site. This building can be flanked from the left quickly.

RECOMMENDED WEAPONS
Sniper Rifle, LMG (supported)

22

Available in Combat Mission, Sector Control, and Hotspot, this sight from the northern spawn point looks down a heavily trafficked path often used as a flank. Go prone with a bipod to lay down suppressive with an LMG or use a sniper rifle for a more precise shot.

COMBAT MISSION

Legend:
- Attacker Spawn
- Defender Spawn
- Bomb Site

During the opening phase of this battle, the attackers start on the far east side of the map, pushing along the coast toward the first bomb site (A). It's easy to get bogged down at the choke points between the spawn point and the bomb site. With few flanking paths, the attackers must simply muscle their way through to gain a foothold near the bomb site. Likewise, the defenders must coordinate to lock down the few paths that can be utilized by the attackers. In the second phase of the battle, the next bomb site (B) is located within the lighthouse. With only two entrances, attacking the lighthouse can be a nightmare, especially if it's well defended. When defending here, keep one Fireteam Buddy on the second floor at all times to serve as a spawn point. This allows the defenders to apply pressure on this location. For the attackers, the best solution for cracking this nut is by establishing a perimeter and conducting aggressive coordinated assaults on the interior—sending one soldier in at a time won't get the job done. If the attackers can take out the first two bomb sites, they'll have a much easier time securing the final one located at the antenna to the north. Still, it's important to sweep the nearby buildings before attempting to plant a charge.

HOTSPOT

Legend:
- ⬤ Attacker Spawn
- ⬤ Defender Spawn
- ✦ Potential Target

During Hotspot, almost the entire map is open for both teams, but the action stays focused around the five potential targets, leading to some intense close-quarters firefights. Early on, the attackers have no clue what the first target will be, but this is no time for the attackers to loiter around their spawn point. Instead, they should try to establish a foothold near the center of the map. Structures like the lighthouse, burning building, and the houses near the supply truck or antenna all serve as good temporary bases from which its easy to respond to any of the potential targets. With the targets spread out across the map, the defenders should focus on guarding the current target instead of trying to lock down any particular portion of the map. Defenders have the easiest time securing the targets at the lighthouse, supply truck, and antenna, since these locations offer great sight lines and overwatch positions that can be leveraged to engage attackers. As the fight shifts from one location to another, don't forget to alter your tactics and weaponry. Long-range weapons are best suited around the antenna and lighthouse, while close-quarters weapons are more effective in the map's center.

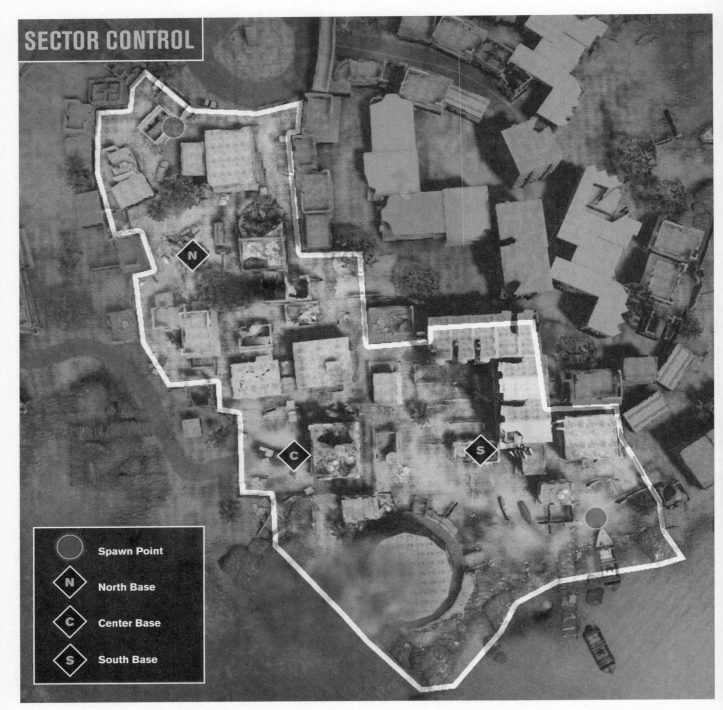

SECTOR CONTROL

Legend:
- ⬤ Spawn Point
- ◈ N — North Base
- ◈ C — Center Base
- ◈ S — South Base

In Sector Control, the bases are spread out among the lighthouse, supply truck, and antenna, making for a highly transient match as both teams race about the map capturing flags. While the North Base and South Base are likely to be held by the teams spawning nearby, the Center Base is always up for grabs, making it the hottest point on the map. Here the flag is located in the courtyard next to the supply truck. Capturing and maintaining control of this base is difficult since all fighting occurs at close range within the cramped courtyard. Watch out for incoming grenades and offensive support actions if you choose to linger here very long. While the battle rages at the Center Base, consider making a move for the North or South Base. The east side of the map isn't necessarily safe, but it's far less congested than the area around the supply truck. By sticking to this less-traveled side of the map, you'll have an easier time capturing the base closest to the opposing team's spawn point. If your team manages to capture all three bases, it's relatively simple to pin the opposing team at their spawn point. Such spawn camping tactics are usually frowned upon, but you must prepare yourself for this possibility.

HOME RUN

In Home Run, the two flags are located on the north side of the map, not far from the antenna. The attacking team spawns to the south, between the lighthouse and supply truck. From here they only have a few options when it comes to approaching the flags. The central path is never a good idea as it's often watched by defenders. Always take one of the flanking paths: west if you're heading for Flag A or east if you're heading for Flag B. Regardless of which direction you choose, gird yourself for some close-quarters engagements as you fight in the narrow alleys between your spawn point and the flags. With only three paths to cover, the defending team is most effective when locking down these approaches. Greet the attackers with proximity mines, remote charges, and focused fire on these narrow choke points surrounding each flag. Due to the tight quarters and minimal approaches, matches here are often decided before anyone touches a flag. Such tactics often work well for the attackers—instead of trying to capture a flag, simply hunt down and wipe out all the defenders.

TEAM DEATHMATCH

Spawn Point

Somalia Stronghold is one of the largest Team Deathmatch maps available, where careful planning and team coordination can often make all the difference. In most instances, teams fighting on this map will tend to pick a location as their "Alamo" and defend it. The most obvious location is the lighthouse to the south. While this is a strong defensive position, it's tough to score too many kills from this structure due to the lack of windows. The nearby burning building is another popular option, offering plenty of great overwatch positions and sight lines, ideal for covering the southern half of the map. But this structure is quite porous and difficult to lock down—if you choose to hold out here, make sure you have enough teammates to secure the numerous entry points. The houses near the antenna or supply truck are too small to serve as your team's base of operations, but they can serve as places of refuge when you need to heal or resupply. If you choose to move about the map during the match, stay near your Fireteam Buddy and a few other teammates at all times so you can support each other. Also, consider staying away from the lighthouse and burning building, especially if they're already occupied—attacking these fortified positions can lead to heavy casualties.

TUNGAWAN JUNGLE

Located on the south Philippines mainland, this jungle section is walled along its shoreline by a dense mangrove forest. The area plays a critical role in the supply route connecting the local region to the north of the country. A small jungle outpost is the only thing that guards the single bridge in the area, and underplays the considerable strategic value of this region.

TACTICAL OVERVIEW

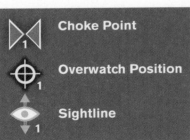

The humidity and threat of malaria are the least of your worries in this sweltering jungle environment. Fighting among the dense foliage and bamboo houses offers a good variety of action across all game modes, requiring constant analysis of your chosen class and weapon. In some areas, close-quarters weapons are best and in other areas you'll want more long-range capability. The abandoned fishing village on the south side of the map is home to some intense house-to-house fighting, particularly during Combat Mission and Sector Control. All paths funnel toward the center of the map where teams often clash near a tank, situated near a few houses—expect a mix of close-quarters and long-range combat here. Then there's the bridge to the north, the site of much fighting during Team Deathmatch and Combat Mission. The long sight lines afforded by this location make it a popular area for snipers and other sharpshooters. If you don't feel like switching classes often, you can never go wrong with the assaulter class on this map. The assault rifles offered by this class are ideal for engaging targets at any range.

	Choke Point
1	

	Overwatch Position
1	

	Sightline
1	

TUNGAWAN JUNGLE TACTICAL

CHOKE POINTS

RECOMMENDED WEAPONS
SMG, Shotgun, Proximity Mines

During Combat Mission, Sector Control, and Hotspot, this space beneath the house creates a tight spot to lay proximity mines or to circle around behind an enemy. It's dark enough to be used as a point of ambush if you've managed to go undetected, but your flanks are exposed enough to be taken out quickly. Use close-quarters weapons to tackle any enemies within or around the house, but try to use mid- to long-range weapons for anyone down range of the water.

RECOMMENDED WEAPONS
LMG, Sniper Rifle (supported)

During Combat Mission, set up the bipod with either a sniper rifle or LMG to take out enemies approaching from the left path. Attackers will have just enough cover to move up, so be patient when taking them out. You can be flanked from the rear, but it's unlikely unless the enemies have already stormed the point, in which case you're probably already dead.

RECOMMENDED WEAPONS
LMG (supported), Grenades, Proximity Mines

This choke point is a path less travelled within Combat Mission, Sector Control, Home Run, and Hotspot, as it's fairly indirect. Assume the prone position within the blades of grass, deploy your bipod, and spray anyone wandering into the opening. Once you've gathered a couple kills, fall back as you are sure to be taken by a volley of grenades.

RECOMMENDED WEAPONS
Explosives, SMG, Shotgun, LMG, Assault Rifle

During Combat Mission, Sector Control, and Hotspot, this building is a high-traffic area primed for proximity mines as it is close quarters and dark, and has two doors with a wall partition in the middle. Move through here with your Fireteam Buddy using primarily short-range weapons to take out any lurking enemies. Do not linger long within as a couple of cooked grenades through the doors will ruin your day.

OVERWATCH POSITIONS

RECOMMENDED WEAPONS
Explosives, SMG, LMG, Assault Rifle

During Combat Mission, there's a space beneath this building just large enough and dark enough to lay an ambush for anyone trying to arm or disarm the bomb site. Spray anyone with any short- to mid-range weapons to dispatch them quickly. You'll have a 90-degree field to protect, so always try to observe your flanks when possible. This is also an extremely good location to place proximity mines.

RECOMMENDED WEAPONS
LMG, Proximity Mines, Grenades

During Combat Mission, deploy your bipod in this window to lay down suppressive fire and mow through attackers. During Sector Control, this looks directly over the South Base. You'll be flanked from the door behind you, so it's important to have your six covered with proximity mines or your buddy watching the bomb site from the door. Have your buddy throw a few grenades into this overwatch to chase enemies out of cover so you can finish them off.

OVERWATCH POSITIONS

RECOMMENDED WEAPONS

Explosives, Sniper Rifle, LMG, Assault Rifle

During Combat Mission and Sector Control, this building is highly trafficked between two objectives. During Hotspot, as a potential target, it is highly contested. Firing prone from the doorway toward the beach offers a longer sight line, but little cover. There are several entrances to the west, north, and east with a small wall division. Place proximity mines near the entrances to cover your flanks. Moving in on this position should often be conducted with a Fireteam Buddy while wielding short- to mid-range weapons from the east, and mid- to long-range weapons from the west. If enemies have advanced on this position, prepare for a close-quarters engagement.

RECOMMENDED WEAPONS

Explosives, LMG, Assault Rifle, Sniper Rifle

During all game modes besides Team Deathmatch, this overwatch is likely to receive enemies passing through the village courtyard often. It's a major thoroughfare between objectives and to be considered a valuable position with adequate cover. Combat Mission, in particular, overlooks the first bomb plant site. Watch for enemies flanking fairly quickly from the western side of the building or through the southern door of the building. Patrol often to ensure this position is a fairly clear place to engage the enemy. Use the LMG or assault rifle to cover the courtyard or possibly a sniper rifle to cover the roads and nearer choke points.

RECOMMENDED WEAPONS

Grenades, Assault Rifle, LMG (supported)

During Combat Mission and Hotspot, this location is a superb elevated defensive position with plenty of cover to protect the bomb site from enemies approaching from the roads. During Sector Control, these positions cover the North Base. The cover is exceptional and deploying your bipod is essential for accuracy. Having a buddy covering the middle road and northern path to protect your flanks would be ideal.

RECOMMENDED WEAPONS

LMG (supported), Assault Rifle

During Combat Mission, in between the house and jungle there is a well hidden in a bit of cover. Climb over the scrap metal, mount an LMG or break out an assault rifle, and wait in ambush. The jungle overgrowth will provide enough camouflage to keep your body hidden until it's too late for the enemy to react.

RECOMMENDED WEAPONS

Explosives, Assault Rifle, LMG (supported)

During Combat Mission, this small house overwatch covers a small path that leads to bomb site C. Shut down this path by setting up the bipod in the window. For further coverage, have your Fireteam Buddy take cover in front of this position to fire down the opposite path. Be aware of the side door, as enemies can flank quickly. Any snipers in the area should booby trap this house to protect anyone holding this position. This spot can also be effective in Team Deathmatch, but don't hang around here too long.

RECOMMENDED WEAPONS

Assault Rifle, Grenades

During Combat Mission, this rock near the defenders' spawn point makes for great cover while defending the last bomb site. Enemies are unable to flank. Hold this position using LMGs and assault rifles. However, it's a tight spot and enemies might try to flush you out of it by lobbing grenades, so be sure everyone is dead before they can target you.

SIGHT LINES

RECOMMENDED WEAPONS
LMG or Sniper Rifle (supported)

13

During all game modes aside from Team Deathmatch, this site line looks directly down the middle lane into the southern spawn area. Deploy a bipod while prone with either the sniper rifle or the LMG to pick off incoming enemies. Cover-wise you are fairly exposed from behind. If anyone is using the other window of this building, there should be a good crossfire going that should cause enemies to consider alternate paths.

RECOMMENDED WEAPONS
LMG, Sniper Rifle (supported)

14

During Hotspot, Sector Control, and Combat Mission, this path is good impromptu prone placement for supported LMGs or sniper rifles looking down into the village to take out any unaware enemies. Since the middle road and village courtyard is an open thoroughfare, this position can be good while advancing or falling back for a couple assists or kills. The major down side is that the rear is totally exposed to flankers.

RECOMMENDED WEAPONS
Sniper Rifle (supported), LMG, Mk19

15

During Combat Mission, Sector Control, and Hotspot, as a defensive position climb up onto the tank, go prone, set up any bipod weapon or perhaps the Mk19, and fire down the center road upon any unsuspecting enemy. Be advised: snipers may pick you off. Your immediate left and the house to your right may flank this position quickly. Use this position with discretion and ensure your teammates are covering those flanks.

RECOMMENDED WEAPONS
LMG, 40mm Grenade Launcher, Sniper Rifle

16

Use this as a fallback position during Combat Mission. If you can manage to get behind these ammo crates you'll be nearly invisible, and provided a fantastic view of anyone attempting to plant a bomb on the northern side of the tank. During Sector Control or Combat Mission, any enemies approaching from the northern path into this open space won't expect to be fired on from here.

RECOMMENDED WEAPONS
Sniper Rifle, LMG

17

This is a great sight line for supported sniper rifles for both the attackers and defenders in Combat Mission or Team Deathmatch. Any sniper in possession of either of these positions is likely to determine the outcome of the match, however they can be flanked from left and right and mortared fairly easily. Snipers can easily take out any enemies rushing or diffusing the bomb site. Have your Fireteam Buddy cover you with LMG suppressive fire to hold these points.

RECOMMENDED WEAPONS
Explosives, Assault Rifle, Sniper Rifle, LMG

18

This line of site is best for protecting the bomb site during Combat Mission. The area will often be contested with your teammates meeting enemy forces during Team Deathmatch as well. Deploy the LMG or sniper rifle bipod on the provided window and fire upon anyone in sight. An assault rifle will also suffice for greater mobility. Proximity mine the door that flanks your six. Have a teammate cover the west window. If your buddy is taken out, quickly dismount and avenge him.

RECOMMENDED WEAPONS
Sniper Rifle, LMG, Assault Rifle

19

Combat Mission's third objective point (bomb site C) and Team Deathmatch will often have people clamoring to take position on the bridge. Each side flank of the bridge has trucks to support your rifle while you take out any snipers and campers. Flanking the bridge leaves your own flanks completely exposed, so get in and get out.

Early during this battle, the attackers start off in water, just off the coast from the fishing village. This gives the defenders a great opportunity to stop the attack before it starts. However, there are many paths the attackers can utilize to infiltrate the village—a frontal assault on bomb site A is not advised. The second bomb site (B) is located near the tank at the center of the map. Once again, the defenders have a good shot at ending the battle here by simply guarding the few approaches from the fishing village. When attacking here, always attempt to flank from the east or west—charging down the main dirt road is suicide. In the final phase of the battle, the defenders must prevent the attackers from destroying the bridge on the north side of the map. Here the bomb must be planted on the vertical supports beneath the bridge, posing yet another challenge for the attackers. This area can be watched by snipers from both sides, making it extremely difficult to arm or disarm a charge in this open area.

COMBAT MISSION

- ◯ Attacker Spawn
- ◯ Defender Spawn
- ✦ Bomb Site

HOTSPOT

Attacker Spawn

Defender Spawn

Potential Target

In Hotspot, the attackers start out near the bridge on the north side of the map while the defenders spawn at the fishing village to the south. The five potential targets are spread out between these two locations. The attackers must move out quickly to avoid being pinned down near their spawn point. When attacking, try to establish an early presence near the tank in the center of the map. Taking control of this area early on grants the attackers easy access to two potential targets. The nearby structures also offer decent overwatch positions as well as cover when your Fireteam Buddy is waiting to spawn. Unless notified of a potential target in the center, the defending team should consider consolidating their forces around the three potential targets near the fishing village. Although it's a rather large area to defend, if the defending team can lock down this area, they can practically guarantee a victory, even if the two targets near the center are destroyed.

This is a relatively large-scale Sector Control map, with the three bases spread over a wide area. This offers plenty of room to maneuver, particularly when moving between the North Base (by the tank) and South Base (at the fishing village). The entire east side of the map is usually clear of threats as most players are drawn to the intense firefights raging around the Center Base to the west. As a result, you and your Fireteam Buddy can spend most of the match shuttling between the North and South Bases along the east side without encountering much resistance. But don't expect to hold the base farthest from your spawn point very long—once you capture it, either dig in and defend the flag or retreat before the inevitable counterattack. If you choose to grind against the hotly contested Center Base, make an effort to attack from the narrow northeastern path. This allows you to flank the cross-traffic funneling in from the north and south.

SECTOR CONTROL

	Spawn Point
N	North Base
C	Center Base
S	South Base

HOME RUN

⬤	**Attacker Spawn**
⬤	**Defender Spawn**
◆	**Flag**

Home Run takes place entirely within the confines of the fishing village, leading to some intense house-to-house fighting as both teams attempt to secure the flags. The attackers start off in the water on the east side, much like Combat Mission. If the defenders hurry, they can intercept the attackers as they emerge from the shallow water, but it's best to consolidate forces around the two flags. Both flags are situated in relatively open areas that can easily be covered from the nearby bamboo houses. By sneaking along the north edge of the map, the attackers have a good chance of securing Flag B without drawing too much attention. Flag A is a much tougher one to approach unless the attackers stage an aggressive frontal assault, sweeping the nearby structures before making a move on the flag. In the event of a flag capture, defenders need to be ready to hunt down the flag carrier. Try to hit the flag carrier before the attacker can enter the maze-like swamp to the east.

TEAM DEATHMATCH

● Spawn Point

During Team Deathmatch, movement is restricted to the area surrounding the bridge. This is a very small area when playing on a server with 20 players. The area is condensed even further due to the no man's land in the center of the map—traveling along this low stream-bed is a bad idea, making you vulnerable to snipers posted on the bridge to the north or the hills to the south. This forces almost all traffic to the perimeter of the map, making these narrow pathways even more congested. Be ready to engage opponents at close range as you and your teammates travel together in a pack—going solo is a very bad idea. The perimeter path wraps around the entire map, giving it the feel of a race track. If you don't feel like running and gunning, camp along the edge of the path and engage the cross-traffic. The structures on the east and northwest sides are popular spots for those seeking to fight from a stationary position. If your team can secure one (or both) of these shack-like buildings, you can control the flow of traffic on the perimeter path and rack up some impressive kills in the process.

[US]
SEAL

[CANADIAN]
JTF-2

[BRITISH]
SAS

[SWEDISH]
SO

[US]
OGA

[US]
SFOD-D

WARFIGHTER COMPENDIUM

HJK

[POLISH]
GROM

[RUSSIAN]
SPETSNAZ
ALFA GROUP

SK

[SOUTH KOREAN]
UDT/SE

[AUSTRALIAN]
SASR

MULTIPLAYER SCORING SYSTEM

ACTION	VALUE	BUDDY VALUE*	DESCRIPTION
Kill	100	—	Kill enemy using primary or secondary weapon.
Avenged by Buddy	50	—	Buddy avenged player's death.
Was Saved by Buddy	50	—	Buddy killed enemy attacking you.
Support Action Kill	20	—	Kill enemy using support action vehicle.
Damage Assist	1–100	—	Assist in the kill of an enemy. Score is 1–100 based on how much damage is caused to target.
Spotting Assist	50	—	Actively spot an enemy that is killed during the spotting duration.
UAV Spotting Assist	10	—	Ally kills enemy that is spotted by the player's UAV.
Fireteam Replenish	100	—	Call in the Fireteam Replenish support action.
Place Jammer	20	—	Place a Radar Jammer in enemy territory.
Destroy Jammer	20	—	Destroy an enemy Radar Jammer.
Jammer Kill Assist	10	—	Enemy is killed while affected by your Radar Jammer.

ACTION	VALUE	BUDDY VALUE*	DESCRIPTION
Disrupt Enemy UAV	100	—	Destroy enemy UAV by shooting it or by using the Radar Jammer.
Smoke Plant Assist	50	—	Ally plants bomb while inside the Smoke Screen area.
Smoke Defuse Assist	50	—	Ally defuses bomb while inside the Smoke Screen area.
Smoke Capture Assist	50	—	Ally captures sector while inside the Smoke Screen area.
Give Ammo	10	—	Ally gets ammo from player.
Heal Ally	20	—	Ally gets healed from player.
Buddy Spawn	10	—	Buddy spawns on player.
Vehicle Force Retreat	200	—	Vehicle was forced to retreat and player caused over 20% of the damage given.
Vehicle Destroy	200	—	Destroyed a vehicle (MUSA Robot).
EOD	50	—	Destroy an enemy's explosive (remote charge or proximity mine).

KILL MODIFIERS

ACTION	VALUE	BUDDY VALUE*	DESCRIPTION
Avenger	20	5	Target recently killed an ally.
Buddy Avenger	50	Faster respawn	Target recently killed Fireteam Buddy.
Savior	20	5	Target recently damaged (but didn't kill) an ally.
Buddy Savior	50	—	Target recently damaged (but didn't kill) Fireteam Buddy.
Defender	50	—	Target is within the radius of a base under ally control.
Attacker	50	—	Target is within the radius of a base under enemy control.
Fireteam Wipe	50	5	Kill both members of an enemy Fireteam before one can respawn.
Headshot	50	5	Kill enemy with headshot.
Humiliation	100	10	Kill enemy with melee attack.
Double Kill	50	5	Kill two enemies at the same time.
Triple Kill	50	5	Kill three enemies at the same time.
Multi Kill	50	5	Kill four or more enemies at the same time.
Marksman	20 (+bonus)	5	As a sniper, kill an enemy with a headshot from over 20 meters away. One bonus point per meter distance.
Booby Trap	20	—	Kill with proximity mine.
Switchblade Kill	20	—	Kill with Switchblade.
RQ-11 Kill	100	10	Kill with the RQ-11 Raven.
Comeback	100	10	Player has died three times without getting a kill prior to making a kill.
Killjoy	50	5	Kill a player that is on a killstreak.
Nemesis Revenge	50	5	Kill enemy that had killed player three times without you killing him

ACTION	VALUE	BUDDY VALUE*	DESCRIPTION
COMBAT MISSION/HOTSPOT			
Bomb Planted	200	—	Plant the bomb in Combat Mission or Hotspot game mode.
Buddy Plant Assist	100	—	Be within 7 meters of the bomb when it is planted by a buddy.
Bomb Exploded	50	—	Planted bomb is detonated.
Bomb Defused	200	—	Disarm the bomb in Combat Mission or Hotspot game mode.
Buddy Defuse Assist	100	—	Be within 7 meters of the bomb when it is disarmed by a buddy.
Smoke Assist	50	—	Use Smoke Screen to cover the arming/disarming of a bomb.
SECTOR CONTROL			
Capture	100	—	Be within the radius of a base when it is captured.
Flag Attack	50	—	Kill an enemy within the radius of an enemy base.
Flag Defense	50	—	Kill an enemy within the radius of a friendly base.
Smoke Assist	50	—	Use Smoke Screen to cover a base from being captured.
HOME RUN			
Stole Flag	100	—	Pick up the flag as an attacker.
Runner Kill	200	—	Kill the flag carrier as a defender.
Home Run	200	—	Return the flag successfully to team's base as attacker.
Survivor	100	—	Survived the round.

* = points earned if action performed within 20 meters of Fireteam Buddy

MULTIPLAYER RIBBONS

RIBBON	NAME	CRITERIA	POINTS
	Combat Mission Attacker Ribbon	In a round of Combat Mission, plant and detonate 2 bombs	500
	Combat Mission Defender Ribbon	In a round of Combat Mission, disarm 2 bombs	500
	Combat Mission Ribbon	Finish a round of Combat Mission	500
	Combat Mission Winner Ribbon	Win a round of Combat Mission	500
	CQB Ribbon	In a round, kill 10 enemies using the Tomahawk	500
	Distinguished Fireteam Ribbon	In a round, finish as the featured Fireteam	500
	Explosives Expert Ribbon	In a round, kill 10 enemies using thrown explosives	500
	Fire Assistance Ribbon	In a round, perform 10 damage assists	500
	Fireteam Wipe Ribbon	In a round, perform 5 Fireteam wipes	500
	Home Run All Star Ribbon	In a round of Home Run, steal the flag 2 times	500
	Home Run Defender Ribbon	In a round of Home Run, kill the flag carrier 4 times	500

RIBBON	NAME	CRITERIA	POINTS
	Home Run Ribbon	Finish a round of Home Run	500
	Home Run Winner Ribbon	Win a round of Home Run	500
	Hotspot Attacker Ribbon	In a round of Hotspot, plant and detonate 3 bombs	500
	Hotspot Defender Ribbon	In a round of Hotspot, disarm 3 bombs	500
	Hotspot Ribbon	Finish a round of Hotspot	500
	Hotspot Winner Ribbon	Win a round of Hotspot	500
	Kill Count Ribbon	In a round, kill 25 enemies	500
	Marksman Ribbon	In a round, perform 10 headshots	500
	Platoon Unity Ribbon	In a round, play as your Platoon's home unit for the majority of the time	500
	Recon Ribbon	In a round, perform 10 spotting assists	500
	Rescue Ribbon	In a round, save your buddy 10 times	500

RIBBON	NAME	CRITERIA	POINTS
	Retaliation Ribbon	In a round, avenge 10 teammates	500
	Sector Control Attacker Ribbon	In a round of Sector Control, capture 4 sectors	500
	Sector Control Defender Ribbon	In a round of Sector Control, defend 8 sectors	500
	Sector Control Ribbon	Finish a round of Sector Control	500
	Sector Control Winner Ribbon	Win a round of Sector Control	500
	Sidearm Ribbon	In a round, kill 10 enemies using sidearms	500
	Team Deathmatch Ribbon	Finish a round of Team Deathmatch	500
	Team Deathmatch Winner Ribbon	Win a round of Team Deathmatch	500
	Warfighter Nations Ribbon	Spend 10 National Pride tokens on the Battlelog website	500

MULTIPLAYER MEDALS

MEDAL	NAME	CRITERIA	POINTS
	Accuracy Medal	Perform 50 headshots	1,000
	Action Commendation	Kill 5 enemies	1,000
	Anti-Vehicle Medal	Get 10 Vehicle Assists	3,000
	Apache Commendation	Spend 5 minutes in the AH-64 Apache	3,000
	Assaulter Medal	Kill 200 enemies as the Assaulter class	3,000
	Assaulter Tier 1 Medal	Kill 2,000 enemies as the Assaulter class	5,000
	Blocker Commendation	Kill 5 flag runners in Home Run	1,000
	Bronze Atlas Medal	Kill 1,000 enemies	1,000
	Campaign Commendation	Be on the winning team 10 times	1,000
	Combat Medal	Kill 300 enemies with primary weapons	3,000
	Combat Versatility Medal	Kill 200 enemies with sidearms	3,000
	Conquest Commendation	Capture 10 sectors	1,000

MEDAL	NAME	CRITERIA	POINTS
	Danger Close Medal	Kill someone from the Danger Close development team or someone that has this medal	5,000
	Defense Commendation	Defend 20 sectors	1,000
	Demolitions Medal	Kill 200 enemies as the Demolitions class	3,000
	Demolitions Tier 1 Medal	Kill 2,000 enemies as the Demolitions class	5,000
	Disarm Commendation	Disarm 5 bombs	1,000
	Distinguished Intelligence Commendation	Perform 200 spotting assists	3,000
	Effectiveness Commendation	Kill 30 enemies with primary weapons	1,000
	Fireteam Commendation	Perform 20 Fireteam wipes	3,000
	Fireteam Defense Commendation	Save your buddy 20 times	1,000
	Force Commendation	Plant and detonate 5 bombs	1,000
	Global Warfighter Medal	Complete a tour with each class	5,000
	Gold Atlas Medal	Kill 10,000 enemies	5,000

MEDAL	NAME	CRITERIA	POINTS
	Heavy Gunner Medal	Kill 200 enemies as the Heavy Gunner class	3,000
	Heavy Gunner Tier 1 Medal	Kill 2,000 enemies as the Heavy Gunner class	5,000
	Heavy Ordnance Medal	Kill 100 enemies by calling in support actions	3,000
	Home Run Commendation	Perform 5 home runs	1,000
	Honorable Service Medal	Be on the winning team 100 times	3,000
	Intelligence Commendation	Perform 20 spotting assists	1,000
	Lead Blocker Medal	Kill 100 flag runners in Home Run	3,000
	Lead Conquest Medal	Capture 200 sectors	3,000
	Lead Defense Medal	Defend 400 sectors	3,000
	Lead Disarm Medal	Disarm 100 bombs	3,000
	Lead Fireteam Medal	Perform 100 Fireteam wipes	3,000
	Lead Force Medal	Plant 100 bombs	3,000
	Lead Home Run Medal	Perform 100 home runs	3,000

WARFIGHTER COMPENDIUM

MEDAL	NAME	CRITERIA	POINTS
	Meritorious Unit Australian SAS-R	Kill 100 enemies as the Australian SAS-R unit	1,000
	Meritorious Unit British SAS	Kill 100 enemies as the British SAS unit	1,000
	Meritorious Unit Canadian JTF-2	Kill 100 enemies as the Canadian JTF-2 unit	1,000
	Meritorious Unit German KSK	Kill 100 enemies as the German KSK unit	1,000
	Meritorious Unit Norwegian FSK/HJK	Kill 100 enemies as the Norwegian FSK/HJK unit	1,000
	Meritorious Unit Polish GROM	Kill 100 enemies as the Polish GROM unit	1,000
	Meritorious Unit ROKN UDT/SEAL	Kill 100 enemies as the ROKN UDT/SEAL unit	1,000
	Meritorious Unit RU Spetsgruppa Alfa	Kill 100 enemies as the RU Spetsgruppa Alfa unit	1,000
	Meritorious Unit Swedish SOG	Kill 100 enemies as the Swedish SOG unit	1,000
	Meritorious Unit US Army SFOD-D	Kill 100 enemies as the US Army SFOD-D unit	1,000
	Meritorious Unit US Navy SEAL	Kill 100 enemies as the US Navy SEAL unit	1,000
	Meritorious Unit US OGA	Kill 100 enemies as the US OGA unit	1,000
	Point Man Medal	Kill 200 enemies as the Point Man class	3,000

MEDAL	NAME	CRITERIA	POINTS
	Point Man Tier 1 Medal	Kill 2,000 enemies as the Point Man class	5,000
	Recon Medal	Launch the RQ-11 Raven 50 times	3,000
	Silver Atlas Medal	Kill 4,000 enemies	3,000
	Sniper Medal	Kill 200 enemies as the Sniper class	3,000
	Sniper Tier 1 Medal	Kill 2,000 enemies as the Sniper class	5,000
	Spec Ops Medal	Kill 200 enemies as the Spec Ops class	3,000
	Spec Ops Tier 1 Medal	Kill 2,000 enemies as the Spec Ops class	5,000
	Stealth Medal	Kill 15 enemies using the Tomahawk	1,000
	Superior Service Duty Medal	Play online for 24 hours	5,000
	Surveillance Medal	Launch the RQ-7B Shadow 10 times	3,000
	Top Performance Medal	Finish in the Top 3 in 15 rounds	3,000
	Valorous Unit Australian SAS-R	Kill 1,000 enemies as the Australian SAS-R unit	3,000
	Valorous Unit British SAS	Kill 1,000 enemies as the British SAS unit	3,000

MEDAL	NAME	CRITERIA	POINTS
	Valorous Unit Canadian JTF-2	Kill 1,000 enemies as the Canadian JTF-2 unit	3,000
	Valorous Unit German KSK	Kill 1,000 enemies as the German KSK unit	3,000
	Valorous Unit Norwegian FSK/HJK	Kill 1,000 enemies as the Norwegian FSK/HJK unit	3,000
	Valorous Unit Polish GROM	Kill 1,000 enemies as the Polish GROM unit	3,000
	Valorous Unit ROKN UDT/SEAL	Kill 1,000 enemies as the ROKN UDT/SEAL unit	3,000
	Valorous Unit RU Spetsgruppa Alfa	Kill 1,000 enemies as the RU Spetsgruppa Alfa unit	3,000
	Valorous Unit Swedish SOG	Kill 1,000 enemies as the Swedish SOG unit	3,000
	Valorous Unit US Army SFOD-D	Kill 1,000 enemies as the US Army SFOD-D unit	3,000
	Valorous Unit US Navy SEAL	Kill 1,000 enemies as the US Navy SEAL unit	3,000
	Valorous Unit US OGA	Kill 1,000 enemies as the US OGA unit	3,000
	Versatility Commendation	Kill 20 enemies with sidearms	1,000

MULTIPLAYER CAREER PROGRESSION

INSIGNIA	NAME	POINTS	AUSTRALIAN SAS-R		BRITISH SAS		CANADIAN JTF-2		GERMAN KSK		NORWAY FSK/HJK	
			Class Unlock	Unit Unlock	Class Unlock	Unit Unlock	Class Unlock	Unit Unlock	Class Unlock	Unit Unlock	Class Unlock	Unit Unlock
	Private 1	0	Assaulter	Australian SAS-R	Assaulter	British SAS	Assaulter	Canadian JTF-2	Assaulter	German KSK	Assaulter	Norway FSK/HJK
	Private 2	2,000	Assaulter Grenade Launcher	—	Assaulter Grenade Launcher	—	Assaulter Grenade Launcher		Assaulter Grenade Launcher	—	Assaulter Grenade Launcher	—
	Private 3	5,000	Heavy Gunner	German KSK	Heavy Gunner	German KSK	Heavy Gunner	German KSK	Heavy Gunner	German KSK	Heavy Gunner	German KSK
	Private 4	8,000	Spec Ops	Canadian JTF-2	Spec Ops	Canadian JTF-2	Spec Ops	Canadian JTF-2	Spec Ops	Canadian JTF-2	Spec Ops	Canadian JTF-2
	Private 5	11,500	Sniper	ROKN UDT/SEAL	Sniper	ROKN UDT/SEAL	Sniper	ROKN UDT/SEAL	Sniper	ROKN UDT/SEAL	Sniper	ROKN UDT/SEAL
	Private First Class 1	15,000	Point Man	Swedish SOG	Point Man	Swedish SOG	Point Man	Swedish SOG	Point Man	Swedish SOG	Point Man	Swedish SOG
	Private First Class 2	19,000	Demolitions	RU Spetsgruppa Alfa	Demolitions	RU Spetsgruppa Alfa	Demolitions	RU Spetsgruppa Alfa	Demolitions	RU Spetsgruppa Alfa	Demolitions	RU Spetsgruppa Alfa
	Private First Class 3	23,000	Assaulter	Polish GROM	Assaulter	Polish GROM	Assaulter	Polish GROM	Assaulter	Polish GROM	Assaulter	Polish GROM
	Private First Class 4	27,000	Heavy Gunner	British SAS	Heavy Gunner	British SAS	Heavy Gunner	British SAS	Heavy Gunner	British SAS	Heavy Gunner	British SAS
	Private First Class 5	31,500	Spec Ops	US OGA	Spec Ops	US OGA	Spec Ops	US OGA	Spec Ops	US OGA	Spec Ops	US OGA
	Corporal 1	36,000	Sniper	US Army SFOD-D	Sniper	US Army SFOD-D	Sniper	US Army SFOD-D	Sniper	US Army SFOD-D	Sniper	US Army SFOD-D
	Corporal 2	41,000	Point Man	Australian SAS-R	Point Man	Australian SAS-R	Point Man	Australian SAS-R	Point Man	Australian SAS-R	Point Man	Australian SAS-R
	Corporal 3	46,000	Demolitions	Norway FSK/HJK	Demolitions	Norway FSK/HJK	Demolitions	Norway FSK/HJK	Demolitions	Norway FSK/HJK	Demolitions	Norway FSK/HJK
	Corporal 4	51,000	Assaulter	US Navy SEAL	Assaulter	US Navy SEAL	Assaulter	US Navy SEAL	Assaulter	US Navy SEAL	Assaulter	US Navy SEAL
	Corporal 5	56,500	Heavy Gunner	Canadian JTF-2	Heavy Gunner	Canadian JTF-2	Heavy Gunner	Canadian JTF-2	Heavy Gunner	Canadian JTF-2	Heavy Gunner	Canadian JTF-2
	Sergeant 1	62,000	Spec Ops	ROKN UDT/SEAL	Spec Ops	ROKN UDT/SEAL	Spec Ops	ROKN UDT/SEAL	Spec Ops	ROKN UDT/SEAL	Spec Ops	ROKN UDT/SEAL
	Sergeant 2	68,000	Sniper	Swedish SOG	Sniper	Swedish SOG	Sniper	Swedish SOG	Sniper	Swedish SOG	Sniper	Swedish SOG
	Sergeant 3	74,000	Point Man	RU Spetsgruppa Alfa	Point Man	RU Spetsgruppa Alfa	Point Man	RU Spetsgruppa Alfa	Point Man	RU Spetsgruppa Alfa	Point Man	RU Spetsgruppa Alfa
	Sergeant 4	80,000	Demolitions	Polish GROM	Demolitions	Polish GROM	Demolitions	Polish GROM	Demolitions	Polish GROM	Demolitions	Polish GROM
	Sergeant 5	86,500	Assaulter	British SAS	Heavy Gunner	US Navy SEAL	Assaulter	British SAS	Assaulter	British SAS	Assaulter	British SAS
	Staff Sergeant 1	93,000	Heavy Gunner	US Navy SEAL	Spec Ops	US Army SFOD-D	Heavy Gunner	US Navy SEAL	Heavy Gunner	US Navy SEAL	Heavy Gunner	US Navy SEAL
	Staff Sergeant 2	100,000	Spec Ops	US Army SFOD-D	Sniper	Australian SAS-R	Spec Ops	US Army SFOD-D	Spec Ops	US Army SFOD-D	Spec Ops	US Army SFOD-D
	Staff Sergeant 3	107,000	Sniper	Australian SAS-R	Point Man	Norway FSK/HJK	Sniper	Australian SAS-R	Sniper	Australian SAS-R	Sniper	Australian SAS-R
	Staff Sergeant 4	114,000	Point Man	Norway FSK/HJK	Demolitions	US Navy SEAL	Point Man	Norway FSK/HJK	Point Man	Norway FSK/HJK	Point Man	Norway FSK/HJK
	Staff Sergeant 5	121,500	Demolitions	US Navy SEAL	Assaulter	German KSK	Demolitions	US Navy SEAL	Demolitions	US Navy SEAL	Demolitions	US Navy SEAL
	Sergeant First Class 1	129,000	Assaulter	German KSK	Heavy Gunner	ROKN UDT/SEAL	Assaulter	German KSK	Heavy Gunner	ROKN UDT/SEAL	Assaulter	German KSK
	Sergeant First Class 2	137,000	Heavy Gunner	ROKN UDT/SEAL	Spec Ops	Swedish SOG	Heavy Gunner	ROKN UDT/SEAL	Spec Ops	Swedish SOG	Heavy Gunner	ROKN UDT/SEAL
	Sergeant First Class 3	145,000	Spec Ops	Swedish SOG	Sniper	RU Spetsgruppa Alfa	Spec Ops	Swedish SOG	Sniper	RU Spetsgruppa Alfa	Spec Ops	Swedish SOG
	Sergeant First Class 4	153,000	Sniper	RU Spetsgruppa Alfa	Point Man	Polish GROM	Sniper	RU Spetsgruppa Alfa	Point Man	Polish GROM	Sniper	RU Spetsgruppa Alfa
	Sergeant First Class 5	161,500	Point Man	Polish GROM	Demolitions	British SAS	Point Man	Polish GROM	Demolitions	British SAS	Point Man	Polish GROM

POLISH GROM		ROKN UDT/SEAL		RU SPETSGRUPPA ALFA		SWEDISH SOG		US ARMY SFOD-D		US NAVY SEAL		US OGA	
Class Unlock	Unit Unlock	Class Unlock	Unit Unlock	Class Unlock	Unit Unlock	Class Unlock	Unit Unlock	Class Unlock	Unit Unlock	Class Unlock	Unit Unlock	Class Unlock	Unit Unlock
Assaulter	Polish GROM	Assaulter	ROKN UDT/SEAL	Assaulter	RU Spetsgruppa Alfa	Assaulter	Swedish SOG	Assaulter	US Army SFOD-D	Assaulter	US Navy SEAL	Assaulter	US OGA
Assaulter Grenade Launcher	—	Assaulter Grenade Launcher	—	Assaulter Grenade Launcher	—	Assaulter Grenade Launcher	—	Assaulter Grenade Launcher	—	Assaulter Grenade Launcher	—	Assaulter Grenade Launcher	—
Heavy Gunner	German KSK	Heavy Gunner	German KSK	Heavy Gunner	German KSK	Heavy Gunner	German KSK	Heavy Gunner	German KSK	Heavy Gunner	German KSK	Heavy Gunner	German KSK
Spec Ops	Canadian JTF-2	Spec Ops	Canadian JTF-2	Spec Ops	Canadian JTF-2	Spec Ops	Canadian JTF-2	Spec Ops	Canadian JTF-2	Spec Ops	Canadian JTF-2	Spec Ops	Canadian JTF-2
Sniper	ROKN UDT/SEAL	Sniper	ROKN UDT/SEAL	Sniper	ROKN UDT/SEAL	Sniper	ROKN UDT/SEAL	Sniper	ROKN UDT/SEAL	Sniper	ROKN UDT/SEAL	Sniper	ROKN UDT/SEAL
Point Man	Swedish SOG	Point Man	Swedish SOG	Point Man	Swedish SOG	Point Man	Swedish SOG	Point Man	Swedish SOG	Point Man	Swedish SOG	Point Man	Swedish SOG
Demolitions	RU Spetsgruppa Alfa	Demolitions	RU Spetsgruppa Alfa	Demolitions	RU Spetsgruppa Alfa	Demolitions	RU Spetsgruppa Alfa	Demolitions	RU Spetsgruppa Alfa	Demolitions	RU Spetsgruppa Alfa	Demolitions	RU Spetsgruppa Alfa
Heavy Gunner	British SAS	Assaulter	Polish GROM	Assaulter	Polish GROM	Assaulter	Polish GROM	Assaulter	Polish GROM	Assaulter	Polish GROM	Assaulter	Polish GROM
Spec Ops	US OGA	Heavy Gunner	British SAS	Heavy Gunner	British SAS	Heavy Gunner	British SAS	Heavy Gunner	British SAS	Heavy Gunner	British SAS	Heavy Gunner	British SAS
Sniper	US Army SFOD-D	Spec Ops	US OGA	Spec Ops	US OGA	Spec Ops	US OGA	Spec Ops	US OGA	Spec Ops	US OGA	Spec Ops	US OGA
Point Man	Australian SAS-R	Sniper	US Army SFOD-D	Sniper	US Army SFOD-D	Sniper	US Army SFOD-D	Sniper	US Army SFOD-D	Sniper	US Army SFOD-D	Sniper	US Army SFOD-D
Demolitions	Norway FSK/HJK	Point Man	Australian SAS-R	Point Man	Australian SAS-R	Point Man	Australian SAS-R	Point Man	Australian SAS-R	Point Man	Australian SAS-R	Point Man	Australian SAS-R
Assaulter	US Navy SEAL	Demolitions	Norway FSK/HJK	Demolitions	Norway FSK/HJK	Demolitions	Norway FSK/HJK	Demolitions	Norway FSK/HJK	Demolitions	Norway FSK/HJK	Demolitions	Norway FSK/HJK
Heavy Gunner	Canadian JTF-2	Assaulter	US Navy SEAL	Assaulter	US Navy SEAL	Assaulter	US Navy SEAL	Assaulter	US Navy SEAL	Heavy Gunner	Canadian JTF-2	Assaulter	US Navy SEAL
Spec Ops	ROKN UDT/SEAL	Heavy Gunner	Canadian JTF-2	Heavy Gunner	Canadian JTF-2	Heavy Gunner	Canadian JTF-2	Heavy Gunner	Canadian JTF-2	Spec Ops	ROKN UDT/SEAL	Heavy Gunner	Canadian JTF-2
Sniper	Swedish SOG	Spec Ops	ROKN UDT/SEAL	Spec Ops	ROKN UDT/SEAL	Spec Ops	ROKN UDT/SEAL	Spec Ops	ROKN UDT/SEAL	Sniper	Swedish SOG	Spec Ops	ROKN UDT/SEAL
Point Man	RU Spetsgruppa Alfa	Sniper	Swedish SOG	Sniper	Swedish SOG	Sniper	Swedish SOG	Sniper	Swedish SOG	Point Man	RU Spetsgruppa Alfa	Sniper	Swedish SOG
Demolitions	Polish GROM	Point Man	RU Spetsgruppa Alfa	Point Man	RU Spetsgruppa Alfa	Point Man	RU Spetsgruppa Alfa	Point Man	RU Spetsgruppa Alfa	Demolitions	Polish GROM	Point Man	RU Spetsgruppa Alfa
Assaulter	British SAS	Demolitions	Polish GROM	Demolitions	Polish GROM	Demolitions	Polish GROM	Demolitions	Polish GROM	Assaulter	British SAS	Demolitions	Polish GROM
Heavy Gunner	US Navy SEAL	Assaulter	British SAS	Assaulter	British SAS	Assaulter	British SAS	Assaulter	British SAS	Heavy Gunner	US Navy SEAL	Assaulter	British SAS
Spec Ops	US Army SFOD-D	Heavy Gunner	US Navy SEAL	Heavy Gunner	US Navy SEAL	Heavy Gunner	US Navy SEAL	Heavy Gunner	US Navy SEAL	Spec Ops	US Army SFOD-D	Heavy Gunner	US Navy SEAL
Sniper	Australian SAS-R	Spec Ops	US Army SFOD-D	Spec Ops	US Army SFOD-D	Spec Ops	US Army SFOD-D	Spec Ops	US Army SFOD-D	Sniper	Australian SAS-R	Spec Ops	US Army SFOD-D
Point Man	Norway FSK/HJK	Sniper	Australian SAS-R	Sniper	Australian SAS-R	Sniper	Australian SAS-R	Sniper	Australian SAS-R	Point Man	Norway FSK/HJK	Sniper	Australian SAS-R
Demolitions	US Navy SEAL	Point Man	Norway FSK/HJK	Point Man	Norway FSK/HJK	Point Man	Norway FSK/HJK	Point Man	Norway FSK/HJK	Demolitions	US Navy SEAL	Point Man	Norway FSK/HJK
Assaulter	German KSK	Demolitions	US Navy SEAL	Demolitions	US Navy SEAL	Demolitions	US Navy SEAL	Demolitions	US Navy SEAL	Assaulter	German KSK	Demolitions	US Navy SEAL
Heavy Gunner	ROKN UDT/SEAL	Assaulter	German KSK	Assaulter	German KSK	Assaulter	German KSK	Assaulter	German KSK	Heavy Gunner	ROKN UDT/SEAL	Assaulter	German KSK
Spec Ops	Swedish SOG	Heavy Gunner	ROKN UDT/SEAL	Heavy Gunner	ROKN UDT/SEAL	Heavy Gunner	ROKN UDT/SEAL	Heavy Gunner	ROKN UDT/SEAL	Spec Ops	Swedish SOG	Heavy Gunner	ROKN UDT/SEAL
Sniper	RU Spetsgruppa Alfa	Spec Ops	Swedish SOG	Spec Ops	Swedish SOG	Spec Ops	Swedish SOG	Spec Ops	Swedish SOG	Sniper	RU Spetsgruppa Alfa	Spec Ops	Swedish SOG
Point Man	Polish GROM	Sniper	RU Spetsgruppa Alfa	Sniper	RU Spetsgruppa Alfa	Sniper	RU Spetsgruppa Alfa	Sniper	RU Spetsgruppa Alfa	Point Man	Polish GROM	Sniper	RU Spetsgruppa Alfa
Demolitions	British SAS	Point Man	Polish GROM	Point Man	Polish GROM	Point Man	Polish GROM	Point Man	Polish GROM	Demolitions	British SAS	Point Man	Polish GROM

INSIGNIA	NAME	POINTS	AUSTRALIAN SAS-R		BRITISH SAS		CANADIAN JTF-2		GERMAN KSK		NORWAY FSK/HJK	
			Class Unlock	Unit Unlock	Class Unlock	Unit Unlock	Class Unlock	Unit Unlock	Class Unlock	Unit Unlock	Class Unlock	Unit Unlock
	Master Sergeant 1	170,000	Demolitions	British SAS	Assaulter	US OGA	Demolitions	British SAS	Assaulter	US OGA	Demolitions	British SAS
	Master Sergeant 2	179,000	Assaulter	US OGA	Heavy Gunner	US Army SFOD-D	Assaulter	US OGA	Heavy Gunner	US Army SFOD-D	Assaulter	US OGA
	Master Sergeant 3	188,000	Heavy Gunner	US Army SFOD-D	Spec Ops	Australian SAS-R	Heavy Gunner	US Army SFOD-D	Spec Ops	Australian SAS-R	Heavy Gunner	US Army SFOD-D
	Master Sergeant 4	197,000	Spec Ops	Australian SAS-R	Sniper	Norway FSK/HJK	Spec Ops	Australian SAS-R	Sniper	Norway FSK/HJK	Spec Ops	Australian SAS-R
	Master Sergeant 5	206,500	Sniper	Norway FSK/HJK	Point Man	US Navy SEAL	Sniper	Norway FSK/HJK	Point Man	US Navy SEAL	Sniper	Norway FSK/HJK
	First Sergeant 1	216,000	Point Man	US Navy SEAL	Demolitions	German KSK	Point Man	US Navy SEAL	Demolitions	German KSK	Point Man	US Navy SEAL
	First Sergeant 2	226,000	Demolitions	German KSK	Assaulter	Canadian JTF-2	Demolitions	German KSK	Assaulter	Canadian JTF-2	Demolitions	German KSK
	First Sergeant 3	236,000	Assaulter	Canadian JTF-2	Heavy Gunner	Swedish SOG	Heavy Gunner	Swedish SOG	Heavy Gunner	Swedish SOG	Assaulter	Canadian JTF-2
	First Sergeant 4	246,000	Heavy Gunner	Swedish SOG	Spec Ops	RU Spetsgruppa Alfa	Spec Ops	RU Spetsgruppa Alfa	Spec Ops	RU Spetsgruppa Alfa	Heavy Gunner	Swedish SOG
	First Sergeant 5	256,500	Spec Ops	RU Spetsgruppa Alfa	Sniper	Polish GROM	Sniper	Polish GROM	Sniper	Polish GROM	Spec Ops	RU Spetsgruppa Alfa
	Sergeant Major 1	267,000	Sniper	Polish GROM	Point Man	British SAS	Point Man	British SAS	Point Man	British SAS	Sniper	Polish GROM
	Sergeant Major 2	278,000	Point Man	British SAS	Demolitions	US OGA	Demolitions	US OGA	Demolitions	US OGA	Point Man	British SAS
	Sergeant Major 3	289,500	Demolitions	US OGA	Assaulter	US Army SFOD-D	Assaulter	US Army SFOD-D	Assaulter	US Army SFOD-D	Demolitions	US OGA
	Sergeant Major 4	301,500	Assaulter	US Army SFOD-D	Heavy Gunner	Australian SAS-R	Heavy Gunner	Australian SAS-R	Heavy Gunner	Australian SAS-R	Assaulter	US Army SFOD-D
	Sergeant Major 5	313,500	Heavy Gunner	Australian SAS-R	Spec Ops	Norway FSK/HJK	Spec Ops	Norway FSK/HJK	Spec Ops	Norway FSK/HJK	Heavy Gunner	Australian SAS-R
	Command Sergeant Major 1	326,000	Spec Ops	Norway FSK/HJK	Sniper	US Navy SEAL	Sniper	US Navy SEAL	Sniper	US Navy SEAL	Spec Ops	Norway FSK/HJK
	Command Sergeant Major 2	339,000	Sniper	US Navy SEAL	Point Man	German KSK	Point Man	German KSK	Point Man	German KSK	Sniper	US Navy SEAL
	Command Sergeant Major 3	352,500	Point Man	German KSK	Demolitions	Canadian JTF-2	Demolitions	Canadian JTF-2	Demolitions	Canadian JTF-2	Point Man	German KSK
	Command Sergeant Major 4	366,500	Demolitions	Canadian JTF-2	Assaulter	ROKN UDT/SEAL	Assaulter	ROKN UDT/SEAL	Assaulter	ROKN UDT/SEAL	Demolitions	Canadian JTF-2
	Command Sergeant Major 5	380,500	Assaulter	ROKN UDT/SEAL	Heavy Gunner	RU Spetsgruppa Alfa	Heavy Gunner	RU Spetsgruppa Alfa	Heavy Gunner	RU Spetsgruppa Alfa	Assaulter	ROKN UDT/SEAL
	Sergeant Major of the Army 1	395,000	Heavy Gunner	RU Spetsgruppa Alfa	Spec Ops	Polish GROM	Spec Ops	Polish GROM	Spec Ops	Polish GROM	Heavy Gunner	RU Spetsgruppa Alfa
	Sergeant Major of the Army 2	410,000	Spec Ops	Polish GROM	Sniper	British SAS	Sniper	British SAS	Sniper	British SAS	Spec Ops	Polish GROM
	Sergeant Major of the Army 3	425,500	Sniper	British SAS	Point Man	US OGA	Point Man	US OGA	Point Man	US OGA	Sniper	British SAS
	Sergeant Major of the Army 4	441,500	Point Man	US OGA	Demolitions	US Army SFOD-D	Demolitions	US Army SFOD-D	Demolitions	US Army SFOD-D	Point Man	US OGA
	Sergeant Major of the Army 5	457,500	Demolitions	US Army SFOD-D	Assaulter	Australian SAS-R	Assaulter	Australian SAS-R	Assaulter	Australian SAS-R	Demolitions	US Army SFOD-D
	Second Lieutenant	474,000	Heavy Gunner	Norway FSK/HJK	Heavy Gunner	Norway FSK/HJK	Heavy Gunner	Norway FSK/HJK	Heavy Gunner	Norway FSK/HJK	Assaulter	Australian SAS-R
	First Lieutenant	491,000	Spec Ops	US Navy SEAL	Spec Ops	US Navy SEAL	Spec Ops	US Navy SEAL	Spec Ops	US Navy SEAL	Heavy Gunner	Norway FSK/HJK
	Captain	508,500	Sniper	German KSK	Sniper	German KSK	Sniper	German KSK	Sniper	German KSK	Spec Ops	US Navy SEAL
	Major	526,500	Point Man	Canadian JTF-2	Point Man	Canadian JTF-2	Point Man	Canadian JTF-2	Point Man	Canadian JTF-2	Sniper	German KSK
	Lieutenant Colonel	544,500	Demolitions	ROKN UDT/SEAL	Demolitions	ROKN UDT/SEAL	Demolitions	ROKN UDT/SEAL	Demolitions	ROKN UDT/SEAL	Point Man	Canadian JTF-2

POLISH GROM		ROKN UDT/SEAL		RU SPETSGRUPPA ALFA		SWEDISH SOG		US ARMY SFOD-D		US NAVY SEAL		US OGA	
Class Unlock	Unit Unlock	Class Unlock	Unit Unlock	Class Unlock	Unit Unlock	Class Unlock	Unit Unlock	Class Unlock	Unit Unlock	Class Unlock	Unit Unlock	Class Unlock	Unit Unlock
Assaulter	US OGA	Demolitions	British SAS	Demolitions	British SAS	Demolitions	British SAS	Demolitions	British SAS	Assaulter	US OGA	Demolitions	British SAS
Heavy Gunner	US Army SFOD-D	Assaulter	US OGA	Assaulter	US OGA	Assaulter	US OGA	Assaulter	US OGA	Heavy Gunner	US Army SFOD-D	Heavy Gunner	US Army SFOD-D
Spec Ops	Australian SAS-R	Heavy Gunner	US Army SFOD-D	Heavy Gunner	US Army SFOD-D	Heavy Gunner	US Army SFOD-D	Heavy Gunner	US Army SFOD-D	Spec Ops	Australian SAS-R	Spec Ops	Australian SAS-R
Sniper	Norway FSK/HJK	Spec Ops	Australian SAS-R	Spec Ops	Australian SAS-R	Spec Ops	Australian SAS-R	Spec Ops	Australian SAS-R	Sniper	Norway FSK/HJK	Sniper	Norway FSK/HJK
Point Man	US Navy SEAL	Sniper	Norway FSK/HJK	Sniper	Norway FSK/HJK	Sniper	Norway FSK/HJK	Sniper	Norway FSK/HJK	Point Man	US Navy SEAL	Point Man	US Navy SEAL
Demolitions	German KSK	Point Man	US Navy SEAL	Point Man	US Navy SEAL	Point Man	US Navy SEAL	Point Man	US Navy SEAL	Demolitions	German KSK	Demolitions	German KSK
Assaulter	Canadian JTF-2	Demolitions	German KSK	Demolitions	German KSK	Demolitions	German KSK	Demolitions	German KSK	Assaulter	Canadian JTF-2	Assaulter	Canadian JTF-2
Heavy Gunner	Swedish SOG	Assaulter	Canadian JTF-2	Assaulter	Canadian JTF-2	Assaulter	Canadian JTF-2	Assaulter	Canadian JTF-2	Heavy Gunner	Swedish SOG	Heavy Gunner	Swedish SOG
Spec Ops	RU Spetsgruppa Alfa	Heavy Gunner	Swedish SOG	Heavy Gunner	Swedish SOG	Heavy Gunner	Swedish SOG	Heavy Gunner	Swedish SOG	Spec Ops	RU Spetsgruppa Alfa	Spec Ops	RU Spetsgruppa Alfa
Sniper	Polish GROM	Spec Ops	RU Spetsgruppa Alfa	Spec Ops	RU Spetsgruppa Alfa	Spec Ops	RU Spetsgruppa Alfa	Spec Ops	RU Spetsgruppa Alfa	Sniper	Polish GROM	Sniper	Polish GROM
Point Man	British SAS	Sniper	Polish GROM	Sniper	Polish GROM	Sniper	Polish GROM	Sniper	Polish GROM	Point Man	British SAS	Point Man	British SAS
Demolitions	US OGA	Point Man	British SAS	Point Man	British SAS	Point Man	British SAS	Point Man	British SAS	Demolitions	US OGA	Demolitions	US OGA
Assaulter	US Army SFOD-D	Demolitions	US OGA	Demolitions	US OGA	Demolitions	US OGA	Demolitions	US OGA	Assaulter	US Army SFOD-D	Assaulter	US Army SFOD-D
Heavy Gunner	Australian SAS-R	Assaulter	US Army SFOD-D	Assaulter	US Army SFOD-D	Assaulter	US Army SFOD-D	Heavy Gunner	Australian SAS-R	Heavy Gunner	Australian SAS-R	Heavy Gunner	Australian SAS-R
Spec Ops	Norway FSK/HJK	Heavy Gunner	Australian SAS-R	Heavy Gunner	Australian SAS-R	Heavy Gunner	Australian SAS-R	Spec Ops	Norway FSK/HJK	Spec Ops	Norway FSK/HJK	Spec Ops	Norway FSK/HJK
Sniper	US Navy SEAL	Spec Ops	Norway FSK/HJK	Spec Ops	Norway FSK/HJK	Spec Ops	Norway FSK/HJK	Sniper	US Navy SEAL	Sniper	US Navy SEAL	Sniper	US Navy SEAL
Point Man	German KSK	Sniper	US Navy SEAL	Sniper	US Navy SEAL	Sniper	US Navy SEAL	Point Man	German KSK	Point Man	German KSK	Point Man	German KSK
Demolitions	Canadian JTF-2	Point Man	German KSK	Point Man	German KSK	Point Man	German KSK	Demolitions	Canadian JTF-2	Demolitions	Canadian JTF-2	Demolitions	Canadian JTF-2
Assaulter	ROKN UDT/SEAL	Demolitions	Canadian JTF-2	Demolitions	Canadian JTF-2	Demolitions	Canadian JTF-2	Assaulter	ROKN UDT/SEAL	Assaulter	ROKN UDT/SEAL	Assaulter	ROKN UDT/SEAL
Heavy Gunner	RU Spetsgruppa Alfa	Heavy Gunner	RU Spetsgruppa Alfa	Assaulter	ROKN UDT/SEAL	Assaulter	ROKN UDT/SEAL	Heavy Gunner	RU Spetsgruppa Alfa	Heavy Gunner	RU Spetsgruppa Alfa	Heavy Gunner	RU Spetsgruppa Alfa
Spec Ops	Polish GROM	Spec Ops	Polish GROM	Heavy Gunner	RU Spetsgruppa Alfa	Heavy Gunner	RU Spetsgruppa Alfa	Spec Ops	Polish GROM	Spec Ops	Polish GROM	Spec Ops	Polish GROM
Sniper	British SAS	Sniper	British SAS	Spec Ops	Polish GROM	Spec Ops	Polish GROM	Sniper	British SAS	Sniper	British SAS	Sniper	British SAS
Point Man	US OGA	Point Man	US OGA	Sniper	British SAS	Sniper	British SAS	Point Man	US OGA	Point Man	US OGA	Point Man	US OGA
Demolitions	US Army SFOD-D	Demolitions	US Army SFOD-D	Point Man	US OGA	Point Man	US OGA	Demolitions	US Army SFOD-D	Demolitions	US Army SFOD-D	Demolitions	US Army SFOD-D
Assaulter	Australian SAS-R	Assaulter	Australian SAS-R	Demolitions	US Army SFOD-D	Demolitions	US Army SFOD-D	Assaulter	Australian SAS-R	Assaulter	Australian SAS-R	Assaulter	Australian SAS-R
Heavy Gunner	Norway FSK/HJK	Heavy Gunner	Norway FSK/HJK	Assaulter	Australian SAS-R	Assaulter	Australian SAS-R	Heavy Gunner	Norway FSK/HJK	Heavy Gunner	Norway FSK/HJK	Heavy Gunner	Norway FSK/HJK
Spec Ops	US Navy SEAL	Spec Ops	US Navy SEAL	Heavy Gunner	Norway FSK/HJK	Heavy Gunner	Norway FSK/HJK	Spec Ops	US Navy SEAL	Spec Ops	US Navy SEAL	Spec Ops	US Navy SEAL
Sniper	German KSK	Sniper	German KSK	Spec Ops	US Navy SEAL	Spec Ops	US Navy SEAL	Sniper	German KSK	Sniper	German KSK	Sniper	German KSK
Point Man	Canadian JTF-2	Point Man	Canadian JTF-2	Sniper	German KSK	Sniper	German KSK	Point Man	Canadian JTF-2	Point Man	Canadian JTF-2	Point Man	Canadian JTF-2
Demolitions	ROKN UDT/SEAL	Demolitions	ROKN UDT/SEAL	Point Man	Canadian JTF-2	Point Man	Canadian JTF-2	Demolitions	ROKN UDT/SEAL	Demolitions	ROKN UDT/SEAL	Demolitions	ROKN UDT/SEAL

INSIGNIA	NAME	POINTS	AUSTRALIAN SAS-R		BRITISH SAS		CANADIAN JTF-2		GERMAN KSK		NORWAY FSK/HJK	
			Class Unlock	Unit Unlock	Class Unlock	Unit Unlock	Class Unlock	Unit Unlock	Class Unlock	Unit Unlock	Class Unlock	Unit Unlock
	Colonel 1	563,000	Assaulter	Swedish SOG	Assaulter	Swedish SOG	Assaulter	Swedish SOG	Assaulter	Swedish SOG	Demolitions	ROKN UDT/SEAL
	Colonel 2	582,000	Heavy Gunner	Polish GROM	Heavy Gunner	Polish GROM	Heavy Gunner	Polish GROM	Heavy Gunner	Polish GROM	Assaulter	Swedish SOG
	Colonel 3	601,500	Spec Ops	British SAS	Spec Ops	British SAS	Spec Ops	British SAS	Spec Ops	British SAS	Heavy Gunner	Polish GROM
	Colonel 4	621,500	Sniper	US OGA	Sniper	US OGA	Sniper	US OGA	Sniper	US OGA	Spec Ops	British SAS
	Colonel 5	641,500	Point Man	US Army SFOD-D	Point Man	US Army SFOD-D	Point Man	US Army SFOD-D	Point Man	US Army SFOD-D	Sniper	US OGA
	Colonel 6	662,000	Demolitions	Australian SAS-R	Demolitions	Australian SAS-R	Demolitions	Australian SAS-R	Demolitions	Australian SAS-R	Point Man	US Army SFOD-D
	Colonel 7	683,000	Assaulter	Norway FSK/HJK	Assaulter	Norway FSK/HJK	Assaulter	Norway FSK/HJK	Assaulter	Norway FSK/HJK	Demolitions	Australian SAS-R
	Colonel 8	704,500	Heavy Gunner	US OGA	Heavy Gunner	US OGA	Heavy Gunner	US OGA	Heavy Gunner	US OGA	Heavy Gunner	US OGA
	Brigadier General	726,500	Spec Ops	German KSK	Spec Ops	German KSK	Spec Ops	German KSK	Spec Ops	German KSK	Spec Ops	German KSK
	Major General	748,500	Sniper	Canadian JTF-2	Sniper	Canadian JTF-2	Sniper	Canadian JTF-2	Sniper	Canadian JTF-2	Sniper	Canadian JTF-2
	Lieutenant General	771,000	Point Man	ROKN UDT/SEAL	Point Man	ROKN UDT/SEAL	Point Man	ROKN UDT/SEAL	Point Man	ROKN UDT/SEAL	Point Man	ROKN UDT/SEAL
	General	794,000	Demolitions	Swedish SOG	Demolitions	Swedish SOG	Demolitions	Swedish SOG	Demolitions	Swedish SOG	Demolitions	Swedish SOG
	General of the Army	817,500	Assaulter	RU Spetsgruppa Alfa	Assaulter	RU Spetsgruppa Alfa	Assaulter	RU Spetsgruppa Alfa	Assaulter	RU Spetsgruppa Alfa	Assaulter	RU Spetsgruppa Alfa

ADVANCED CAREER PROGRESSION – ALL UNITS

INSIGNIA	NAME	POINTS
	Atlas Major Bronze 1	841,500
	Atlas Major Bronze 3	891,000
	Atlas Major Silver 1	916,500
	Atlas Major Silver 2	942,500
	Atlas Major Silver 3	969,500
	Atlas Major Gold 1	997,000
	Atlas Major Gold 2	1,025,000
	Atlas Major Gold 3	1,053,500
	Atlas Colonel Bronze 1	1,083,000
	Atlas Colonel Bronze 2	1,113,500
	Atlas Colonel Bronze 3	1,145,000
	Atlas Colonel Silver 1	1,177,000
	Atlas Colonel Silver 2	1,209,500

INSIGNIA	NAME	POINTS
	Atlas Colonel Silver 3	1,243,000
	Atlas Colonel Gold 1	1,278,000
	Atlas Colonel Gold 2	1,313,500
	Atlas Colonel Gold 3	1,350,000
	Atlas General Bronze 1	1,387,500
	Atlas General Bronze 2	1,426,000
	Atlas General Bronze 3	1,466,000
	Atlas General Silver 1	1,506,500
	Atlas General Silver 2	1,548,000
	Atlas General Silver 3	1,591,000
	Atlas General Gold 1	1,635,500
	Atlas General Gold 2	1,681,000
	Atlas General Gold 3	1,727,500

WARFIGHTER COMPENDIUM

POLISH GROM		ROKN UDT/SEAL		RU SPETSGRUPPA ALFA		SWEDISH SOG		US ARMY SFOD-D		US NAVY SEAL		US OGA	
Class Unlock	Unit Unlock	Class Unlock	Unit Unlock	Class Unlock	Unit Unlock	Class Unlock	Unit Unlock	Class Unlock	Unit Unlock	Class Unlock	Unit Unlock	Class Unlock	Unit Unlock
Assaulter	Swedish SOG	Assaulter	Swedish SOG	Demolitions	ROKN UDT/SEAL	Demolitions	ROKN UDT/SEAL	Assaulter	Swedish SOG	Assaulter	Swedish SOG	Assaulter	Swedish SOG
Heavy Gunner	Polish GROM	Heavy Gunner	Polish GROM	Assaulter	Swedish SOG	Heavy Gunner	Polish GROM	Heavy Gunner	Polish GROM	Heavy Gunner	Polish GROM	Heavy Gunner	Polish GROM
Spec Ops	British SAS	Spec Ops	British SAS	Heavy Gunner	Polish GROM	Spec Ops	British SAS	Spec Ops	British SAS	Spec Ops	British SAS	Spec Ops	British SAS
Sniper	US OGA	Sniper	US OGA	Spec Ops	British SAS	Sniper	US OGA	Sniper	US OGA	Sniper	US OGA	Sniper	US OGA
Point Man	US Army SFOD-D	Point Man	US Army SFOD-D	Sniper	US OGA	Point Man	US Army SFOD-D	Point Man	US Army SFOD-D	Point Man	US Army SFOD-D	Point Man	US Army SFOD-D
Demolitions	Australian SAS-R	Demolitions	Australian SAS-R	Point Man	US Army SFOD-D	Demolitions	Australian SAS-R	Demolitions	Australian SAS-R	Demolitions	Australian SAS-R	Demolitions	Australian SAS-R
Assaulter	Norway FSK/HJK	Assaulter	Norway FSK/HJK	Demolitions	Australian SAS-R	Assaulter	Norway FSK/HJK	Assaulter	Norway FSK/HJK	Assaulter	Norway FSK/HJK	Assaulter	Norway FSK/HJK
Heavy Gunner	US OGA	Heavy Gunner	US OGA	Assaulter	Norway FSK/HJK	Heavy Gunner	US OGA	Heavy Gunner	US OGA	Heavy Gunner	US OGA	Heavy Gunner	US OGA
Spec Ops	German KSK	Spec Ops	German KSK	Heavy Gunner	US OGA	Spec Ops	German KSK	Spec Ops	German KSK	Spec Ops	German KSK	Spec Ops	German KSK
Sniper	Canadian JTF-2	Sniper	Canadian JTF-2	Spec Ops	German KSK	Sniper	Canadian JTF-2	Sniper	Canadian JTF-2	Sniper	Canadian JTF-2	Sniper	Canadian JTF-2
Point Man	ROKN UDT/SEAL	Point Man	ROKN UDT/SEAL	Sniper	Canadian JTF-2	Point Man	ROKN UDT/SEAL	Point Man	ROKN UDT/SEAL	Point Man	ROKN UDT/SEAL	Point Man	ROKN UDT/SEAL
Demolitions	Swedish SOG	Demolitions	Swedish SOG	Point Man	ROKN UDT/SEAL	Demolitions	Swedish SOG	Demolitions	Swedish SOG	Demolitions	Swedish SOG	Demolitions	Swedish SOG
Assaulter	RU Spetsgruppa Alfa	Assaulter	RU Spetsgruppa Alfa	Demolitions	Swedish SOG	Assaulter	RU Spetsgruppa Alfa	Assaulter	RU Spetsgruppa Alfa	Assaulter	RU Spetsgruppa Alfa	Assaulter	RU Spetsgruppa Alfa

ASSAULTER WEAPON PINS

MEDAL	NAME	CRITERIA	POINTS
	EBR JTF-2 Marksman	Score 20 kills with weapon.	1,000
	EBR JTF-2 Sharpshooter	Score 200 kills with weapon.	3,000
	EBR JTF-2 Expert	Score 500 kills with weapon.	5,000
	EBR SAS-R Marksman	Score 20 kills with weapon.	1,000
	EBR SAS-R Sharpshooter	Score 200 kills with weapon.	3,000
	EBR SAS-R Expert	Score 500 kills with weapon.	5,000
	M14 EBR Spetsnaz Marksman	Score 20 kills with weapon.	1,000
	M14 EBR Spetsnaz Sharpshooter	Score 200 kills with weapon.	3,000
	M14 EBR Spetsnaz Expert	Score 500 kills with weapon.	5,000
	AG3 FSK/HJK Marksman	Score 20 kills with weapon.	1,000
	AG3 FSK/HJK Sharpshooter	Score 200 kills with weapon.	3,000
	AG3 FSK/HJK Expert	Score 500 kills with weapon.	5,000

MEDAL	NAME	CRITERIA	POINTS
	G3KA4 KSK Marksman	Score 20 kills with weapon.	1,000
	G3KA4 KSK Sharpshooter	Score 200 kills with weapon.	3,000
	G3KA4 KSK Expert	Score 500 kills with weapon.	5,000
	G3 AK4 SOG Marksman	Score 20 kills with weapon.	1,000
	G3 AK4 SOG Sharpshooter	Score 200 kills with weapon.	3,000
	G3 AK4 SOG Expert	Score 500 kills with weapon.	5,000
	Greko's HK416 GROM Marksman	Score 20 kills with weapon.	1,000
	Greko's HK416 GROM Sharpshooter	Score 200 kills with weapon.	3,000
	Greko's HK416 GROM Expert	Score 500 kills with weapon.	5,000
	HK416 SFOD-D Marksman	Score 20 kills with weapon.	1,000
	HK416 SFOD-D Sharpshooter	Score 200 kills with weapon.	3,000
	HK416 SFOD-D Expert	Score 500 kills with weapon.	5,000

MEDAL	NAME	CRITERIA	POINTS
	HK416 Navy SEAL Marksman	Score 20 kills with weapon.	1,000
	HK416 Navy SEAL Sharpshooter	Score 200 kills with weapon.	3,000
	HK416 Navy SEAL Expert	Score 500 kills with weapon.	5,000
	M4V1 OGA Marksman	Score 20 kills with weapon.	1,000
	M4V1 OGA Sharpshooter	Score 200 kills with weapon.	3,000
	M4V1 OGA Expert	Score 500 kills with weapon.	5,000
	M4V1 SAS Marksman	Score 20 kills with weapon.	1,000
	M4V1 SAS Sharpshooter	Score 200 kills with weapon.	3,000
	M4V1 SAS Expert	Score 500 kills with weapon.	5,000
	M4V1 UDT/SEAL Marksman	Score 20 kills with weapon.	1,000
	M4V1 UDT/SEAL Sharpshooter	Score 200 kills with weapon.	3,000
	M4V1 UDT/SEAL Expert	Score 500 kills with weapon.	5,000

DEMOLITIONS WEAPON PINS

MEDAL	NAME	CRITERIA	POINTS
	AA-12 SAS-R Marksman	Score 20 kills with weapon.	1,000
	AA-12 SAS-R Sharpshooter	Score 200 kills with weapon.	3,000
	AA-12 SAS-R Expert	Score 500 kills with weapon.	5,000
	AA-12 SOG Marksman	Score 20 kills with weapon.	1,000
	AA-12 SOG Sharpshooter	Score 200 kills with weapon.	3,000
	AA-12 SOG Expert	Score 500 kills with weapon.	5,000

MEDAL	NAME	CRITERIA	POINTS
	AA-12 Navy SEAL Marksman	Score 20 kills with weapon.	1,000
	AA-12 Navy SEAL Sharpshooter	Score 200 kills with weapon.	3,000
	AA-12 Navy SEAL Expert	Score 500 kills with weapon.	5,000
	HK416C GROM Marksman	Score 20 kills with weapon.	1,000
	HK416C GROM Sharpshooter	Score 200 kills with weapon.	3,000
	HK416C GROM Expert	Score 500 kills with weapon.	5,000

MEDAL	NAME	CRITERIA	POINTS
	HK416C JTF-2 Marksman	Score 20 kills with weapon.	1,000
	HK416C JTF-2 Sharpshooter	Score 200 kills with weapon.	3,000
	HK416C JTF-2 Expert	Score 500 kills with weapon.	5,000
	HK416C KSK Marksman	Score 20 kills with weapon.	1,000
	HK416C KSK Sharpshooter	Score 200 kills with weapon.	3,000
	HK416C KSK Expert	Score 500 kills with weapon.	5,000

DEMOLITIONS WEAPON PINS (CONTINUED)

MEDAL	NAME	CRITERIA	POINTS
	HK416C SAS Marksman	Score 20 kills with weapon.	1,000
	HK416C SAS Sharpshooter	Score 200 kills with weapon.	3,000
	HK416C SAS Expert	Score 500 kills with weapon.	5,000
	Mk16 PDW FSK/HJK Marksman	Score 20 kills with weapon.	1,000
	Mk16 PDW FSK/HJK Sharpshooter	Score 200 kills with weapon.	3,000
	Mk16 PDW FSK/HJK Expert	Score 500 kills with weapon.	5,000

MEDAL	NAME	CRITERIA	POINTS
	Mk16 PDW OGA Marksman	Score 20 kills with weapon.	1,000
	Mk16 PDW OGA Sharpshooter	Score 200 kills with weapon.	3,000
	Mk16 PDW OGA Expert	Score 500 kills with weapon.	5,000
	Mk16 PDW SFOD-D Marksman	Score 20 kills with weapon.	1,000
	Mk16 PDW SFOD-D Sharpshooter	Score 200 kills with weapon.	3,000
	Mk16 PDW SFOD-D Expert	Score 500 kills with weapon.	5,000

MEDAL	NAME	CRITERIA	POINTS
	AKS-74U Spetsnaz Marksman	Score 20 kills with weapon.	1,000
	AKS-74U Spetsnaz Sharpshooter	Score 200 kills with weapon.	3,000
	AKS-74U Spetsnaz Expert	Score 500 kills with weapon.	5,000
	AA-12 UDT/SEAL Marksman	Score 20 kills with weapon.	1,000
	AA-12 UDT/SEAL Sharpshooter	Score 200 kills with weapon.	3,000
	AA-12 UDT/SEAL Expert	Score 500 kills with weapon.	5,000

HEAVY GUNNER WEAPON PINS

MEDAL	NAME	CRITERIA	POINTS
	M240 FSK/HJK Marksman	Score 20 kills with weapon.	1,000
	M240 FSK/HJK Sharpshooter	Score 200 kills with weapon.	3,000
	M240 FSK/HJK Expert	Score 500 kills with weapon.	5,000
	M240 SAS Marksman	Score 20 kills with weapon.	1,000
	M240 SAS Sharpshooter	Score 200 kills with weapon.	3,000
	M240 SAS Expert	Score 500 kills with weapon.	5,000
	M240L Navy SEAL Marksman	Score 20 kills with weapon.	1,000
	M240L Navy SEAL Sharpshooter	Score 200 kills with weapon.	3,000
	M240L Navy SEAL Expert	Score 500 kills with weapon.	5,000
	Mk43 Mod1 SFOD-D Marksman	Score 20 kills with weapon.	1,000
	Mk43 Mod1 SFOD-D Sharpshooter	Score 200 kills with weapon.	3,000
	Mk43 Mod1 SFOD-D Expert	Score 500 kills with weapon.	5,000

MEDAL	NAME	CRITERIA	POINTS
	M249 JTF-2 Marksman	Score 20 kills with weapon.	1,000
	M249 JTF-2 Sharpshooter	Score 200 kills with weapon.	3,000
	M249 JTF-2 Expert	Score 500 kills with weapon.	5,000
	M249 UDT/SEAL Marksman	Score 20 kills with weapon.	1,000
	M249 UDT/SEAL Sharpshooter	Score 200 kills with weapon.	3,000
	M249 UDT/SEAL Expert	Score 500 kills with weapon.	5,000
	M249 GROM Marksman	Score 20 kills with weapon.	1,000
	M249 GROM Sharpshooter	Score 200 kills with weapon.	3,000
	M249 GROM Expert	Score 500 kills with weapon.	5,000
	Ksp90 SOG Marksman	Score 20 kills with weapon.	1,000
	Ksp90 SOG Sharpshooter	Score 200 kills with weapon.	3,000
	Ksp90 SOG Expert	Score 500 kills with weapon.	5,000

MEDAL	NAME	CRITERIA	POINTS
	Mk46 Mod1 OGA Marksman	Score 20 kills with weapon.	1,000
	Mk46 Mod1 OGA Sharpshooter	Score 200 kills with weapon.	3,000
	Mk46 Mod1 OGA Expert	Score 500 kills with weapon.	5,000
	MG4KE KSK Marksman	Score 20 kills with weapon.	1,000
	MG4KE KSK Sharpshooter	Score 200 kills with weapon.	3,000
	MG4KE KSK Expert	Score 500 kills with weapon.	5,000
	MG4 SAS-R Marksman	Score 20 kills with weapon.	1,000
	MG4 SAS-R Sharpshooter	Score 200 kills with weapon.	3,000
	MG4 SAS-R Expert	Score 500 kills with weapon.	5,000
	PKM Spetsnaz Marksman	Score 20 kills with weapon.	1,000
	PKM Spetsnaz Sharpshooter	Score 200 kills with weapon.	3,000
	PKM Spetsnaz Expert	Score 500 kills with weapon.	5,000

POINT MAN WEAPON PINS

MEDAL	NAME	CRITERIA	POINTS
	AK-103 GROM Marksman	Score 20 kills with weapon.	1,000
	AK-103 GROM Sharpshooter	Score 200 kills with weapon.	3,000
	AK-103 GROM Expert	Score 500 kills with weapon.	5,000
	AK-103 OGA Marksman	Score 20 kills with weapon.	1,000
	AK-103 OGA Sharpshooter	Score 200 kills with weapon.	3,000
	AK-103 OGA Expert	Score 500 kills with weapon.	5,000
	AK-103 Spetsnaz Marksman	Score 20 kills with weapon.	1,000
	AK-103 Spetsnaz Sharpshooter	Score 200 kills with weapon.	3,000
	AK-103 Spetsnaz Expert	Score 500 kills with weapon.	5,000
	Ak5C SOG Marksman	Score 20 kills with weapon.	1,000
	Ak5C SOG Sharpshooter	Score 200 kills with weapon.	3,000
	Ak5C SOG Expert	Score 500 kills with weapon.	5,000

MEDAL	NAME	CRITERIA	POINTS
	Austeyr F88 SAS-R Marksman	Score 20 kills with weapon.	1,000
	Austeyr F88 SAS-R Sharpshooter	Score 200 kills with weapon.	3,000
	Austeyr F88 SAS-R Expert	Score 500 kills with weapon.	5,000
	F88 SAS Marksman	Score 20 kills with weapon.	1,000
	F88 SAS Sharpshooter	Score 200 kills with weapon.	3,000
	F88 SAS Expert	Score 500 kills with weapon.	5,000
	F88 FSK/HJK Marksman	Score 20 kills with weapon.	1,000
	F88 FSK/HJK Sharpshooter	Score 200 kills with weapon.	3,000
	F88 FSK/HJK Expert	Score 500 kills with weapon.	5,000
	OBR 5.56 JTF-2 Marksman	Score 20 kills with weapon.	1,000
	OBR 5.56 JTF-2 Sharpshooter	Score 200 kills with weapon.	3,000
	OBR 5.56 JTF-2 Expert	Score 500 kills with weapon.	5,000

MEDAL	NAME	CRITERIA	POINTS
	OBR 5.56 KSK Marksman	Score 20 kills with weapon.	1,000
	OBR 5.56 KSK Sharpshooter	Score 200 kills with weapon.	3,000
	OBR 5.56 KSK Expert	Score 500 kills with weapon.	5,000
	OBR 5.56 SFOD-D Marksman	Score 20 kills with weapon.	1,000
	OBR 5.56 SFOD-D Sharpshooter	Score 200 kills with weapon.	3,000
	OBR 5.56 SFOD-D Expert	Score 500 kills with weapon.	5,000
	OBR 5.56 UDT/SEAL Marksman	Score 20 kills with weapon.	1,000
	OBR 5.56 UDT/SEAL Sharpshooter	Score 200 kills with weapon.	3,000
	OBR 5.56 UDT/ SEAL Expert	Score 500 kills with weapon.	5,000
	OBR 5.56 Navy SEAL Marksman	Score 20 kills with weapon.	1,000
	OBR 5.56 Navy SEAL Sharpshooter	Score 200 kills with weapon.	3,000
	OBR 5.56 Navy SEAL Expert	Score 500 kills with weapon.	5,000

SNIPER WEAPON PINS

MEDAL	NAME	CRITERIA	POINTS
	OBR 7.62 SFOD-D Marksman	Score 20 kills with weapon.	1,000
	OBR 7.62 SFOD-D Sharpshooter	Score 200 kills with weapon.	3,000
	OBR 7.62 SFOD-D Expert	Score 500 kills with weapon.	5,000
	OBR 7.62 SAS-R Marksman	Score 20 kills with weapon.	1,000
	OBR 7.62 SAS-R Sharpshooter	Score 200 kills with weapon.	3,000
	OBR 7.62 SAS-R Expert	Score 500 kills with weapon.	5,000

MEDAL	NAME	CRITERIA	POINTS
	SC5 FSK/HJK Marksman	Score 20 kills with weapon.	1,000
	SC5 FSK/HJK Sharpshooter	Score 200 kills with weapon.	3,000
	SC5 FSK/HJK Expert	Score 500 kills with weapon.	5,000
	SC5 OGA Marksman	Score 20 kills with weapon.	1,000
	SC5 OGA Sharpshooter	Score 200 kills with weapon.	3,000
	SC5 OGA Expert	Score 500 kills with weapon.	5,000

MEDAL	NAME	CRITERIA	POINTS
	SC5 SAS Marksman	Score 20 kills with weapon.	1,000
	SC5 SAS Sharpshooter	Score 200 kills with weapon.	3,000
	SC5 SAS Expert	Score 500 kills with weapon.	5,000
	TAC-300 SOG Marksman	Score 20 kills with weapon.	1,000
	TAC-300 SOG Sharpshooter	Score 200 kills with weapon.	3,000
	TAC-300 SOG Expert	Score 500 kills with weapon.	5,000

SNIPER WEAPON PINS (CONTINUED)

MEDAL	NAME	CRITERIA	POINTS	MEDAL	NAME	CRITERIA	POINTS	MEDAL	NAME	CRITERIA	POINTS
	TAC-300 Spetsnaz Marksman	Score 20 kills with weapon.	1,000		TAC-300 Navy SEAL Marksman	Score 20 kills with weapon.	1,000		TAC-50 JTF-2 Marksman	Score 20 kills with weapon.	1,000
	TAC-300 Spetsnaz Sharpshooter	Score 200 kills with weapon.	3,000		TAC-300 Navy SEAL Sharpshooter	Score 200 kills with weapon.	3,000		TAC-50 JTF-2 Sharpshooter	Score 200 kills with weapon.	3,000
	TAC-300 Spetsnaz Expert	Score 500 kills with weapon.	5,000		TAC-300 Navy SEAL Expert	Score 500 kills with weapon.	5,000		TAC-50 JTF-2 Expert	Score 500 kills with weapon.	5,000
	TAC-300 UDT/SEAL Marksman	Score 20 kills with weapon.	1,000		TAC-50 GROM Marksman	Score 20 kills with weapon.	1,000		TAC-50 KSK Marksman	Score 20 kills with weapon.	1,000
	TAC-300 UDT/SEAL Sharpshooter	Score 200 kills with weapon.	3,000		TAC-50 GROM Sharpshooter	Score 200 kills with weapon.	3,000		TAC-50 KSK Sharpshooter	Score 200 kills with weapon.	3,000
	TAC-300 UDT/SEAL Expert	Score 500 kills with weapon.	5,000		TAC-50 GROM Expert	Score 500 kills with weapon.	5,000		TAC-50 KSK Expert	Score 500 kills with weapon.	5,000

SPEC OPS WEAPON PINS

MEDAL	NAME	CRITERIA	POINTS	MEDAL	NAME	CRITERIA	POINTS	MEDAL	NAME	CRITERIA	POINTS
	AK-103 Bullpup GROM Marksman	Score 20 kills with weapon.	1,000		G36 SAS-R Marksman	Score 20 kills with weapon.	1,000		Mk18 SOG Marksman	Score 20 kills with weapon.	1,000
	AK-103 Bullpup GROM Sharpshooter	Score 200 kills with weapon.	3,000		G36 SAS-R Sharpshooter	Score 200 kills with weapon.	3,000		Mk18 SOG Sharpshooter	Score 200 kills with weapon.	3,000
	AK-103 Bullpup GROM Expert	Score 500 kills with weapon.	5,000		G36 SAS-R Expert	Score 500 kills with weapon.	5,000		Mk18 SOG Expert	Score 500 kills with weapon.	5,000
	AK-103 Bullpup Spetsnaz Marksman	Score 20 kills with weapon.	1,000		Mk18 JTF-2 Marksman	Score 20 kills with weapon.	1,000		MP7 UDT/SEAL Marksman	Score 20 kills with weapon.	1,000
	AK-103 Bullpup Spetsnaz Sharpshooter	Score 200 kills with weapon.	3,000		Mk18 JTF-2 Sharpshooter	Score 200 kills with weapon.	3,000		MP7 UDT/SEAL Sharpshooter	Score 200 kills with weapon.	3,000
	AK-103 Bullpup Spetsnaz Expert	Score 500 kills with weapon.	5,000		Mk18 JTF-2 Expert	Score 500 kills with weapon.	5,000		MP7 UDT/SEAL Expert	Score 500 kills with weapon.	5,000
	G36 FSK/HJK Marksman	Score 20 kills with weapon.	1,000		Mk18 SAS Marksman	Score 20 kills with weapon.	1,000		MP7 Navy SEAL Marksman	Score 20 kills with weapon.	1,000
	G36 FSK/HJK Sharpshooter	Score 200 kills with weapon.	3,000		Mk18 SAS Sharpshooter	Score 200 kills with weapon.	3,000		MP7 Navy SEAL Sharpshooter	Score 200 kills with weapon.	3,000
	G36 FSK/HJK Expert	Score 500 kills with weapon.	5,000		Mk18 SAS Expert	Score 500 kills with weapon.	5,000		MP7 Navy SEAL Expert	Score 500 kills with weapon.	5,000
	G36 KSK Marksman	Score 20 kills with weapon.	1,000		Mk18 SFOD-D Marksman	Score 20 kills with weapon.	1,000		MP7 OGA Marksman	Score 20 kills with weapon.	1,000
	G36 KSK Sharpshooter	Score 200 kills with weapon.	3,000		Mk18 SFOD-D Sharpshooter	Score 200 kills with weapon.	3,000		MP7 OGA Sharpshooter	Score 200 kills with weapon.	3,000
	G36 KSK Expert	Score 500 kills with weapon.	5,000		Mk18 SFOD-D Expert	Score 500 kills with weapon.	5,000		MP7 OGA Expert	Score 500 kills with weapon.	5,000

ACHIEVEMENTS & TROPHIES

IMAGE	NAME	DESCRIPTION	GAMER SCORE	TROPHY
	Warfighter	Complete the campaign on any difficulty	40	Silver
	Tier 1	Complete the campaign on Tier 1 difficulty	50	Silver
	Unexpected Cargo	Complete Unintended Consequences	15	Bronze
	Know the Enemy	Complete Through the Eyes of Evil	15	Bronze
	Hit the Beach	Complete Shore Leave	15	Bronze
	Pit and Pin	Complete Hot Pursuit	20	Bronze
	Rain of Terror	Complete Changing Tides	15	Bronze
	Monsoon Lagoon	Complete Rip Current	15	Bronze
	One Shot, Three Kills	Complete Hat Trick	15	Bronze
	Non-Official Cover	Complete Finding Faraz	20	Bronze
	Class Dismissed	Complete Connect the Dots	20	Bronze
	Pedal to the Medal	Complete Hello and Dubai	20	Bronze
	Closing Ceremony	Complete Old Friends	20	Bronze
	One Man Mutiny	Complete Bump in the Night	20	Bronze
	Let Him Rot	Complete Shut it Down	20	Bronze
	Preacher's Path	Finish all the Preacher Missions	30	Silver
	Stump's No Chump	Finish all the Stump Missions	30	Silver
	Double Header	Kill two enemies with one bullet in the Changing Tides mission	10	Bronze
	Release the Kraken!	Kill 25 enemies during the boat exfil in Rip Current	15	Bronze

IMAGE	NAME	DESCRIPTION	GAMER SCORE	TROPHY
	Hardcore	Complete the campaign on Hardcore difficulty	80	Gold
	Tag, You're It	Catch Faraz within 15 minutes in Finding Faraz	10	Bronze
	Leftover Lead	Complete the sniping section in Shore Leave without missing a shot	15	Bronze
	On the Clock	Complete the training in Through the Eyes of Evil in under 18 seconds	10	Bronze
	Target Practice	Shoot down the targets in the training camp caves in Connect the Dots	10	Bronze
	Storm Watch	Get through the sandstorm without hitting any vehicles in Hello and Dubai	10	Bronze
	Vender Bender	Destroy 90 market stalls in Hot Pursuit	10	Bronze
	Dirty Laundry	Find the grenades in the laundry room in Bump in the Night	15	Bronze
	Room Service	Unlock all door breach options	20	Bronze
	Master Locksmith	Use each breaching option at least once	15	Bronze
	Extreme Realism	Recover from near-death 5 times without dying	10	Bronze
	Tier 1 Imports	Kill 50 enemies using disposable weapons	15	Bronze
	Peek-a-Boo	Kill an enemy while using peek and lean	5	Bronze
	Lean With It	Kill 25 enemies while using peek and lean	15	Bronze
	It's Dangerous to go Alone!	Request ammo from an ally	5	Bronze
	Lead Farmer	Request ammo from an ally 25 times	10	Bronze
	Tactical Toggler	Kill 25 enemies while using Combat Toggle	15	Bronze
	Unstoppable	Complete any combat mission on hardest difficulty setting without dying	30	Silver
	The Axeman	Kill 25 enemies with melee	20	Bronze

MULTIPLAYER ACHIEVEMENTS

IMAGE	NAME	DESCRIPTION	GAMER SCORE	TROPHY
	MVP	Finish in first place in any online match	20	Silver
	All In	Call in Apache support	20	Silver
	There IS an I in Fireteam	Finish a round as part of the featured Fireteam	15	Bronze
	Brothers in Arms	Win a round with a friend as a Fireteam Buddy	20	Bronze
	Warchief	Unlock all soldiers in multiplayer	35	Silver
	Jack of all Guns	Earn the Marksman Badge for all weapons	20	Silver
	Back in the Fight	Complete a tour with any class	50	Gold

IMAGE	NAME	DESCRIPTION	GAMER SCORE	TROPHY
	Honey Badger	Use your Fireteam Buddy to re-arm or heal	10	Bronze
	Squad Leader	Unlock a soldier of each class	20	Bronze
	Downrange	Play online for 15 minutes	20	Bronze
	Job Done	Complete 3 Combat Mission objectives	20	Bronze
	Global Warfighters	Unlock a soldier from each unit	25	Silver
PS3 EXCLUSIVE				
	For Honor For Country	Collect all other **Medal of Honor Warfighter** Trophies	N/A	Platinum

PREACHER
1/6 SCALE COLLECTIBLE FIGURE

HYPER-REALISTIC
FULLY ARTICULATED ACTION FIGURE

MEDAL OF HONOR™ WARFIGHTER

Official Game Guide
Written by: David Knight & Michael Knight

Prima Games
An Imprint of Random House, Inc.
3000 Lava Ridge Court, Suite 100
Roseville, CA 95661
www.primagames.com

Product Manager: JJ Zingale
Design & Layout: Red Sheet Studio
Copyeditor: Julia Kilmer
Screenshots and additional MP text: Loren Gilliland
Support Team: Russell Ewell, Garrit Rocha and Paul Bernardo

Prima Games and the authors would like to thank Kevin O'Leary, Geoff Bent, Brian Austin, Ryan Hamlyn, Daniel Chin, Thad Sasser, Alan Hadaya, Luke Thai, Michael Tamura, Esmeralda Perez, Antonio Trama, Kevin Hendrickson, Dan Moditch, Craig Owens, Ben Jones, Chris Salazar, Daniel Wiksten, Marc Janas, Michael Roth, David Sirland, Salvador Delgado, Kristoffer Bergqvist, Christian Grass, Elisabetta Silli, Dave Fox, Mike Cook, Warren Buss, Chase Swanson, Lorraine Honrada, Daniel Davis and Jim Stadelman for their support throughout this project.

Important:
Prima Games has made every effort to determine that the information contained in this book is accurate. However, the publisher makes no warranty, either expressed or implied, as to the accuracy, effectiveness, or completeness of the material in this book; nor does the publisher assume liability for damages, either incidental or consequential, that may result from using the information in this book. The publisher cannot provide any additional information or support regarding gameplay, hints and strategies, or problems with hardware or software. Such questions should be directed to the support numbers provided by the game and/or device manufacturers as set forth in their documentation. Some game tricks require precise timing and may require repeated attempts before the desired result is achieved.

ISBN: 978-0-307-89538-7

Printed in the United States of America.

Australian warranty statement:

This product comes with guarantees that cannot be excluded under the Australian Consumer Law. You are entitled to a replacement or refund for a major failure and for compensation for any other reasonably foreseeable loss or damage. You are also entitled to have the goods repaired or replaced if the goods fail to be of acceptable quality and the failure does not amount to a major failure.

This product comes with a 1 year warranty from date of purchase. Defects in the product must have appeared within 1-year, from date of purchase in order to claim the warranty. All warranty claims must be facilitated back through the retailer of purchase, in accordance with the retailer's returns policies and procedures. Any cost incurred, as a result of returning the product to the retailer of purchase - are the full responsibility of the consumer.

AU wholesale distributor: Bluemouth Interactive Pty Ltd, Suite 1502, 9 Yarra Street, South Yarra, Victoria, 3141. (+613 9646 4011)

Email: support@bluemouth.com.au